# Powerful Profits from

# INTERNET POKER

ALSO BY THE AUTHOR

*Casino Magazine's Play Smart and Win*
(Simon & Schuster/Fireside, 1994)

*Casino Games Made Easy* (Premier, 1999)

*Powerful Profits from Blackjack* (Kensington, 2003)

*Powerful Profits from Slots* (Kensington, 2003)

*Casino GambleTalk: The Language of Gambling and New Casino Games* (Kensington, 2003)

*Powerful Profits from Craps* (Kensington, 2003)

*Powerful Profits from Video Poker* (Kensington, 2003)

*Powerful Profits: Winning Strategies for Casino Games* (Kensington, 2004)

*Powerful Profits from Keno* (Kensington, 2004)

*Powerful Profits from Casino Table Games*
(Kensington, 2004)

*Powerful Profits from Internet Gambling*
(Kensington, 2005)

*Powerful Profits from Video Slots* (Kensington, 2005)

*Powerful Profits from Poker* (Kensington, 2005)

# Powerful Profits from

# INTERNET POKER

## VICTOR H. ROYER

LYLE STUART
Kensington Publishing Corp.
www.kensingtonbooks.com

LYLE STUART BOOKS are published by

Kensington Publishing Corp.
850 Third Avenue
New York, NY 10022



All Kensington titles, imprints, and distributed lines are available at special quantity discounts for bulk purchases for sales promotions, premiums, fund-raising, educational, or institutional use. Special book excerpts or customized printings can also be created to fit specific needs. For details, write or phone the office of the Kensington special sales manager: Kensington Publishing Corp., 850 Third Avenue, New York, NY 10022, attn: Special Sales Department; phone 1-800-221-2647.

Lyle Stuart is a trademark of Kensington Publishing Corp.

First printing: January 2006

10 9 8 7 6 5 4 3 2 1

Printed in the United States of America

ISBN 0-8184-0654-2

This book is gratefully dedicated to

**Jiřinka Lukášová**

"Veni, Vidi, Vici"—I came, I saw, I conquered.

—JULIUS CAESAR

Remember this each time you go to a casino.

# Contents

# Foreword

This is a book about Internet poker. It is intended as a companion to my other books, in particular *Powerful Profits from Internet Gambling, Powerful Profits from Tournament Poker,* and *Powerful Profits from Poker.* Although I hope that you purchase these books and read what I have written in them, I do not assume that you will do so, nor assume that you will purchase any of my other books to which some of this text also refers. Wherever possible, I will describe this incredible phenomenon of Internet poker in as much detail as I can within the scope of this book's intended purpose. That purpose is to help you navigate through the world of Internet poker. To accomplish this, I will also use several examples of poker sites that I myself patronize, and those that I have selected as examples of everything that is the best in the world of Internet poker. There are many different sites on the Internet dedicated to gambling. Many of these are online casinos that are profiled in my book *Powerful Profits from Internet Gambling,* as well as many others that are both online casinos and online poker rooms. The explosion of Internet poker, and poker in general, has been so enormous in the past few years that even online casinos that previously did not offer poker as one of their games now do so. This is in direct response to, and a testimonial to, the worldwide interest in the phenomenon we all know as poker.

The world of Internet poker has exploded exponentially to that of real poker in the real-world brick-and-mortar casinos. In 2004 there were thousands of Internet gambling sites, of which about 1,000 operate exclusively and only as poker sites. As technology improves and interest in poker continues to grow, the entire cyberworld of the Internet will continue to expand and improve; this will have the inevitable result of spawning an ever-increasing number of Internet gambling sites, and especially Internet poker sites. Even today as I write this book, there are already too many such sites. It is becoming increasingly difficult for a player to navigate the world of the Internet gambling experience without at some point being exposed to something unscrupulous, or at least not quite right. As I mentioned in my book on Internet gambling, the world of cyberspace is not regulated by anything or anyone anywhere. It is, therefore, eminently possible that you may expose yourself to an unpleasant experience if you venture into the world of Internet poker without knowing at least something about what it is that you are actually getting into. It is for this reason that I wrote my previous books, including the books on poker, on Internet gambling, and now on Internet poker. In those pages, as well as here, it is my intent to provide you with a guide that you can use to safely navigate the world of cyberspace, and to guide you to those experiences that will be wonderful, profitable, and safe and secure. I also want to provide you with the means and methods of being able to choose the best or better games to play and the necessary knowledge and ammunition to play them as profitably and as successfully as possible. Naturally, as with all skill-based games, of which poker is the preeminent one, exactly how profitable you become playing online poker will vary significantly based on your own abilities, skills, and knowledge of the games. In this book, I provide you with a map to make your navigation of cyberspace and the world of Internet poker easier and the information necessary in order to make you a good, solid, experienced, and profitable Internet poker player.

During the 2004 WSOP (World Series of Poker), famed poker player and legend Doyle Brunson was asked during an ESPN interview what he thinks about the new crop of young players that performed so well during that particular World Series. His reply was both insightful and prophetic. He said (I paraphrase this quote as nearly as I can remember it), "These young Internet poker players can learn in one year what took me ten years." In the modern twenty-first-century world of playing poker, be it on the Internet or in real-world casinos, no truer statement has ever been given. As usual, Doyle got this square-on. Internet poker is such a wonderful phenomenon that, indeed, you can learn more in one month than it took this old-time road gambler so many years to learn. The point was so absolutely true and correct that it could easily befuddle the mind, especially when you think that the world of Internet poker is such an extraordinarily recent phenomenon. Because we quickly become used to new technology, and because this technology is expanding everywhere exponentially and influencing so many aspects of our lives, it is easy to forget that less than ten years ago, there were barely a handful of online poker rooms that ran barely a few games, and most of them not for real money. In such a short time, this has changed incredibly and dramatically. Today, we not only have so many Internet poker rooms, and so many Internet casinos, but we also have an explosion in land-based casinos, poker rooms, and card rooms, in almost every state in the United States and almost every country in the world.

Naturally, with so many choices the question becomes obvious: just which online poker rooms are the best? Along with this question come many other questions: How do I play? How do I make a deposit? How do I get my money? How do I withdraw money? Is it better to play for play money or real money? How do I know that the site is secure? How do I play the games? Although I cannot possibly hope to answer every question that every player might have, what I can do in this book is to try to steer you toward what I consider to be the best, the safest, and the most popular online casinos that play poker as their primary games. In this book, I have chosen to show you several online poker rooms, those that I have personally investigated as closely as I could, on whose sites I have played for at least a year, and whose services I have experienced personally. I have selected these online poker rooms because I consider them the best, the safest, and the most enjoyable poker-playing experience to be found on the Internet at this time. This does not mean that there are not others that are equally as good. It simply means that in this book, I chose those listed here because I like them and find them to be true, honest, and secure. Therefore, in addition to those sites that I mention in detail in the body of this book, I created the Featured Directory of Online Poker Rooms, in which I give you a few more online poker rooms that I personally have reviewed so that you can have a greater profile and selection. Additionally, I have created the General Directory of Online Poker Rooms—a more extensive listing of some of the other poker rooms that I also consider to be pretty good. Both directories are located in the back of the book. Naturally, I have my favorites, and the reason why I have favorite poker rooms is because I consider those to be the best and on whose sites I have personally had the best experiences. These favorites are examined in the body of this book and can be found as well in the Featured Directory of Online Poker Rooms. Their selections are really arbitrarily up to me only, and I put them in my book in no particular order. I actually begin by first mentioning PartyPoker.com primarily because their site is part of the WPT (World Poker Tour). PartyPoker.com is also a reputable poker site and one where the experience of playing poker is about as good and as easy as it gets. This site also offers the Party Millions Poker Cruise, of which the championship event is televised on the WPT. My other reason for selecting this particular online poker room as the first in my book is perhaps more personal, and that is because I happen to like the WPT host Shana Hiatt.*

My personal preferences aside, PartyPoker.com stands out among the clutter of Internet casinos and Internet poker rooms precisely because it offers good games, a good range of games, good service, and the absolute confidence in strict security, featuring the latest of Internet encryption software. I also mention several other sites throughout this book, those that are identified in my chapter profiles, as well as those in the Featured Directory of Online Poker Rooms. Those other poker rooms have also been selected for the same reasons as those that I just

*Since I originally wrote this, Shana has left the WPT as host, to pursue personal matters. We all miss you, Shana!

described for PartyPoker. com, although perhaps without Shana Hiatt. It is, therefore, very important that readers of this book understand that every Internet poker room I mention in my book is one that I consider to be top notch. This particularly applies to PokerStars.com, which is probably the world's biggest online poker room. If you have watched the WSOP on television, you probably know that in 2003 and 2004, PokerStars.com produced the world champions of poker. In 2003, Chris Moneymaker turned a $40 entry fee in an online tournament into $2.5 million when he won the WSOP. In 2004, Greg Raymer parlayed his $160 satellite buy-in into the record prize of $5 million as that year's WSOP champion. Both of these players were Internet poker players, and both of them are also PokerStars.com champions. I have therefore selected PokerStars. com as my featured Internet poker room, not only because they are the world's largest online poker room, but primarily because they provided those two world champions. In my book, I profile PartyPoker.com as well as PokerStars.com because they are both instrumental in leading the Internet poker boom. PartyPoker.com is the only Internet poker site featured on the WPT and PokerStars .com is the site featured in the WSOP, through the presence of their two world champions, Chris Moneymaker and Greg Raymer.

One of the privileges of being an author of gambling books is that I can pick and choose from among casinos, and in this case Internet poker rooms, and choose those that I wish to actually describe in detail. My selection process consisted primarily of my playing on those sites and experiencing everything they have to offer for myself, as well as my desire to strike a balance between the two most popular televised poker championships—the WPT and WSOP. I was able to achieve all those goals by profiling PartyPoker.com and PokerStars.com. In addition, I have been playing at various online casinos for as long as they have been in existence. And I have been playing in Internet poker rooms for as long as they have been available, from when all they offered were a few games for play money, all the way to today where real money play is available. I consider all this to have been extraordinarily worthwhile, and I continue to play on these sites. I play on them both in ring games as well as in tournaments. I have played in the very smallest of games to the very highest of stakes. I have won my fair share of online poker tournaments, and I have also won my fair share of online poker games. All these experiences put together have allowed me to develop a broad perspective and a large tapestry of knowledge about the world of Internet poker and how to succeed in it. And now, this information is contained in this book.

I wish to provide you with the opportunity to learn Internet Poker quickly and to become successful even more quickly. Just like Doyle Brunson said, if you learn to play Internet poker you can learn in one year what would have taken you probably about ten years in the real world. I have been playing in casinos for many decades and I can tell you firsthand that if I had access to this kind of Internet poker–learning experience twenty-five or thirty years ago, I could have and would have saved a large portion of time and expense because I would not have had to spend several decades in casinos learning the skills necessary to be a winning poker player. Instead, I would have used all the wonderful resources available on these great Internet poker sites to learn my craft, the games, the structure, the betting, the discipline, and money management, as well as everything else that goes hand-in-hand with the establishment and the building of a successful poker player. I have no regrets, because mine has been a wonderfully exciting life, and all that I have experienced in it has now made it possible for me to write all of these books in my series of many books on casino games and gaming, including land-based poker, and here in this book on Internet poker. Everything that has been part of my life I have put into all of these books, and I have invested in them all that I can say.

The world of Internet poker is still a relatively young and new experience for many people and, therefore, by following what I have provided you in this book will make it easier for you to be able to get ahead much faster and with less stress, risk, and with greater and faster success. You will learn not only how to navigate through the various sites and select the best ones that fit your playing profile and your interest, but you also will learn how to do this well and how to play the ring cash games and how to play tournaments, and basically how to maximize the yield from this experience, both from the enjoyment perspective as well as the financial rewards. There is no substitute for experience, and eventually you will have to invest some time and real money to experience all of this before you become good; however, the knowledge that you can gain from this book and actually applying what you learn here to your own continuing education as you play will together create for you the profile and map by which you can create for yourself the kind of Internet poker–playing success that meets with your desires and objectives. If you also choose to read my other books, so much the better, but it is not a prerequisite. In the pages that follow you will find all that you will need to know in order to enter the world of cyberspace poker and make it an enjoyable and profitable experience.

# Preface

This is the twelth book in my series of gambling books, under the general series title of *Powerful Profits*. All of these books were written and conceived as one single unit, to work together, in order to provide for those who wish to read them with a complete, total, and detailed profile and analysis of every kind of contemporary modern casino gambling game and casino gambling experience now available. With the explosion of Internet gambling, and in particular the worldwide phenomenon of poker, both as a game for real-world casinos and poker rooms and especially the Internet, it was only natural that my books on Internet gambling and poker would evolve into this book specifically about Internet poker. This book, therefore, combines the experience of Internet gambling along with the phenomenon of poker. Traditional poker, as that may have been understood up to this point, particularly in reference to the grand and great old road gamblers of history, has also evolved into many new games, and variations of traditional games. Advances in communication technology, multimedia, and computer technology all combined in the twenty-first century to create from the World Wide Web the communion of cybergamblers who can all now gather as frequently as they wish at any Internet poker table and game of their choice, and do so completely from the comfort of their own home. What would have appeared entirely futuristic to most people as recently as twenty years ago, now seems commonplace. What is even more remarkable is that an entire generation of young poker players have grown up in the game of poker along with the Internet and computers, seemingly oblivious to the facts of history or any knowledge or appreciation of the often long decades of learning that those who are now expert poker players have had to undergo in order to reach such a level of professionalism and expertise. Although it is true that many of the young poker players have become more familiar with the history of poker, primarily by watching the WSOP and WPT on television, it is nevertheless true that the majority of them are nonetheless unaware that there was once a world of poker in which computers and Internet poker rooms did not exist. Such perceptions aren't failings, because each generation grows up in a world where everything looks precisely the way it should be, and they quickly come to accept circumstances and situations that to the previous generation appeared to be miraculous.

What has remained as a constant, spanning generations, has been humankind's interest in gambling and gambling games, and in the past several years in particular this worldwide interest in poker. Many older forms of poker have died out, as is usually the case when evolution takes over and new generations become used to new games. When in years past poker players have cut their teeth on games like Five Card Stud, California Lowball, Seven Card Stud, Razz and Deuce to Seven Lowball, with perhaps some other lesser-known games also thrown into this historical mix, modern twenty-first-century poker players primarily play Texas Hold'Em as their main game of choice, in structured limits, pot-limit, and in many cases—such as just about every Texas Hold'Em tournament—in the no-limit version. Significantly due to exposure on television, Texas Hold'Em has quickly overtaken the world as the most commonly played game anywhere, including in all the Internet poker rooms. As you read this book, you will see that I place greater emphasis on Texas Hold'Em, as was indeed the case with my earlier poker book. I designed it this way because most of the games that you will play in the real world, and as far as this book is concerned in Internet poker rooms, will be Texas Hold'Em games. Although it is important for any poker player to also gain knowledge and perhaps mastery of other poker games, the successful poker player will pick one game they wish to master and then select a second game in which they will become quite proficient but will always remain only as their second game. Knowledge of the other games is also important because it can exercise your brain and allow you to be able to better juxtapose playing principles and experienced skills from one situation to the other. Adapting to circumstances as they occur, and as a result digging deep into your well and arsenal of knowledge, is an important aspect of poker-playing success. No situation you encounter is always identical to any other. This is an important concept, and one that is often misunderstood, or not understood at all, by many poker players, and particularly the millions of newbie Internet poker players. Unlike perhaps some other gambling games, poker is a game that is in a constant state of flux. Although the game and its rules and playing principles and structures may be the same, each hand in the game, and each time you play on any one table, will always be different to anything else you have ever experienced. Just because most of the time it is correct to raise with pocket Aces in late positions in Texas Hold'Em, for example, it is not correct to always do so and disregard the circumstances of that particular moment and that particular hand in progress. Sometimes it may be better for your value to not advertise the strength of your hand in these positions or under these circumstances. The point is, of course, that being successful in poker, and primarily in Texas Hold'Em, it is important to appreciate the concept of change and variability. Although you should play a solid game in which you will have good discipline and a solid sense of the best starting hands, as well as the ability to analyze and appreciate situations and circumstances as they unfold, your best tools in order to become a profitable poker player—and this is particularly applicable to the Internet poker phenomenon—will be your powers of observation and your ability to adapt to circumstances in that very instant. Situations of all kinds possible occur in Internet poker rooms and games with a far greater frequency than in land-based casino poker rooms and card rooms, primarily because of the speed of Internet games. In the real world you might be lucky to get forty hands per hour, but in Internet poker rooms, and in particular in shorthanded games, you often find from fifty hands per hour to as many as eighty hands per hour being dealt. This is a pace for poker unheard of in the annals of poker history, and is made possible only because the Internet poker games are being dealt by software and not by human dealers, and all poker players are forced by the software to always act in turn, and there are never any other distractions such as may be in real-world casino poker rooms and card rooms. This allows for greater speed in all aspects of the Internet playing experience. Naturally, it also means that you are not participating in the overall experience of the community of live human beings who exchange social intercourse over a poker table, as is the case with games in real-world poker. But it also means that you have absolute anonymity, and as a result you can use that to your benefit by carefully observing the games as they are played and learning everything that you can about your opponents and their playing patterns. This allows you to better yourself in a multitude of situations and circumstances, not the least of which is the ability to experience Texas Hold'Em, as well as the many other games offered in Internet casinos and poker rooms, for limits that would be unheard of in the real world. You can cheaply experience games that in the real world could cost you many thousands of dollars over many years, with the outcome being that you truly can learn more in one year of playing on the Internet than you probably would in ten years of playing in the real world (as Doyle Brunson so succinctly put it), and do this for about one-tenth the cost.

Perhaps the greatest advantage of all is just that—the ability to be able to learn and experience and actually play these poker games against real live players instead of just the computer program, as was the case for the simulations available for home computers prior to the advent of the Internet. The second greatest advantage to Internet poker is the fact that you can gain this experience by playing for free money, in Internet poker rooms called "play money." Every poker site that I mention in this book offers free play money with which to experience their games, and they will replenish that free money as many times as you need after each twenty-four hours. When you are finally ready to play for real money, all of the poker sites I mention in this book offer very low limits, often structured games for just pennies, nickels, and dimes, all the way up to whatever structured limits players wish to play, including private tables, shorthanded tables, heads-up matches, and as many varieties thereof as players care to play. All of this information is available by looking at those various sites in ring game menus, as well as tournament menus, and in the multitude of information about themselves and their games as is offered on their sites. To make it even easier for you to gain this experience and expertise, I profile two of the best poker sites currently on the Internet—PartyPoker.com and PokerStars.com. You are probably familiar with PartyPoker.com because they host the PartyPoker Million WPT tournament seen on television every year. You are probably familiar with PokerStars.com also because they produced the incredible winners of the 2003 and 2004 WSOP championships—Chris Moneymaker in 2003 and Greg Raymer in 2004. Most of these champions won their entries into the WSOP main event on PokerStars.com. I have therefore selected these two great poker sites for individual profiles in their own chapters in this book, because I wanted to show you the very best that the world of Internet poker currently has available. The section Featured Directory of Online Poker Rooms also shows you other poker sites that I personally like, and the Directory of Online Poker Rooms lists other poker sites that can provide you with valuable comparisons between the various experiences. I encourage you to patronize these sites because they are the best that the world of the Internet has to offer to date, especially so for PartyPoker.com and PokerStars.com.

I would also like to give an honorable mention to PokerRoom.com, on which site I also play quite frequently and which I profiled in detail in my earlier book *Powerful Profits from Poker*. This excellent poker site appears in my Featured Directory of Online Poker Rooms at the end of this book, and you can read more details about it in my earlier poker book.

Your overall poker-playing experience on the Internet will be governed primarily by two significant factors:

- The quality of your computer and your Internet connection
- Your knowledge, skills, and abilities, and expertise in the poker games of your choice

Quality of your computer and Internet connection are absolutely essential ingredients if you want to play Internet poker. Without a good computer, and equally good Internet connection, you will still be able to play, but your experience will not be nearly as good as it could be if you upgraded your system and ISP (Internet Service Provider). To achieve a quality experience playing Internet poker in the twenty-first-century, as minimum requirements for your computer you should have at least the following:

- Microsoft Windows XP 2000 home edition
- Minimum Intel Pentium 4 processor, or comparable AMD
- 40 Gb hard drive
- 1GHz of speed
- Minimum 256 RAM (preferably at least 512)
- Broadband access to a cable modem at a minimum of 128 Kbps upstream and 256 downstream

If you don't have at least this for your computer, you should upgrade it immediately if you plan to play on the Internet on a frequent basis. Of course, these recommendations are for PCs. If you have a Macintosh, then I'm sorry for you, but you have to make do. Macintosh computers are great for designing graphics, such as in the world of advertising and marketing, but they are not ideal for Internet poker. If you want to play on the Internet as a frequent poker player you should acquire a PC with at least the above minimum specifications, and preferably considerably more than that.

Knowledge, skills, abilities, and expertise in poker are powers you can acquire not only from reading this book and my earlier poker book—as well as my earlier book on Internet gambling—but also from the various information available on the poker sites that I recommend in my books, as well as the many magazine articles and other great books on poker that now abound everywhere. The sum total of the knowledge that you acquire will together contribute toward enriching your mind with the necessary and required information, which you will then need to translate into your actual experience and the doing of it. Theoretical knowledge and its practical applicability are two vastly different sides of the same success coin. Many people may have great theoretical knowledge, but that in itself isn't enough for them, because they are pretty lousy at applying it to the real-world experiences, including cyberexperiences in Internet poker games. On the other hand, there are players who have gained a great deal of "streetwise" knowledge by playing various poker games without actually studying any books or texts about them, and practically little or no theory of the games, but who are able through this experience acquired over many years to play quite well, and often profitably. However, many such players are usually limited by their lack of overall knowledge, and as a result their combined experience-based skills usually lead them to only advance up to a certain point. Ideally, you will take all of the information that I offer in this book, and my previous books, and from all of it together create the overall general tapestry of that which constitutes your knowledge of poker games and the Internet playing experience. Thereafter, whether or not you will be able to actually translate that knowledge into real-world success and do so well and profitably largely depends on yourself and the person you are. Some readers of this book will find it easy to translate this knowledge into real-world success, whereas others may not find it as easy, and perhaps some may not find it easy at all. I have gone to great lengths to try to make everything as clear and as easy as possible, but because I don't know you and your circumstances, I cannot possibly anticipate how well you will take what I have created and apply it to your own personal success rates. But one thing I do know for sure: You will be far better as an Internet poker player for having read this than those who have not. And that, dear friends, is the ultimate purpose of this as well as all of my other books.

# *Powerful Profits from*

# *INTERNET POKER*

# Cyberspeak

In order to get you prepared and prepped, this short chapter introduces you to some of the online language that you will find commonly used as you play Internet poker. You can witness the comments made by other players through the chat box windows. Cyberspace poker has a language of its own and most of it is in a very abbreviated form. It is quite a unique language that has evolved from the need for speed and the ability to transmit comments and observations from one player to another without the necessity of spending a great deal of time at the computer keyboard. Although voice-recognition technology is already available, it is not yet available or applicable to Internet poker rooms. Therefore, in order to chat through the chat box windows, players have to use the computer keyboard to type their messages. Sometimes this can be very distracting and it can also be a problem, especially if you are one of those who are digitally challenged and whose fingers may be able to do the walking, but typing is a considerably more difficult proposition. In order to overcome this, cyberspace poker players have developed a language all their own, and one that consists of several symbols used on the keyboard that, when read, communicate a person's message quite clearly, although you first have to know what it means. Such cyberlanguage is composed of many hundreds of characters, but only very few of them are actually useful to this discussion in this book. As you play Internet poker, you will become exposed to many more such expressions, since newer ones are being created on almost a daily basis.

## CYBERSPEAK DICTIONARY

Following is a list of the most commonly occurring expressions in cyberlanguage, as they apply to Internet poker.

| **Symbol** | **What It Means** |
|---|---|
| nh | Nice hand |
| n1 | Nice one |
| gg | Good game |
| gh | Good hand |
| gl | Good luck |
| ty | Thank you |
| tu | Thank you |
| yw | You're welcome |
| ur | You are |
| nf | Nice fold |
| np | Nice play |
| tx | Thanks |
| np | No problem |
| u2 | You too, meaning You also *or* You as well |
| gf | Good fold |
| ck | Sick, *meaning something really bad* |
| zzzzzz | *means someone is falling asleep and acting very slow* |
| LOL | Laugh out loud—*when something is funny* |
| LMAO | Laugh my ass off—*when something is very, very funny* |
| ROFL | Rolling on floor, laughing—*when it is really funny!* |

This list provides you with the basics of cyberspeak and allows you to communicate with your fellow Internet poker players in a manner acceptable and immediately identifiable by them, especially those who are more familiar with playing in cyberspace. It will also immediately demonstrate to every player that you have familiarity with the Internet, and particularly in playing Internet poker. Therefore, even if you are very new to Internet poker and are only now starting to play, by putting in a few comments like this soon after you sit at the game, you will be able to showcase your expertise in Internet poker simply by knowing this language. This can help mask your newness and help you gain faster acceptability by the cyberspace poker–playing community. You can thereafter forgo the option to chat with your other fellow players and take more advantage of the recommendations and suggestions about the preservation of your anonymity which I will describe later in this book.

It is now time to jump headlong into the discussion of Internet poker by beginning with the most popular Internet poker game of all—Texas Hold'Em.

# Texas Hold'Em

If you have read my earlier book *Powerful Profits from Poker*, you already know the depths of discussion to which I have taken the game of Texas Hold'Em in that book. Although that book was written primarily for playing the game in real-world casino poker rooms and card rooms, nevertheless many of those playing principles and items of knowledge leading to skill, as well as the principle of transference of knowledge into skill and experience, also apply to cyberspace poker. If you have not yet read *Powerful Profits from Poker,* I encourage you to do so because this chapter is a continuation of the discussion begun in that book, as it applies to Internet poker. I am not going to duplicate the many great details that I have presented in that book, but instead I supplement those discussions with additional commentary, observations, and recommendations as they apply to play of Texas Hold'Em specifically for the Internet.

## INTERNET TEXAS HOLD'EM

The first thing you will notice about Internet Texas Hold'Em is that there is a huge variety of games and limits from which to choose. Internet poker rooms offer something that land-based casinos cannot, and that is a choice of games that cannot only be played for free money—which is basically virtual play money supplied by the Internet poker room for you to play with for free, and which can be refilled on a twenty-four-hour basis each time you lose it up to the usual amount of about 1,000 play money dollars—but also games that can be played for real money from as low as one-cent to two-cent limits. Even if you are an absolute novice in the game, and you do not wish to practice with free money, but instead wish to enter the world of real-money play and gain the experience and thrills while doing so without it costing you an arm and a leg, you can easily enter a multitude of such games at these extremely low limits. Although not all Internet poker sites offer games in these penny ante limits, just about every Internet poker site available, including those that I feature in this book, offer games from at least $.25 to $.50 limits or, more commonly, limits from $.50 to $1 and up. At these small limits anyone can experience the thrill of playing this great poker game for real money, while at the same time investing very little in gaining such education. Prior to the availability of the Internet, poker experience such as this usually took many years to acquire, and almost always at great expense. If you have watched any of the television broadcasts of the WPT and WSOP championship games, you probably have noticed that they all play the game of Texas Hold'Em in such major tournaments, and you probably have taken notice of the many interviews conducted with the grand and great old road gamblers. People like Doyle Brunson and Amarillo Slim, to name just two among the surviving great road gamblers, often take time to talk during those interviews about how long it took them to acquire the great level of expertise they now possess. They often mention the fact that during the age of the Internet, a great many of the new poker players are able to play more hands in one month than they could in a year and as a result can gain years' worth of experience in playing no-limit Texas Hold'Em. In fact, Doyle Brunson at the recent World Series of Poker commented on just such a thing as a great crop of Internet poker players descended upon the World Series and made such a huge impact on this time-honored championship. His were truly prophetic and insightful words whose meaning should not be lost on you, either while reading this book or thereafter. What you are about to learn concerning Internet Texas Hold'Em, as well as all the other Internet poker games that will be mentioned—and in general acquire Internet poker–playing expertise—was impossible for those great traditional players of this game in years past. As you enter the world of Internet poker, and specifically Internet Texas Hold'Em, you will be able to learn in just one year what would have taken you several years on the road in the olden days, and do so for the price of nickels and dimes, and perhaps merely dollars, instead of hundreds and thousands and tens of thousands of dollars in those days past. You will gain familiarity with how the game is played, and you will gain familiarity with how to play for real money under a variety of situations and circumstances, including a great range of opponents in limit cash games, and also a multitude of tournaments.

To accomplish this and provide you with a lasting benefit that spans not only the Internet, but also extends to the real-world poker rooms and card rooms, and the real world's tournaments, you first have to realize that the world of cyberspace poker is completely different from the world of poker in real-world casinos. There are substantial differences, many of which I will discuss later on in this book, and particularly in the chapters on strategy. However, the first thing you should notice is that Texas Hold'Em played on the Internet is not only considerably faster than in the real world, but also vastly more volatile. It is faster because in cyberspace everything is dealt by the program and not by a human dealer, and also because you are facing your opponents and your game only in cyberspace and not in real world and, therefore, there are no distractions, no mistakes in chip handling, no errors in shortchanging the pot by putting in the wrong amount of the call or raise, no discussions among players other than in the chat box—which does not detract from the speed or efficiency of the game—and generally none of the procedural problems that often distract from the speed and efficiency of dealing the game in the real world. You will face hands at about the rate of double that of the real-world Texas Hold'Em games, which means that you will face twice the cost, twice the blinds, and twice as many decisions. Volatility will increase commensurately not only with all these factors but also with the multitude of and variety of opponents you will be facing. Circumstances like this, particular only to Internet poker, will provide you not only with the opportunity to experience profitability at an equally higher rate commensurate to real-world poker rooms, but also the danger of losing your bankroll twice as fast. In addition, you may experience attrition of your bankroll twice as fast due to increased frequency of blinds, antes, as well as pots lost to inexperienced players who got lucky on you. In fact, one of the most important aspects of your experience on the Internet (as I will mention in my chapters on strategy) will be your ability to discipline yourself and overcome adversity. There is nothing worse than learning how to play well, setting up a situation where you have the best of everything, and have your players trapped in a pot that is huge, only to lose this on the very last card when you discover that one of your opponents stayed in with all that expense of betting and wagering with absolutely no hand whatsoever, and then pulled out a one-card miracle that made him a hand that defeats you.

This is something that you will experience over and over again on the Internet, particularly in the low-limit games. You will also experience this in the lower buy-in tournaments because these games are largely populated by players who are new to the game and are experiencing how to play it—and often play horrendously and with really bad cards that have absolutely no hope, or very little hope. Under such circumstances, some of these players will get lucky on you and defeat the very good hands with which you play. And because the Internet poker rooms are populated with a majority of such players, you often face not just one such volatile opponent, but several. It is not unusual in these small-limit games to find yourself in a situation of having to face five opponents on the very last card, all of whom you know to have substandard holdings up to that point, as well as drawing nearly dead, or entirely dead. What you always have to fear in these lower-limit games are not those players who are drawing absolutely dead, but those who still have at least a glimmer of hope. In higher-limit games, and particularly in real-world poker games, you often have to face only one such volatile opponent, someone who obviously knows little or nothing about the game. But in the world of cyberspace—and in particular in these lower-limit games and small buy-in tournaments—you will often face at least two, perhaps three, of the five opponents that stay with you down to the river no matter what they have and no matter how much it costs. Under such conditions, you have to defeat the one least knowledgeable opponent *and* all the others, most of whom will also fall into this category. This means that while in real-world poker rooms, or at least in the higher-limit games, you usually would have to worry about only one opponent and therefore have the possibility of only 1:1 against you in such circumstances, now you may face an average of five opponents who are chasing you down, and therefore your odds are now 5:1 against you no matter what hand you have and no matter what its winning percentage may be inherent in the mathematics of the game. What is often missed in all of the analysis of various Internet poker games is the volatility formula of inexperienced and unknowledgeable opponents willing to invest any amount of money to see the very last card even when their hope is only a one card out, whose odds of appearance may be thousands to one against. Now multiply that by the fact that you may face an average of five such players, and you quickly discover than in Internet poker the tried-and-true principles of how to play your hands may not always be so when facing such a multitude of opponents who simply don't care about the money or anything else and will pay any price to see if they get lucky. Now you have to face five players trying to get lucky as opposed to one, which would normally be the case.

You also have to recognize and understand that you are now facing the possibility in any one hand of having at least five random hands playing against you, and this will make it very difficult for you to put other players on a hand. Since you are also unable to see the opponents themselves, and therefore picking up on any potential tells will also be very difficult (as I will discuss further later on in the chapters on strategy) your difficulties are now compounded by this volatility and the very nature of Internet poker that preserves anonymity among combatants. All of this discussion so far has led up to one simple piece of advice, and something that you absolutely must learn before you begin playing Internet Texas Hold'Em, or any Internet poker game, and advice that will be invaluable to you no matter how long you play and at no matter what limits you play. And that is this: don't get rattled—remember your discipline.

Where most Internet poker players fail the most often is precisely in this one area, and that is the loss of self-discipline. When facing situations of protracted losses as well as horrendous beats, they become rattled, lose confidence, start playing loose, and lose more money, which then leads them to get more agitated and lose even more confidence, and all of this leads to their loss of self-discipline. Acquiring such discipline, and then being able to maintain it as you continue to play Internet poker, and particularly Internet Texas Hold'Em, will be the hardest thing you ever have to learn to do. Very few poker players ever have it to an extent where they can consistently maintain their focus and concentration to a point of continued profitability. There are examples of such players who have made their way into the WPT tournaments, in particular WPT champion Eric Lindgren who is known by his Internet moniker "E-Dog." There are, of course, many others, including players who play exclusively on the Internet and do extremely well. You do not have to be a world champion, or be on television, or be famous at all in order to be a successful and profitable poker player. If you enjoy playing Texas Hold'Em, and you enjoy playing in cyberspace, you can easily enjoy yourself in a multitude of levels of profitability without ever having to publicize this or extend your success any further than where you wish to be. Many play purely for the enjoyment, while others play for supplementary income, and some even reach the rarefied atmosphere of professional poker players and play for a living. It really doesn't matter at which level you wish to play. Even if your interest is only to play for the entertainment aspect, recognizing that you are sitting in the comfort of your own home and are able to interact with players from all over the world, then this is perfectly fine for you. I hope that your interest is also to play a very good game, and to make money at it, no matter at which level you have selected to play.

Even if you only play at the $.50 to $1 level, or at any level where you invest real money, it would be foolhardy to assume that you simply wish to lose your money. Instead, we all assume that you wish to win, even if it is only a few cents or a few dollars. Even if you play at stakes where your buy-in is only $10 and your stakes are only $.25 to $.50, I think I will be correct in assuming that you will enjoy the game far more if you win $5 at the end of your session as opposed to losing $5 at the end of your session. Although the swing of $5 in profit versus $5 in losses is probably not very high, and the loss of the money will probably not impact you negatively, nor will the profit of $5 alter your lifestyle, I think that if you chose to play Internet poker for real money you have most likely done so not only because you wish to be entertained by this hugely popular game, but also to make it profitable no matter what the level. To play otherwise is perhaps something that some players may do, but I don't think you are one of them, particularly if you are reading this book. By making an effort to improve your game, and to learn something about Internet poker, and in this chapter about Internet Texas Hold'Em in particular, it is pretty clear that no matter what you do in your choices of games, your intent is to improve your game, and that means to improve your profitability while playing Internet poker. It is to these ends that this book is written, and to no other. While it is possible to enjoy yourself purely for the entertainment aspect of playing Internet poker, regardless of the amount of money that it may cost you, I assure you that playing profitably on a consistent basis is far more entertaining and enjoyable, even at the lowest of all limits. Therefore, to conclude this first piece of Internet Texas Hold'Em advice, simply remember that no matter how bad things get for you, the foundation of your success in Internet Texas Hold'Em, as well as in all of the Internet poker games you may choose, is a very strong sense of self-discipline. This will help you to overcome all of those volatilities and adversities and directly lead to not only your increased confidence in your game and abilities, but also to increased profitability over all.

## THE BEGINNING

At the beginning of everything there are always choices. Playing Internet Texas Hold'Em is no different. There are good choices and bad choices. The good choices will result in profitability, and the bad choices will not. The first thing you need to learn is that you *have* choices, and that everything you do depends on the very *first* choices you make. Naturally, your first choice is whether or not to play at all, but we assume here that you have already made that decision. Once you make the decision to play Internet Texas Hold'Em, your next decision is where. As mentioned previously, I recommend that you play on those poker sites that I feature in great detail, particularly PartyPoker.com and PokerStars.com. Both poker sites have a great many games to choose from and offer some of the best Texas Hold'Em games, as well as other poker games, on the Internet. At PartyPoker.com, you can participate in many games and also participate in tournaments where you can win your entry into that famous poker cruise that is called Party Poker Million, and which is featured on the WPT tour.

PokerStars.com is the home of the two recent WSOP champions. Both Chris Moneymaker in 2003 and Greg Raymer in 2004 have won their entry into the WSOP championship by playing at this site. I have selected it not only because they have great games and a great variety of games and terrific and secure customer support, but also because it is the home of champions in the WSOP. You can read more about PokerStars.com in the chapter devoted to it in this book.

I recommend both of these sites because they offer complementary varieties of Texas Hold'Em games as well as other Internet poker games and tournaments. You can very easily accommodate play on both of these sites as well as take advantage of their very liberal deposit bonuses and numerous player incentives as well as free tournaments. Playing on both sites also allows you to experience the varieties of players whom you will encounter, and this will build for you your sense of discipline and confidence so that you can become a great Internet poker player at anytime and in any game.

Your second choice is, of course, which game to play. Since we are discussing Texas Hold'Em here, you would first scroll down to the menu that lists games in Texas Hold'Em. You then have to decide at which limit you wish to play, or if you wish to play pot-limit or no-limit cash games, or if you wish to play tournaments. If you wish to play tournaments, you have to click on the corresponding tab, as opposed to the one that says "Cash Games" or "Ring Games." I will talk about tournaments in just a little bit, so for right now we will concentrate on limit cash games. Which limit you select will depend on the amount of money you have available. Here I'm talking about real-money games and not play-money games, because I am assuming that by the time you get to read this far into this book you have already understood what is meant by play money and have already tried that out for yourself. Now that you are ready to play in real cash games, what you can afford will be determined by how much money you have available. Remember that Internet poker is considerably more volatile than land-based poker. Although when I play land-based poker I can very easily approach a \$4–\$8 limit in a half kill* Texas Hold'Em game with a \$100 buy-in, in Internet poker games a \$100 buy-in would be nowhere nearly enough for this level of action. This is largely because you will often be facing

*In a kill game, if a player meets certain criteria (such as winning two pots in a row), the stakes are doubled for the next hand. In a half kill game, the stakes are increased 50 percent.

more than twice the number of hands that you would in real games, but also because of the other factors that contribute to the volatility of Internet poker, such as the fact that you cannot see your opponents and therefore cannot adjust your game according to any perceived personal habits, such as tells. The volatility of your opponents also has to be added into the equation, as we have already discussed here and as I will discuss again in greater detail later on, particularly in the chapters on strategy.

A $100 buy-in in Internet poker will provide you with a good bankroll for a $.50 to $1 limit game, and perhaps a $1–$2 limit game. Higher limits than that will require commensurately higher bankrolls. The reason why I'm mentioning this is the important adage of poker: don't play undercapitalized. It is far better to approach a game with a higher bankroll than would perhaps be recommended, than to do so with a lesser amount. You must remember that whatever game you choose in cyberspace, the fluctuations in your bankroll will be much higher than anywhere else, particularly in comparison to similar games in the real-world casino poker rooms and card rooms. For reasons already explained earlier, and those that follow later on in this book, your choice in the selection of game limits must be determined by the amount of your available cash on deposit at the poker site. For land-based poker games, in real-world casino poker rooms and card rooms, the generally accepted formula for calculating the amount of bankroll that you need in order to sit at any game is fifty times the amount of the big blind. Therefore, if you approach a land-based $4–$8 limit cash game, your bring-in bankroll should be $400. Although this may appear to be inordinately high for the limits as stated, the point is not that you will spend that much money or invest that much money in your buy-ins, but that you have that bankroll available. Sometimes you may find yourself in a terrific game, but as is the case with all such games, the swings in the volatility of them mandate not just the monster pots available for you to collect, but also the cost to contest such pots become commensurately higher, and sometimes you may not actually win them. In such circumstances, having the available bankroll at your disposal can provide you with the confidence factor necessary to be able to overcome such fluctuations, and therefore provide you with the opportunity to exploit such great games to full and great profit. This same formula can easily be applied to Internet Texas Hold'Em games, as well as to other poker games, and this brings us to your next choice.

How much money do you have available? If you are going to play a Texas Hold'Em game on the Internet at the $.50 to $1 limits, then your buy-in should be $50 out of that $100 bankroll that you have. This is following the same formula described above. The same applies to whatever limits you have chosen for yourself, and that is determined by the amount of money you are able to deposit at that particular Internet poker site. I will discuss how to make deposits, how to make withdrawals, and how to manage your money safely and securely in the chapters about my two favorite Internet poker sites, which as you by now know are PartyPoker.com and PokerStars.com. For right now, let's focus on the fact that you have learned how to make such deposits, and that you have made a deposit commensurate with the kinds of limits you have chosen to play.

Your next decision now becomes which table to choose.

Do this by scrolling to the menu of the games that are available at the limits of your choice. Again, the chapters on PokerStars.com and PartyPoker.com will show you not only the welcome screens but also the various menus and game screens, as well as the table screen for the games themselves. It is from one such menu that offers games of Texas Hold'Em in your limits of choice where you will select the game you wish to play.

You will find the selection of games that are either ten-handed, or shorthanded, with anywhere from heads up tables, up to five or six players per table, all the way up to ten players per table. Once you determine that there is an available seat at the table, you simply double-click on the highlighted table and proceed to that particular game table. Or, which is also quite common, you can simply click on the on-screen icon that says something like "Go to table." (The image of such a game table is shown in the chapters that follow later on in this book.) If no seat is available at the game of your choice, you can click on an icon near this menu that says Waiting List. By clicking on this icon your screen name will automatically be entered into the waiting list, which may or may not already have several other players waiting for a seat. If other players are waiting for a seat, then your name will be placed in the next order to the others. Then as seats become available, that list will grow progressively shorter until it becomes your turn, and when the next seat becomes available you will automatically be taken to that particular game table by the game software, where you will be asked to click on the available seat. Once you click on an available seat, you will receive a prompt asking you to select the amount from your available remaining bankroll with which you want to buy in to this game at this table. If, for example, you have $100 available in your bank at that poker site, and you have selected a $.50 to $1 limit Texas Hold'Em game, you can simply enter the amount of $50 in whole amounts and no cents and then click OK, and the software will then deduct $50 from your available playing bankroll that is deposited on that site, and add it to your buy-in chip amount for that particular game table. Once this is accomplished, you will then be prompted to click the button that says Sit-In, and once you do that you are now active at the table. You will then be further prompted to select a small box on the display in the game table window that says something like Auto Post Blinds and Antes. If this icon is not automatically selected by the site, you should always select it because this will allow the software to automatically post for you all your blinds and antes, and do so in turn. However, if it is not immediately your turn to post such blinds, and you wish to wait for the big blind before you enter the game, you should also click the icon: Wait for the Big Blind. This means that although you will be sitting at the table as an active player, you will not be dealt in until it becomes your turn to post the mandatory big blind. Sometimes this is to your advantage, such as when you enter just before the big blind, while at other times it is not to your advantage to wait because you are in late position, and therefore it becomes worthwhile for you to post the big blind at that time.

Therefore, my recommendation is that if you are playing at the lower limits you should always post the big blind after sitting down to a game table if you are in late position, or at least in late-middle position, and to *not* post the big blind but *wait* for the big blind if you are in early-middle position, middle position, and particularly early position. When sitting down at the table, choosing to post the big blind when the available seat was in late position provides you the opportunity to be able to witness the action and perhaps reap some early profits. It is worth the investment in the lower-limit games, although I would not recommend this for the higher limits because the cost of the blind is not worth the receiving of the random hand for which you have to pay first. I also do not recommend making this play in middle or early middle position, and especially not so in early position when you are just one or two off the big blind anyway. Wait to see those few hands, and observe what everybody is doing, and how they are playing, and only commit your money when you are in the mandatory bet anyway. This will be particularly useful when you go to higher limits because there a bet saved becomes more important than a bet invested in order to capture some early profitability.

Once you have made it to the table, your next choice becomes your starting hand selection. In order for you to decide exactly which hands are playable and which aren't, as well as in which position they should be played and how, I will first refer you to my earlier book *Powerful Profits from Poker*, in which I have spent a lot of time presenting precisely these kinds of hands, as well as their rank of importance. In that book I present not only a modified top ten starting hands selection for Texas Hold'Em, but also the top forty starting hands for Texas Hold'Em. Although that book is primarily for play in real-world casino poker rooms or card rooms, the principles of Texas Hold'Em are universal, no matter where they are played. This means that they apply equally well to Internet Texas Hold'Em.

Although there are differences between Internet Texas

Hold'Em and land-based Texas Hold'Em games as they are found in real-world casino poker rooms and card rooms, the principles that form the basis for the selections that constitute the top starting hands for the game follow the same mathematical principles, and are therefore equally applicable to both situations. Consequently, assuming that you have now read and learned those starting hands for Texas Hold'Em as described in those relevant chapters in that book, I will now supplement those discussions with the following list of playable Texas Hold'Em hands as created specifically for the Internet:

**Texas Hold'Em Hands You Can Play from Late Position**

Ace-5 suited
Ace-4 suited
Ace-3 suited
Ace-2 suited
King-8 suited
King-7 suited
King-6 suited
King-5 suited
King-4 suited
King-3 suited
King-2 suited
Queen-9 suited
Jack-7 suited
10-7 suited
9-6 suited
9-7 suited
8-6 suited
8-7 suited
7-5 suited
7-6 suited
6-5 suited
5-4 suited
4-4
3-3
2-2
King-9 offsuit
Queen-9 offsuit
Jack-8 offsuit
Jack-9 offsuit
10-8 offsuit
10-9 offsuit
9-8 offsuit
9-7 offsuit
8-7 offsuit

**Texas Hold'Em Hands You Can Play from Early Position**

Ace-King suited
Ace-Queen suited
Ace-Jack suited
Ace-10 suited
King-Queen suited
King-Jack suited
King-10 suited
Queen-Jack suited
Queen-10 suited
Jack-9 suited

**Texas Hold'Em Early Position Hands (cont.)**

| | |
|---|---|
| Jack-10 suited | 7-7 |
| 10-9 suited | Ace-King offsuit |
| Ace-Ace | Ace-Queen offsuit |
| King-King | Ace-Jack offsuit |
| Queen-Queen | Ace-10 offsuit |
| Jack-Jack | Queen-10 offsuit |
| 10-10 | Queen-Jack offsuit |
| 9-9 | King-Jack offsuit |
| 8-8 | King-Queen offsuit |

**Texas Hold'Em Hands You Can Play in Middle Position**

| | |
|---|---|
| Ace-9 suited | 10-8 suited |
| Ace-8 suited | 9-8 suited |
| Ace-7 suited | 6-6 |
| Ace-6 suited | 5-5 |
| King-9 suited | King-10 offsuit |
| Queen-8 suited | Queen-10 offsuit |
| Queen-9 suited | Queen-Jack offsuit |
| Jack-8 suited | Jack-10 offsuit |

Naturally, you can play all top 10 hands in any position, so it's not necessary to list them again in each category. This also applies to some extent to the top 40 hands. How you play them in those positions, however, depends on a number of factors specific to that individual situation.

Learning these hands and playing them as indicated can provide you with a strong foundation for your continued success playing Texas Hold'Em on the Internet. They are particularly useful for play in cash games, including the lower-limit games, although playing them strictly and appropriately in the higher limits will provide for you even greater profitability. This is not only because such hands play very well in these positions, as listed, but also because the majority of your Internet poker opponents will simply not recognize the value of playing hands of this nature in these positions. Of course, knowing that you should play these hands in the stated positions does not immediately mean that you know *how* to play them *well*. To help you with this aspect of your poker game, I have included chapters on strategy not only in my earlier poker book, but also several chapters on strategy specifically for Internet poker later in this book. Suffice it to say for right now that selecting these hands in these positions will provide you with the best starting hand requirement discipline. Knowing these hands and the positions to which they apply also can allow you to best practice the strategy advice that you will learn, and adapt as your experience grows, as well as provide you with the opportunity to relinquish and get away from these hands accordingly. To give you a heads-up on strategy, I offer the following hints and tips and recommendations as they apply to these hands in particular, and to your overall approach to Texas Hold'Em games—cyberspace style:

## FIT OR FOLD

Remember that about two-thirds of all decisions concerning your hand after flop will happen on the flop. This occurs because the betting at the beginning is at the lower end of the limit range, and therefore you usually will see the first five cards for just the cost of that first round of wagers, even if you have to call a raise or two. Your two cards in the hole plus the three cards that are the flop consist of five cards total, and with only two more cards to come in this particular style of poker, that means that you have just seen more than two-thirds of the available potential of your hand. You can now not only gauge the potential value of what *you* have but also the potential value of your opponents' hands. Therefore, if your hand fits the flop you can continue, but if not, you can relinquish it cheaply.

## SELECTIVE AGGRESSION

I talk about this more in the chapters on strategy that follow later in this book (and I have also discussed this in greater lengths in my other poker books). Suffice it to say that selective aggression means that you have made a conscious and rational decision to continue with your hand in accordance with the value and playing principles embodied within its potential, and have done so by direct commitment and focus to a specifically identified goal, and not without it. Many players mistake naked aggression for selective aggression, and many more players have heard the word *aggression* spoken on television as something that is employed by successful poker players. What most of these Internet opponents forget is the simple fact that aggression alone will not succeed because such aggressive players will soon be discovered as blustering aggressive players and not ones who practice selective aggression with a purpose. Aggression without purpose is not selective aggression. Aggression without purpose is blustering aggression, often known as naked aggression, and inevitably leads to disaster. Even though such naked aggression may succeed in the short term, it will never succeed in the long term, and the long term may not necessarily be measured by numbers of hours. It can be as short as a few hands at that very game and table. Selective aggression, therefore, means purposeful aggression toward the desired and consciously conceived purpose.

## PLAY YOUR POSITION

Remember that in Texas Hold'Em, position is just as important as your proper and correct selection of starting hands and their play thereafter. The mistake that most Internet poker players make, and one that you may encounter most frequently, is not knowing what to play in which position and how to play it. The above list of hands that are playable from the positions indicated provides you with the knowledge of what to play in which position. Now remains the knowledge of *how* to play them, which you will acquire not only from the strategy sections later on in this book (as well as in my other poker books), but also from your continued experience as you grow and improve your skills. For right now, remember that late position in

Texas Hold'Em is tantamount to a golden opportunity and that it therefore should be exploited to its fullest possibility and potential. In late position you can easily play not only a greater variety of hands, but hands that you would throw away in early position. Such hands can now easily become raising hands. In late position in Texas Hold'Em games you can often win pots uncontested even if you don't have a hand, simply because you are last to act. Even when playing on the Internet, late position can allow you to fully exploit the few potential tells that you might be able to gain from the pattern play of your opponents. (You will learn more about what I mean by pattern play in the later sections on strategy, in those chapters of this book.)

Remember that just because you are in late position doesn't mean you should be foolhardy. Automatically entering the pot with inferior hands just because you are in late position is not the recommended strategy. Particularly if you are facing several raises before it is your turn to act. Just because you are in late position does not mean that your opponents acting before you do not have any hand with which to play. This is another mistake that many Internet players make; they assume that just because they are in late position they can control the action at the table, completely disregarding the very significant possibility that the opponents in front of them in the turn of action actually have a hand. Assuming that your opponents don't have anything just because you are in late position is a prescription for disaster and inevitably results in your opponents checking to you and letting you do their betting for them, then hammering you on later streets, causing you to lose far more money than you can ever hope to regain by playing your position well thereafter. Once you are caught as a late-position bluffer you will thereafter be so identified and it will take you a long time indeed to convince your opponents that you are now playing better. Nevertheless, this much said, you are still in the driver's seat when in late position in Texas Hold'Em, and in Internet Texas Hold'Em games in particular you can usually exploit this to great advantage. Just remember to do this well, not recklessly.

## PLAY TIGHT IN EARLY POSITION

Just as it is important to play your late position well, it is equally important to play your early position hands equally as well. In early position it is far more important to *save* money than to be overly aggressive and risk being raised by a player yet to act behind you, especially when you don't have hands that can stand the heat. This is another mistake that Internet poker players often make—playing too many hands in early positions. Whenever you find yourself in early position, which you inevitably will as the game goes round and round, significantly tighten your starting-hand standards. Try to see cheap flops without the cost of additional bets if you can, then continue with the hand only if it really hits you. Never play a hand from early position that saw a cheap flop and only hit middle or bottom pair (unless the entire round was checked and you saw a free card on the turn, and that card made you either trips or two pair). Be wary of hitting the flop with top pair and weak kicker, and even be careful when you hit two pair. How you play the hands from that point on depends on your observation of your opponents and the pace of that game, as well as your skills and the remainder of the strategy advice that I will get to in the chapters on strategy. For right now, remember that in early position you are far better advised to throw away the vast majority of your starting hands, if for nothing else but to avoid becoming trapped in a pot that you will eventually lose. Being in early position means that you are trying to save money, instead of trying to win it as you would in late positions. Saving money in first and early positions is just as important as winning money in late positions. Money saved here means that you will not have to recover it later, and it will save the attrition of your bankroll. Although sometimes you discover that you threw away hands that would have won, it is far better for you to see that *without* having invested in the risk that is the factor in continuing with such hands than it would be in you committing so many bets only to discover that you did not win. For every one hand that you throw away that you would have won, it is far more likely that you would have lost ten or more hands in which you would have invested multiple bets that would have quickly depleted your bankroll. This is yet another mistake that many Internet poker players make, and particularly so Internet Texas Hold'Em players at the lower limits and small buy-in tournaments. Such players risk too much with substandard hands in early positions and therefore cause themselves to lose their bankroll faster, or to gain a quick exit out of tournaments. Remember: Whenever you find yourself in early position, you are faced with the choice of saving your money, and money saved here will mean money that you do not have to recover later; that means that when playing in late positions the money you win will now be money that is profit, instead of money that has to recover the costs of bad choices in early positions.

## DON'T FALL IN LOVE WITH BIG SLICK

As you play more Internet Texas Hold'Em, you eventually encounter a wonderful phenomenon that you can exploit for profitability in many situations and circumstances. In Texas Hold'Em games on the Internet, especially in the lower limits, but also extending to middle and higher limits, you often find players who fall in love with "big slick," suited or not. Just because the hand of Ace-King looks so wonderful, suited or not, you still have to remember that big slick is nothing but a drawing hand. It is not a made hand, and it needs to hit the flop to improve, and certainly to hit the turn or the river to continue to be the powerhouse hand, or for the turn or the river to miss your opponents entirely thereby preserving the value of the hit on the flop. Many Internet poker players make the big mistake of playing big slick as if it were a pair of Aces or Kings. Pairs of Aces and Kings are the top two powerhouse starting hands in Texas Hold'Em, not only because they win comparatively the majority of times, but primarily because before the flop they are *made hands*, and therefore considerable favorites against drawing hands. The hand of Ace-King, suited or not, is still nothing more than a drawing hand, no matter how pretty it looks. As obvious as this observation may be, many Internet Texas Hold'Em players simply do not recognize it, or do not pay attention to it even if they do know it. Sometimes they even argue with you over it, particularly when you play against them with pocket Aces and Kings, and they hit two pair with their big slick only to discover that they are facing a set. In such situations, more often than not they are drawing all but dead. They lament and argue their bad luck and even write messages to you in the chat box telling you how lucky you were, completely oblivious to the fact that *they* were significant underdogs prior to the flop, and even more so following the flop. Therefore, you should remember not to fall in love with big slick because big slick is not a made hand, and needs to hit the flop to improve, and then needs to continue to improve on the turn and river either by hitting additional cards, or for the flop to avoid hitting cards that would benefit your opponents.

## TEXAS HOLD'EM IS NOT LIKE OTHER POKER GAMES

What many Internet poker players also fail to understand is that Texas Hold'Em is not like other poker games, particularly not Seven Card Stud. Often players who venture into the world of cyberspace to play poker have had some experience playing in various venues, mostly at home or in social clubs. Usually the games played there are stud-style games, most often either Five Card Stud or Seven Card Stud. In fact it is a known truth that the majority of poker players who now play Texas Hold'Em got their start by playing Seven Card Stud. Texas Hold'Em became such a hugely popular game primarily because players who had familiarity with Seven-Card Stud found that Texas Hold'Em looked very similar to them. Just like Seven Card Stud, Texas Hold'Em uses a total of seven cards, from which the best five cards constitute the winning hand. However, that is about as much similarity as there is between the two games, and even this similarity is misleading. In Seven-Card Stud, every player receives his own seven cards, and he has to compete against the seven cards being dealt to his opponents. This makes it considerably easier to keep track of the cards that are exposed, and thus make calculations as to which cards are left, leading you to be able to determine the viability of the hand that you are still hoping to get, as well as the hands that your opponents may be drawing to. In Texas Hold'Em, such determinations are more difficult to make, primarily because you can see only the two cards that are your hole cards, and then only the three cards that are the flop, and then only two more remaining cards on the turn and the river. Therefore, you see only a total of seven cards, if you proceed all the way to the river. In that event, your judgment as to the potential value of your hand as well as the potential holdings of your opponents depends in great amount not only on your ability to be able to calculate the mathematical probabilities and odds of such hands—your own as well as those of your opponents—but also your analysis of the methods and play of your opponents, the pace of the game, the potential knowledge and value and quality of the opponents whom you are facing, as well as the inherent and implied pot odds. All of these calculations have less to do with the cards you are holding and much more to do with the circumstances of the game at hand, and in particular with the value of the pot and the quality of your opponents. This is considerably different from Seven Card Stud; there you get to see so many more cards because every player will have four exposed cards before the final 7th-street river card is dealt. This makes it easier for you to be able to determine the value of the hands based on the cards, and less so on your opponents', or the situational analysis of the game in progress, although all these are equally important and contribute to your overall analysis and your end profitability in Seven Card Stud. In Texas Hold'Em you are committed to playing the situation and your opponents more than the cards themselves. This is what makes Internet Texas Hold'Em particularly difficult, because you have to analyze those situations without having the benefit of looking at your opponents. Therefore, it is very important that you remember that playing Internet Texas Hold'Em is not only highly dependent on the situations and circumstances that surround each and every decision in each and every game, as well as each and every hand, but also that the game is nothing like Seven Card Stud.

## RAISING AND FOLDING

Another situation that is a considerable problem to Internet Texas Hold'Em players is exactly when to raise and when to fold. As I mentioned in the immediately preceding paragraphs, Internet Texas Hold'Em in particular is situationally dependent. Your analysis of the game compared with your opponents' most likely hands is very important, as are your own experience and skills in the game. It is only based on the circumstances that you see as perceived in a particular hand in progress, as well as the totality of your analysis that has occurred prior to this hand being played, that will allow you to correctly determine when to raise and when to fold. Remember that the decision to raise or fold is far more position dependent in Texas Hold'Em and far less dependent on the cards that you happen to be holding. It is hard to create an accurate profile of your Internet opponents because you cannot see them as you would in real-world casino poker rooms or card rooms; nevertheless, it is possible for you to make determinations as to their particular playing acumen by observing how they do what and when they do it, as well as what kinds of hands they show down when they do. From all of this information you can then make the determination in the hand in progress, and only then make the appropriate decision of when to raise and when to fold.

In simplest terms, the best advice I can offer you about when to raise and when to fold is to pay attention to the starting-hand requirements listed earlier in this chapter and the positions to which they apply (as well as those I listed in my other poker books). Any of the hands identified for play in late positions, particularly those that contain higher pairs, and those that contain Ace-anything suited, can be considered raising hands. From early positions, only pocket Aces or pocket

Kings would be raising hands, with perhaps also Queens and Jacks depending on the circumstances, and especially on the number of likely opponents who will call such early position raises. Such early position raises are usually performed with these hands, as well as perhaps other hands of lesser values, if from your observational analysis of this particular game you can safely assume that the vast majority of your opponents yet to act behind you are likely to fold their hands to such early position raises, making your raise likely to significantly limit the field. It is for the purpose of limiting the field, and thus enhancing the potential win value of your hand, that most such early position raises are made. In middle positions, it is also your situational analysis that will make that determination.

Specifically, even better advice is what to do with your hands *before* the flop. Before the flop happens, the mathematics of poker—and in particular Texas Hold'Em—govern your decisions far more acutely because the variable circumstances have not yet happened. Therefore, before there is a flop, your decisions on when to raise and when to fold are far more clear-cut. In such situations, you can always raise with high pocket pairs all the way from a pair of 10s through a pair of Aces. Additionally, if you have pairs of Aces, pairs of Kings, or pairs of Queens, you can also re-raise if somebody else raises before it becomes your turn to act. Or, if somebody else raises your raise. In such situations, no matter in which position you happen to be, raising and re-raising allows you to shut out other players who may have wanted to see cheap flops with mediocre or substandard hands, and this therefore increases the value of your holdings, just like I described a little earlier for the situations pertaining to early position raising. Your chances of having the winning hands with these high pocket pairs by raising and/or re-raising improve exponentially as you are able to shut out other players, and thus prevent their hands from hitting the flop. Although this is difficult to do in Internet Texas Hold'Em—particularly in the small-limit games—it will nonetheless work the majority of the time. If you do not have such high pocket pairs, you can usually raise if you have a suited big slick, and even if you have an offsuit Ace-King, although only cautiously and only in middle to late positions.

In other positions you can also safely raise with Ace-Queen suited, Ace-Jack suited, Ace-10 suited, and even with King-Queen suited. Of course, in late positions you can also re-raise with any King-Queen, any King-Jack, any King-10, and even King-9, just about any pair, an Ace with any kicker, and even Queen-Jack, Queen-10, Jack-10, Jack-9, or Queen-9. These latest listings are far more playable when you are facing only the blinds and progressively less so if other players also call the blinds before it is your turn to act; this is especially so if there are players yet to act behind you and they either call your bet or, which is a significant danger sign, call your raise or re-raise you. As a simple rule, the more players that call the blinds before it is your turn to act in late position, the higher your standards of holdings need to be in order for you to put in a raise. If there is already a raise before it becomes your turn to act, then your play thereafter, including your option to re-raise the raiser, is determined by the strength of your hand. To make that decision and that determination, look again at the list of good starting hands for play in late position and act accordingly.

As far as throwing your hands away, that should be relatively easy given what we have just discussed, as well as given the list that was provided for play in late position, or for the other positions available in Texas Hold'Em Internet–style poker games. If you don't have a hand that fits those that were identified here, and the positions to which they apply, throw it away. And that is how you make your decisions prior to the flop, both to maximize your wins, your odds of winning, and to minimize your exposure to losses and expenses of playing.

For more strategy advice on Texas Hold'Em, I now again refer you not only to my other books on poker, but also to the chapters on strategy that follow later in this book. It is now time to move on to chapter 3 and discuss the second most popular Internet poker game—Seven Card Stud.

# Seven Card Stud

Seven Card Stud is probably the most popular poker game in the world, and it is played just about everywhere. But with the advent of the popularity of Texas Hold'Em games, Seven Card Stud games are beginning to go the way of the dinosaur. Especially so in the real-world casino poker rooms and card rooms, where Seven Card Stud has all but disappeared, with some exceptions in the very small limits, and in the middle to higher limit range. Even some of the major tournaments are now dealing exclusively Texas Hold'Em, leaving out all other games, particularly Seven Card Stud. The WSOP is the only remaining major tournament that also includes Seven Card Stud, as well as Stud/8 and other poker games. It is not hard to understand why. In the real world of casino poker rooms and card rooms, speed equals profitability because the casino charges a rake on each pot played. Although some of the higher-limit games charge a collection fee, or such a fee may be charged in card rooms where the various regulations do not permit rake-based games, the situation is all about equivalence. Casinos make money from the frequency of hands, and the faster the game the more money the casino makes if it is a raked game, and the more fun the patrons will have. By the nature of the game, in the real world Seven Card Stud games are notoriously slow. Even the fastest Texas Hold'Em games can average only about forty hands per hour, but Seven Card Stud games are usually only half that. At only twenty hands per hour or so, a great many of the players at the Seven Card Stud table will be doing a lot of sitting and waiting for hands to play, while two or three other players are involved in hands whose resolution may take many minutes. In today's fast-paced environment, not only in the casino business but in life in general, few players are willing to tolerate such a snail's pace in their poker game. Equally so, few casino poker rooms or card rooms are willing to tolerate a game that takes so long to play, with so few hands per hour, while requiring so much labor-intensive dedication and expense that produces such poor results in profitability. As a Seven Card Stud player, I personally find the demise of good Seven Card Stud games quite unfortunate, but understandable.

Fortunately for us all, we now have the Internet where there are many Seven Card Stud games available, in all limits and all varieties, including various derivatives like the Stud/8 or better, which I will describe next.

In my earlier book *Powerful Profits from Poker,* I have written chapters on both Seven Card Stud and Stud/8 or better. As I mentioned in chapter 2, it is not my intent here to duplicate those efforts. Instead, I again refer you to that book where much of these discussions are explained in great detail, while those that appear in this book are a continuation thereof, with specific modifications as they apply directly to Internet poker games. Playing Seven Card Stud on the Internet is better and faster than playing it in the real world. Not only because you are able to find a greater variety of games from which to choose, but primarily because of the speed of the game. Because cyberspace poker is dealt by the computer program, the actual shuffling and dealing of the cards is incredibly quick—and done at a speed that no human dealer could ever approximate. The result is an extremely enjoyable experience for playing poker, at least for something which can sometimes be considerably better than Texas Hold'Em. Although I like Texas

Hold'Em as well as everyone else these days, I have many fond remembrances of playing Seven Card Stud in casinos in Las Vegas when that was the game of choice among most players. Now in cyberspace I can experience the thrill of playing Seven Card Stud while at the same time remain comfortably in my home and enjoy a game at a speed that makes the game both exciting and enjoyable.

## BEGINNING CHOICES

As with all cyberspace poker games, your first choices are among the most important. When choosing to play Seven Card Stud, the first thing you will have to do is select the Seven Card Stud games from the on-screen menu of available games. Not many Seven Card Stud tournaments exist, so most of the games you will play will be ring games, commonly known as cash games. After you have selected the Seven Card Stud icon from the on-screen menu, the next thing you have to do is select the kinds of limits that you wish to play. There are two kinds of Seven Card Stud games commonly available in cyberspace:

- Nonstructured limit games
- Structured limit games

Having a game posted as "nonstructured limits" simply means that whatever the posted range of limits might be, at any time during any round of wagering you can bet from the smallest limit up to the highest. For example, the most common nonstructured limit games for Seven Card Stud are those that are $1–$5 nonstructured limits. This means that you can bet as low as $1 or as high as $5 during any round of wagering, as well as any amount in between. You do not have to bet or raise by a single structured amount, but can vary the amount that you wish to wager. You may wish to wager anywhere from $1 to $5 at any time. You can also raise by any such amount, as long as the raise matches the previous bet or exceeds it. For example, if someone in front of you before your turn to act wagers $2 and you wish to raise, when it comes your turn to act you do not have to raise only by matching bets to that $2 wager, which would be a raise of $2 for a total of $4 wager and would be so mandatory for structured games. In such a nonstructured game you can actually raise by any amount higher than those $2. You could raise by $3 to make it a $5 total bet, or you can raise by $4 to make it a $6 bet, or you can raise by the maximum $5 limit to make it a total of $7 to go. Such nonstructured spread limit games are common in casinos and poker rooms and card rooms everywhere in the real world, as well as in cyberspace. However, in cyberspace you find a different range of limits as well, from as low as $.05 to $.25, all the way up to whatever the amount can conceivably be. Most of the games played at the poker sites I feature in this book usually have limits starting as low as $.50 to $1 and up. The general range is from the small limits up to about $25-$50, and often higher depending on interest from players.

The second kind of Seven Card Stud limits are what is called "structured limits." Structured limit simply means that you have to bet one amount or the other and are not permitted to make wagers in increments in between these limits. To use the same example of the $1–$5 range as shown above, if this was a structured limit game this would mean that you would be permitted to bet only $1 on 3rd street, which is the first round of wagering after the posting of the antes and the bring-in, as well as permitted to wager only $1 on 4th street (unless there was an open pair on the board in which case the wagers would allow for the possibility of higher wagers up to the higher range of the limits), with the wager increasing to the maximum range of $5 bets on 5th street and thereafter. Although most Seven Card Stud games will not be of this particular structured range, I wanted to use this example just to show you the difference between a nonstructured and a structured range limit. Nonstructured Seven Card Stud games are usually found in the real-world casino poker rooms and card rooms, while structured limit games are usually found in cyberspace.

Such structured limits at the poker sites I feature in this book for Seven Card Stud usually begin with $.50 to $1, meaning that you are permitted to wager only $.50 on 3rd street and 4th street, and then only $1 on 5th street and thereafter, and are permitted to raise only by those structured amounts. The same applies to higher-limit structured Seven Card Stud games, the most common of which will be $1–$2 limits, $2–$4 limits, $3–$6 limits, $4–$8 limits, $5–$10 limits, $10–$20 limits, $15–$30 limits, and higher thereafter based on demand from players. All of these are structured limits, and they are so by design because in cyberspace most poker players are familiar with the structured games as those applied to Texas Hold'Em. Since in cyberspace just about every Texas Hold'Em game that has a limit posted is a structured game, Seven Card Stud games in cyberspace are usually played in such structured limits, as opposed to nonstructured methods. Cyberspace Seven Card Stud games are far better played in such structured limits because this not only speeds up the betting but also the decision making among players, and makes it a lot easier to program the game to play more efficiently and quickly. It also doesn't confuse the players who have learned to play structured games first, because they were never exposed to nonstructured games. Especially players who have begun their poker-playing experiences online where nonstructured games are practically nonexistent. Playing structured games makes your decisions much easier, and as a result the wagering methods and procedures, including raising and re-raising, are much more easily accomplished with the use of the Internet action buttons and icons, including the auto play in turn buttons provided on any table game screen. This significantly assists the popularity of Seven Card Stud poker in cyberspace, because it makes these procedures identical to those with which players are familiar from playing Texas Hold'Em. Even though cyberspace Seven Card Stud is just as different from Texas Hold'Em as Seven Card Stud games played in the real world are different from the real world Texas Hold'Em games, the standardization of the procedures and the structured limits makes it more familiar to a great variety and majority of cyberspace poker players, and if for nothing else but this I applaud these poker sites for making Seven Card Stud in cyberspace playable in this manner. It is a lot better game the way it is structured in cyberspace than it would be if it was a nonstructured game. Therefore, I will confine all of my discussions of Seven Card Stud to such structured games only.

Now that you have selected which game to play, and understand the difference between nonstructured and structured games, you are ready to sit at a Seven Card Stud game table with your choice of structured limits. Once you sit at the table and deposit whatever amount of money you have chosen to commit to this particular game table, the procedures for which are identical to those described in the chapter for Texas Hold'Em, what happens now are three things:

- You will be charged a mandatory ante.
- The invisible cyberspace dealer will deal cards to every active player.
- The lowest card by ranking value will be the mandatory forced bring-in.

The mandatory ante bet is just that, mandatory. The amount of this is commensurate with the limits you have chosen. For a game such as $1–$2 limits the mandatory ante bet is $.10. Generally, such a forced ante bet is either 10 percent of the smallest range of the limit, or $1 in most small-limit games. As you progress higher in limits, mandatory ante bets may increase and you will determine for yourself what this is. You can usually obtain this information from the on-screen instructions and game table menus that will tell you exactly what such ante bets are for this particular game. (For more discussion about the value of antes, and how they might increase, I refer you to my other poker books.)

The amount of the bring-in is usually half the smallest limit bet, or $1 in most small-limit games. The amount of such a bring-in may also vary depending on the limits you have chosen, and once again you will need to determine that from the information provided for you for the limits you have chosen at that particular game table. All of this information is readily available from the information page for each game table selection, or from the general instructions that can be accessed from the "How to play" tab on each of the poker sites I mention in this book. Seven Card Stud tables generally contain no more than eight players, as opposed to the ten players that are common in Texas Hold'Em games. In real-world casino card rooms and poker rooms, the Seven Card Stud table usually accommodates nine players, while Texas Hold'Em tables generally accommodate ten players, but may accommodate up to fourteen players. The standard fifty-two-card deck can easily accommodate up to fourteen Texas Hold'Em players but is unable to accommodate more than nine players in Seven Card Stud, because in Seven Card Stud each of the nine players receive their own seven cards, so if all nine players stayed to the bitter end there would not be enough cards to handle all of this action. In such a circumstance, there will be community cards dealt in order to accommodate this many players still in the hand. Fortunately, such situations almost never happen with all nine players remaining to the very end. Usually, in the small-limit games in the real world, there are about four or five players that continue with the action all the way to showdown. This can still often result in the deck running short, in which case the burn cards and the muck and the stub of the remaining deck are shuffled together and the remaining cards dealt. If there are still not enough cards for all players left in the action, one or more community cards are then turned and belong to every player still in the action up to that point, similar to those community cards as played in Texas Hold'Em.

In cyberspace, the limitations of the deck allow usually only about eight seated players at a table. Since it is extremely rare for all eight players to make it all the way to showdown, situations of the virtual dealer running out of cards are equally rare. But because the cyberspace deck does not display the burn cards, and does not display the muck, in the event of too many players left the virtual dealer would automatically reshuffle the virtual burns and virtual muck and continue with the dealing, and in extreme circumstances will display a community card. Don't worry about this, because such situations practically never occur, and I can attest to this from personal experience. In all those years I have played on Internet poker sites I have only experienced this a few times.

What you will experience is the inevitable occurrence of being the forced bring-in. This is determined simply by the lowest card by value and rank. If this happens to you, and it will, remember this is part of the game and put it down to the cost of the game itself, just like the forced blinds in Texas Hold'Em games. Being first to act in this manner in Seven Card Stud is not nearly as bad as being first to act in Texas Hold'Em, although being in early position is generally not a good thing in any poker game. In Seven Card Stud, however, you are better able to gauge the position and the value of your hand if you choose to continue with it, because on all streets your opponents' exposed cards provide you with a window to their potential holdings, as well as an assessment of the likely value of your hand relative to theirs. Sometimes the randomness of the dealing appears as if you are almost always the forced bring-in, and this often leads inexperienced Seven Card Stud players to have the erroneous perception and opinion that they are somehow being targeted. This is absolutely not the case, not in the real world and not in cyberspace.

In cyberspace poker, the computer algorithms that determine the randomness of the shuffled deck absolutely do not know you and do not know whether or not you are the forced bring-in. The computer program simply shuffles and deals strings of binary numerals, then cues the graphic interface portion of the application to display representations of the cards that the program matches up to the binary numerals that the program selected randomly to represent the cards that you happen to get in the position you occupy at that table. No one is out to "get you" and no one is trying to force you into more bring-ins than would ordinarily be your turn to post due to the randomness of the selection process. Many new cyberspace Seven Card Stud players who find themselves in the position of the forced bring-in, in what appears to be to them as an inordinate frequency, often form this wrong opinion and as a result consider cyberspace Seven Card Stud as somehow an unplayable game. This is a wrong opinion indeed, and usually formed only by the very uninformed and inexperienced. The dealing of the cards by the cyberspace dealer is really not a mechanical procedure like it is in the real-world casino poker rooms and card rooms, but is a natural outcome of the random shuffle of the software that plays the game.

In the real world, the dealer always deals to his or her left to right clockwise around the table, with the player in the first seat always receiving the first card and the player in the nine seat, or last seat, always receiving last card. This procedure is also upheld in cyberspace, but in cyberspace you do not see the dealer and therefore you do not see the actual hands and being dealt in that order. As soon as you become active at the table of your choice you will automatically be charged the ante for the next round, and this means that the cyberspace invisible dealer deals you the cards to which you are entitled by the randomness of the shuffle at that point. Once this is accomplished, the game then continues in the normal order of process for Seven Card Stud games.

Your next decision comes when your cards are dealt to you. In Seven Card Stud you are dealt two hole cards and one up card. This is the beginning of the first round of wagering, and it is called 3rd street. You now have several choices to make. Your first choice is whether or not to continue with the hand past this point. You will make this choice based on your knowledge of the game and strategy applicable to Seven Card Stud and the hand rankings and requirements. You can learn those by reading my other poker books, as well as focusing on some of the hints that I provide later in this chapter. Your choice, therefore, becomes whether to call the bets made before it becomes your turn to act (assuming you are not the forced bring-in), complete the bet of the forced bring-in if that had not already been made before it becomes your turn to act, raise, or fold the hand. Only folding the hand at this point will not cost you any money, other than your forced ante. Any action after the 3rd-street stage can only mean that you have chosen to continue with this hand and have therefore invested more money. Your next choices are determined on the remaining turns, which are 4th street, 5th street, 6th street, and 7th street, which is followed by the showdown. Whether or not you consider continuing with your hand past 4th street is directly dependent on the value of your hand and the relative value of your opponents' hands as you are able to gauge and judge them. For the proper assessment of such actions and strategy recommendations particular to the play of Seven Card Stud on this street, I again refer you to my earlier book *Powerful Profits from Poker* because in that book I have gone to great lengths to outline just precisely which are the best starting hands, and how to play hands on each of these streets. However, to provide you with some other examples here, consider the following.

In Seven Card Stud you will see many exposed cards. Therefore, it is important for you to play the cards far more than the players, particularly in cyberspace where you cannot gauge the potential strength and value of your opponents' hands by their physical mannerisms or reactions to previous acts and actions by other players.

Seven Card Stud offers the opportunity to learn and observe which cards are still active and which cards have been folded, simply by looking at the exposed cards from players not only among those who are still active, but in particular those that have folded their hands. Being able to remember which cards are "live" and which cards are "dead" will provide you with invaluable information that is not only relative to the hand that you have, or still hope to make, but in particular allows you to better assess the potential holdings of your opponents.

In Seven Card Stud it is very important for you to keep a mental track of which cards have already been used, such as those that are falling among the exposed cards of your opponents, in addition to those that have already been folded by players that are no longer participating in this hand. For example, suppose you are hoping to hit a straight, such as when in the first four cards you have an open-ender (which is one of the better early round hands in Seven Card Stud), and you therefore know that you need at least one of the remaining eight cards that can assist your hand (those being the four cards that can complete your straight to the highest card and four cards that can complete your hand by hitting the lowest end of it), but you have seen from among the exposed cards of your opponents, including those who have folded their hands up to this point, that all of the cards that you require to complete your straight to the highest have already been dealt out, and that two of the cards you require to complete the low end of the straight are already visible and among those cards that have fallen into hands of your opponents. This means that you are drawing dead to the high end of the straight because those cards are no longer live, and that you are drawing near-dead to the low end of the straight because you now have only two remaining cards that can possibly help you. In such a situation, unless you are drawing to a high straight with overcards to the board, or are at least suited with a live suit, you would now know that it is inappropriate for you to continue with this hand because your chances of making it are slim indeed, and even if you do catch that lucky card you will only make the low end of the straight and therefore might find yourself in a situation where you make your hand but still lose with it.

This example is often used in many texts and magazine articles, as well as in online discussion groups and in the help columns available on many poker sites, as it applies to flush draws. Since you know that there are only thirteen of each suit available, if you start on 3rd street with three to a suit but you see that the exposed cards of your opponents also contain a smattering of the suit that you require to complete your hand, you can now easily calculate exactly how many cards of your suit are still left for you to catch. In this example, since you have three of the cards to that suit and you see that five of your opponents are also showing one card to your suit each, that means that a total of eight cards from the available thirteen have already been used. Therefore only five available cards to that suit still remain, or at least are still left unknown to you.

In such a circumstance it is quite likely that one or more of your opponents also have matching cards of this suit among their hole cards, so this makes your suit all but dead for all intents and purposes. Unless those cards that you have as your starting three cards also have potential to make a hand other than this flush, you now know that you are drawing to a dead suit and therefore should relinquish your hand. Similar such considerations apply if this situation happens on 4th street or 5th street if your suit was considered by you to be live up to that point, but now you have seen the majority of the suit dealt out elsewhere. This is often called having your cards "fall elsewhere," meaning that whenever cards you might need are instead falling in the hands of your opponents and not yours, regardless of whether or not they help their hands or not, your draw to that suit is now all but dead. Sometimes, however, you can also use this knowledge and this method of calculating the value of your hands to your advantage, by also knowing that your opponents themselves do not have what they are perhaps representing. Oftentimes this happens when one or more players are drawing to the same flush. You may be one such player, and you may observe that one of your opponents appears to also be drawing to the same flush. If you have carefully analyzed the exposed cards, and remember those cards that were folded by those players who have not continued past whatever point in this particular game you now happen to be, you may now know something that your opponent does not. If your opponent is not a knowledgeable and experienced player, or not able to possess this kind of memory skills, he may consider his flush draw to still be live, while you already know that his flush draw is dead. Even though your opponent may now show three or four of the flush cards exposed on his board, assuming of course that you have continued up to 6th street at this point, he may be betting very aggressively in order to represent that flush, while you already know that he cannot have it. It is in circumstances such as this that you can play back at your opponent if you have any kind of a hand, including hands that could have normally been beaten by flush and which you would have thrown away if you were facing a board such as this and known that flush to still be potentially live. This is the advantage of Seven Card Stud, because it permits you to be able to study your opponents' holdings much more carefully, and make more accurate determinations not only to the value of your hand, but the potential risk value of your opponents' holdings. Since in cyberspace the cards are clearly displayed on your computer screen, and the game is played entirely in anonymity, it is easy for you to simply make notes even on a piece of paper rather than remembering all those cards in your hand if you cannot do so. I would encourage you, however, to practice your mental skills because this will keep you sharp and focused on the game. Nevertheless, if you are just beginning and are trying to train yourself and your mind to keep track of those cards, being at home in front of your computer allows you to jot down anything you want. Just remember that the cards that are still displayed as part of the active hands of your opponents are clearly visible on the screen, and therefore you can look at them at any time and don't have to remember them right then and there. All you have to do is remember, or write down, those exposed cards that were folded by players as they fold their hands. Being able to track cards successfully in this manner can substantially add to your profitability and expertise in playing cyberspace Seven Card Stud. This is the greatest advantage of cyberspace Seven Card Stud, because it is not only a much faster game than in the real world, but also a lot easier to keep track of the cards that you need in order to be able to make the proper playing decisions.

Other than choosing with which hands to begin, which are your starting hand choice decisions, your other most important decision will come on 5th street. This is because by that time there are five cards dealt to each active player remaining, and it is therefore possible that one or more of your opponents already have a made hand. If you do not have a made hand, and are still drawing to a hand, it is by this time that you should have paid close attention to those cards which are still remaining among the exposed cards of your opponents' holdings, and in particular those cards that have already been folded. Now you have to make the crucial determination whether or not your hand is still live, or if it is dead, as well as the determination of whether or not your live hand will indeed become the winning hand if it so improves. For example, if you see yourself drawing to a Queen high flush in hearts, and you see another player apparently drawing to an Ace high flush in spades, and you have observed carefully and know that both suits are still live, you now face the unenviable task of having to perhaps throw your flush draw away because it is clear that even if you get there and the contest comes down to the choice between your flush and your opponent's flush, it is obvious that yours will be the loser. Therefore, if on 5th street you do not have a made hand and therefore still have only a drawing hand, your determination and decisions are now very simple: You must be drawing to the nut hand, or risk the potential of actually making your hand and investing a great many bets only to see that it is the second nuts, or even worse, simply the losing hand.

Just as in any other poker game, and in cyberspace in particular, knowing the potential winning or losing value of your hand relative to the potential strength of your opponents' is extremely important because it allows you to get away from a hand that may cost you. Remember that saving bets is just as important as winning them. The game of Seven Card Stud, and indeed any other poker game, is not about winning the most pots, but winning the most money. A caveat to this is also an important adage, and that is this: Money saved in bets not invested is equally as important as the bets that now do not have to be recovered. And that, therefore, directly leads to increased profitability in both the short term and long run. Since in cyberspace Seven Card Stud games go by quickly, you need not be exposed to the extraordinary boredom that often plagues Seven Card Stud players in the real world due to the slowness of the game and thus the necessity to often wait long hours before finding a playable hand.

Starting with rolled-up trips is the best starting hand in Seven Card Stud, and the best of all of these are three Aces, of course. However, in Seven Card Stud any rolled-up trips are excellent starting hands, even though they do not always improve to a full house, or quads, and sometimes not to a winning hand. Nevertheless, in Seven Card Stud rolled-up trips are tantamount to pocket Aces or high pocket pairs in Texas Hold'Em. Known as "rolled up" or "wired," the higher the trips the more playable the hands. Small trips, however, such as deuces through 8s, are hands that are vulnerable to a variety of potential higher holdings. (For more information on this I again refer you to my other poker books and the chapters on Seven Card Stud.) For right now, just remember that getting rolled-up trips happens only once in about each 425 hands. That's a long time to wait, and therefore for you to be able to make Seven Card Stud in cyberspace profitable you will also need to play other hands, and you can learn which hands by reading the Seven Card Stud chapters in my earlier poker book.

Many players used to playing Texas Hold'Em try to approach Seven Card Stud from the same perspective. This is particularly so for cyberspace poker players, most of whom have experienced Texas Hold'Em first and only later discovered Seven Card Stud. In particular such errors of perception most commonly apply to what is normally an advanced skill in all poker games—bluffing. Although successful bluffing is very important to the overall profitability of any serious poker player, it is something that is highly overused by just about all cyberspace poker players, particularly in the lower limits. This is because most of those players have come to cyberspace poker by first learning about poker from television, and they fail to recognize the fact that television consists of only highly edited highlights. Such highlights often involve enormous bluffs by players at the final stages of tournaments, because they make for good television. This unfortunately produces the wrong perception among many poker players, particularly the Internet newbies, that bluffing is something that has to be done all the time and that it always wins the pots. This is absolutely not so, because bluffing is a skilled art and it is useful and valuable only if it is done very well and very seldom, and is a much more useful skill in the real world than in cyberspace.

As this applies to Seven Card Stud, bluffing is almost never an option in this game. This advice applies to real-world Seven Card Stud games, and it is also crucially important for you to understand this particularly for cyberspace Seven Card Stud. In Seven Card Stud you can't bluff until after 5th street because only then it is possible for you to actually have made the hand that you might be representing. Unfortunately, in Seven Card Stud you're quite likely to face at least three or four opponents who may actually have drawing hands that can potentially beat what you might represent, or already have a made hand themselves. There are also the other players who might be drawing to a hand that might beat you, or at least beat what you appear to be representing, even though such players may not actually have a hand as yet. The problem with all of this is precisely the open potential of several live hands facing your bluff. If any one of them improves to a made hand, than you will be unlikely to ever lose that opponent, and in Internet Seven Card Stud—no matter what limit you will choose—it is almost never the case that you would be able to bluff so strongly and so consecutively throughout 5th street betting and then 6th street betting and then 7th street betting, all the while pressing your bluff and then having it succeed because you will force all of your remaining opponents to fold their hands at that point. A simple rule of Seven Card Stud is that if you have committed wagers at the 5th-street level, you will usually call almost anything and everything all the way to the 7th-street showdown. Your opponents will play against you with this same mind-set, particularly in cyberspace. Therefore, trying any kind of a bluff is a very low percentage play indeed, especially in cyberspace. Even though there are circumstances, as rare as they are, where such plays can and do succeed, they are so few and far between that you will lose many times more money than you could ever hope by winning any one such bluff. Probably the most valuable advice that you can gain from this particular section of this discussion about cyberspace Seven Card Stud is to remember that bluffing is almost never an option. Unless you are an extraordinarily skilled Seven Card Stud player, and unless you are playing in the highest of limits where you are likely to be facing opponents who are equally as knowledgeable, and therefore capable of folding a hand, just stay away from bluffs altogether. It will save you lots of money.

## ODDS IN SEVEN CARD STUD

Finally, it is time to explain to you some of the odds against you when you are facing drawing hands. Also, the odds against you, or the odds in your favor, depending on some of the holdings with which you might start. I again refer you to my earlier book on poker, because there I have listed much more information about this subject. However, in the spirit of continuing that discussion and showing you some very useful information in this particular section, as this specifically applies to Internet Seven Card Stud games, you can note the following, which describes the mathematical analysis of the likelihood of occurrence and the implied odds of the stated events:

- 4:1 against you to make a full house if you hold trips on 6th street.
- 1½:1 against you to make a flush if you catch a flush card on 4th street to your three flush on 3rd street.
- 8½:1 against you to make that flush if you do *not* catch your flush card on fourth street.
- 1½:1 in your *favor* to make at least two pair if you start with three connectors to a straight flush
- 1½:1 against your making two pair if you start with any pair among your first three cards
- 4:1 against your turning that pair into a three of a kind or better
- 425:1 against your being dealt rolled up trips
- 4½:1 against your making a flush if you start with three suited cards
- 5:1 against your being dealt any pair among your first three cards
- 5:1 against your being able to make a straight if your first three cards are in sequence

- 18:1 against your being dealt any three suited cards among your first three cards
- 3½:1 against your making a full house if you make two pair on 4th street.

As you can see, Seven Card Stud is not just a kid's game; it is a very serious poker game, and among the hardest games to master and play profitably with continued success. For many years it was the game of choice among professional poker players primarily because of all of the factors discussed here, but mostly because of their ability to be able to more accurately gauge the value of their opponents' hands relative to theirs. By simply being aware of everything that was identified for you in this chapter, as well as the information I have presented in such exhausting detail in my earlier poker book, you will be able to enjoy this wonderful game in cyberspace and do so with far more success and certainly a great deal more knowledge than the vast majority of Internet poker players currently possess, and are able to apply to their games. It is now time to talk briefly about some of the other games that are also available in cyberspace, specifically Omaha, Omaha/8, and the game that will now naturally progress from this chapter about Seven Card Stud, the high-low split version of Seven Card Stud commonly known as Stud/8, the subject of the next chapter.

# Seven Card Stud/8 or Better High-Low Split

Seven Card Stud/8 or Better High-Low Split—to which I shall hereafter refer in its short form as Stud/8—is a game whose procedures are identical to those of its high only cousin, Seven Card Stud. However, other than the procedures of how the game is played, such as the dealing of cards, the number of cards that you receive, the order of wagering, and the rest of the procedures pertaining to betting and raising and calling and/or folding, Stud/8 is an entirely different poker game. Here are several key differences:

- You can't make a double bet on an open pair on 4th street as you can in the high only version of Seven Card Stud.
- You are playing for both the high and the low end of the pot.
- There is a qualifier of 8 or better in order for there to be a low.
- High pocket pairs and high starting cards lose much of their value in this game as opposed to the high only Seven Card Stud.

- Low cards are much more prized because a good starting low hand can very often also make a very good high hand and thus scoop the pot.
- Any Ace can be used both as a low card as well as a high card and therefore Aces substantially increase in value in Stud/8.

Clearly, playing Stud/8 is really nothing like playing just the plain Seven Card Stud. This version of Seven Card Stud, often commonly referred to as the high-low split game, is yet another of those traditional poker games that used to enjoy a great deal of popularity in the real-world casino poker rooms and card rooms. But just as with the old-style Seven Card Stud games, this high-low version of Seven Card Stud split pot game has also substantially lost popularity, and has become all but extinct in the real-world casino poker rooms or card rooms, with some, but very few, noted exceptions. One of the problems associated with this game is that it is extremely slow to play in the real world, even slower than Seven Card Stud itself. This is not only because of the procedures, and the requirements to deal all those cards to all those players, but also because of the nature of this game. Because it is a high-low split game, this means that many times the pot will be split between the winner of the high hand and the winner of the low hand. This also means that the real world dealers have to constantly split the pot between the competing sides, and this not only slows down the dealing procedures themselves, but also slows down the paying procedure after the winners of each pot have been determined, because now the money has to be split between those winners. The second reason why this game has lost much of its old popularity is the popularity of Texas Hold'Em. Texas Hold'Em has taken the world by storm and has become the premier game of choice just about everywhere. Not surprisingly, other forms of poker have quickly waned, resulting in the attrition of players because new players have not cut their poker-playing teeth on this particular game, but have instead begun their poker-playing life's journey with Texas Hold'Em. You would be hard-pressed to find any Seven Card Stud players, and particularly Stud/8 players, below the age of fifty in most current card rooms. New players are simply not learning this game and therefore it is not that popular anymore. I am no fan of this form of poker, indeed no fan of any high-low split poker game, or any poker derivative other than the traditional Texas Hold'Em, Seven Card Stud, Omaha High only, Five Card Stud, and Five Card Draw (except perhaps Omaha/8 and the traditional Lowball and Razz). Just like the games of Five Card Stud and Five Card Draw have all but been relegated to history, high-low split games are sure to follow sooner or later. I hold this opinion not only because such games are so incredibly slow to play, but primarily because the inherent volatility requires one to use mental juxtaposition to great and tiring ends, often only to achieve half the result for which you were aiming. Perhaps this is my own particular prejudice, and I'm fully willing to admit it, but when I play poker I want to focus on one goal, and one goal only, and that is to win the whole pot and nothing but the whole pot. Although winning the whole pot is also the objective of Stud/8, as indeed with all the other split games such as Omaha/8, which I will discuss shortly, nevertheless the mental gymnastics that you have to go through in order to achieve this, and the expense that it will cost you in order to get there, simply do not warrant the effort relative to the profit potential you might gain, as little as that may be.

This much said, I am fully aware that many poker players still enjoy high-low split games, and that Internet poker has made the play of high-low split games a great deal more enjoyable than those found in the real world. Once again the wonderment of cyberspace, and the quickness and ease with which software programs can deal out those cards, as well as automatically split the pots, results in split games that are dealt much faster than any human dealer in the real world could possibly hope to accomplish, as well as with much greater efficiency because the software automatically takes into account the splitting of the money without requiring the human dealer to fumble around with chips and make those splits. If for no other reason than this, playing Stud/8 in cyberspace makes it possible to find enjoyment, and even profitability, in playing this game.

## MANY DECISIONS

The object of playing any high-low split game, and in this discussion in particular Stud/8, is to scoop both sides of the pot by having the best possible high hand and at the same time the best possible low hand. Since the Ace card can be used both to make a high hand as well as to make a low hand, possessing an Ace among your cards provides you with a distinct advantage in this game. The best possible hand in Stud/8 is the five-card hand of Ace-2-3-4-5 all suited, thereby making a straight flush as well as the best possible low hand. Any straight so ordered, even when it is not a straight flush, is an incredibly powerful hand in this game, not only because it is an unbeatable low hand but also because it is the powerhouse straight. Having this hand scoops the pot most of the time, and if it is not a straight flush you can only lose to a higher straight for the high end of the pot. In that case you can lose the high end of the pot, but you are still guaranteed the low end. Naturally, there are a great many other potential hands that are also great starting hands, and great finishing hands, in this game. (For those I refer you to my earlier book *Powerful Profits from Poker* in which I discuss the play of Stud/8 in greater detail, as well as showing the best possible starting hands and their play thereafter.) For this chapter, as it applies to the play of this game in cyberspace, I will continue that discussion and provide some hints and tips on how you can make this game entertaining and profitable as played on Internet poker sites.

Assuming that by now you have learned how to find the game and table of your choice, and how to select your game and how to make a deposit, some of which I will again discuss in greater lengths in later chapters, this means that you now find yourself at a Stud/8 table ready to play. Your first decision, therefore, is whether or not to play with the starting hands you received. As in Seven Card Stud, in Stud/8 you will begin with three cards, two cards in the hole, and one exposed up card. The same, of course, applies to all your opponents. You must determine not only whether or not you should proceed with this hand, but also whether this hand can make a high hand, a low hand, both, or neither. You therefore have many more decisions to make at the very beginning than you would have in traditional Seven Card Stud games, and this directly means that you will have to have much more stringent starting hands standards, and a great deal more discipline. The greatest mistake that most high-low split game players make is to assume that just because they can win half the pot this automatically means that they can relax their starting hand standards and therefore play many more hands. This is absolutely not so, and is an extraordinarily foolhardy approach to any high-low split game. The *direct contrary* is the case. In any high-low split game you absolutely must refine your starting-hand standards extremely stringently and absolutely dedicate yourself to a great and unwavering discipline before you ever commit any money to continuing with any such starting hand. The volatility of this game means that whenever you enter into any round after the first three cards are dealt to you, including the cost of the antes, you will thereafter be likely exposed to a great many bets and raises and re-raises on each subsequent round of wagering. So great is the expense of this that if you do not have such stringent starting standards and an equally stringent sense of discipline, you will find yourself exposing your money and your bankroll to horrendous and enormous losses at a pace that is so fast as to make your head spin and your bank account leak as if it were being sucked into a black hole. Unless you are enormously wealthy and such attrition of money means little or nothing to you, you are well advised to only play this game, as well as any other high-low split game, with extreme caution.

In addition to all those decisions that you have to make regarding your own hand at 3rd street, in Stud/8 as well as any other high-low split game you now also have to make these assessments about the potential holdings of your opponents. Since in high-low split games you face a great many more opponents than you do in traditional games, such as traditional Seven Card Stud where you might face only three or four opponents, in Stud/8 you are far more likely to face almost the entire field at the 3rd-street stage. Most players who play this game, and particularly in the lower limits, or in cyberspace, almost never throw away anything that looks like it has some kind of a possibility. This is precisely what makes this game so volatile and so costly. Although the pots are huge, and the prospect of winning them by scooping them is enticing, remember that it is equally so enticing to all of your opponents. That is precisely why many of them will chase with their hands to the bitter end no matter how much it costs them, because if they perceive any kind of hope at all, even the hope of only sharing in half of the pot, they will continue to throw their money in trying to catch a miracle. Many times one of your opponents actually catches such a miracle and defeats what was the best possible hand that you were playing up to that point, only to see it so crushed by such a lucky draw. That is the greatest danger of high-low split games, because chasers in these games abound, and chasing the pot for a miracle is the norm rather than the exception.

Consequently, your starting hand analysis for your own hand should include a double possibility, such as hands that can scoop the pot by winning both the high and low. Remember that if your hand does not look like it can make the nuts, somebody else's hand will. Once you have determined the potential strength and value of your own hand, you now immediately have to focus on your opponents' hands and classify them into three basic categories:

1. Players who appear to be going for both the high and the low
2. Players who appear to be going for only the high hand
3. Players who do not appear to have any hope at all

Naturally, many of these decisions are hard to make with just the first three cards in your own hand, and only the one exposed up card from among all of your opponents. However, since you already know the three cards that you can see because they are in your own hand, you can now make reasonable assumptions and judgments about the potential value of your opponents' hands. If you start with such cards as Ace-2-3, preferably suited but even offsuit, then the first thing you already know is that one of each of the four cards that make up the four possible cards to each of these values are now in your hand, and therefore cannot be among your opponents' hands. If you see two other Aces, and two other 2s, and two other 3s, then you know that most of these cards are already out, leaving only one of each remaining that are yet unseen. So now you know that two of your opponents are potentially drawing to both the high and the low hand, those with the exposed Aces, and four of your other opponents may potentially be drawing to a low hand worse than yours. Since there will be eight players in a traditional Internet Stud/8 poker table, and you have now accounted for seven players, yourself plus the six others we have just identified, you now have one more opponent to look at, and perhaps you will dismiss that player as being among those who have no chance. Of course, this example is quite extreme, and I have used it only for illustration purposes. I show it here simply to give you an idea about the kind of mental gymnastics and thinking processes that you have to undergo even at the very beginning, starting with your first three cards. Be sure to have a ready supply of headache pills, because it will get worse from now on.

The kinds of hands that are good among your starting hands (as shown in my earlier poker book) are not only hands that contain one Ace, such as the example of the Ace-2-3, but also hands that contain one Ace with a pair, two Aces with a low card, such as a 2, or a 3, or a 4, or a 5, but also hands that can only make a one-way low, as well as the hands that can make only a one-way high, and, of course, the winning hands that can make both high and a low. Also the well hidden hands with deceptive value, such as hands that look like you're going for a low hand but you are actually going for a powerhouse high hand, or hands that look like you are going for a high hand but in reality you are going for a low hand, or a two-way hand, as well as huge hands such as rolled-up trips, especially if the rolled-up trips are with small cards. Rolled-up trips with cards such as 2s, 3s, 4s, and 5s are powerhouse starting high hands that are well hidden because they look like you are going for a low. Although it is always important for you to realize that going for the scoop is the real object of playing any high-low split game, sometimes you have a hand that is a powerful high hand only, and therefore you are trying to push it as much as you can, particularly if it looks like that you are also going for a low hand. This is even more important and profitable if it also looks like that the low hand will be a scoop-type hand, because when your hand appears as such to your opponents, you can play it aggressively and try to convince your opponents to throw their hands away thereby assuring yourself of scooping the pot, even though you were only going for the high end of it. All of these details and nuances of the game you will learn as you experience them (and as I have described in my earlier poker book in those chapters).

If you decide to play past 3rd street, on receiving your 4th-street card you should already know whether you are going for the low, the high, or for a potential scoop, as well as be able to determine whether or not your opponents are doing exactly the same as you, have better draws than you, or are going for one or the other side of the pot. You now need to take a very close look at the kind of card that you did catch on 4th street and also pay very close attention to the cards that fell in the exposed hands of your opponents. If you are going for a low, and caught a good card, make sure you think carefully and look at the cards that fell in your opponents' hands, and compare their potential values to yours. In Stud/8 you are quite likely to be facing several players who are also hoping for a low, and you therefore have to determine not only whether or not your low cards are still live, but whether or not your low hand, if made, will actually be the winning hand for the low side of the pot, versus the potential low card holdings of your opponents. The same applies to the high end.

If you are going for only the high end of the pot, make sure that your cards are live, and preferably press your high hand as much as you can all the away to 5th street, trying to drive out as many of your low-handed opponents, thereby giving yourself an opportunity to win not only the high hand, but also scoop the pot by forcing the action to be only between opponents who cannot make a low, or whose hands will eventually be busted due to a nonqualifier.

The next thing to remember on 4th street is that just because you have low-suited cards, all of which may be of the rank of 8 or lower, doesn't mean you automatically have the winning low. Although you have what can be considered a very playable hand, its actual value depends on the holdings of your opponents, as well as whether or not your hand and the remaining cards that you still require are still live. Very often, and particularly so in high-low split games, you may find yourself drawing to a hand that looks good, but unfortunately will lose even when made because you did not pay careful attention to the cards as they fell in the hands of your opponents. Your inattention causes a failure to recognize that your drawing cards are no longer live as well as the fact that your opponents were actually drawing to a hand that was going to be better than the one you were hoping to make. However, if your hand is the only low holding against one or two opponents who are obviously going for the high end of the pot, then even a mediocre hand can win. For example, 8-7-3, or any such variation of a marginally playable hand, even if it fails to improve by hitting, say, a 6 on 4th street, can still be a very playable hand because it is now likely to be the only low. Nevertheless, against multiple opponents—any one of whom may also look like he is drawing to a low hand—such a hand as this loses much of its potential value. Playing it past 4th street is likely to cost you more money by chasing it, because even if made it is unlikely to be the winning low hand against multiple opponents. If you are playing any such hand heads-up, the best you can hope for is to split the pot and get half of your money back, less the rake. Therefore, whenever you find yourself in a heads-up situation in any high-low split game, and you do not have a two-way scoop potential, your only choice is to either try to get your opponent to fold his hand, or for you to fold yours. Anything other than this will cost you money, even if you do win half the pot. You will not get all of your own money back, because cyberspace games are all rake-based games and therefore you will have lost the amount of the rake percentage by continuing to bet into this pot. In such situations either try to drive out your opponent, or be ready to throw your hand away and relinquish your side of the pot knowing that you spent only little and that chasing this pot will result in you absolutely losing money. Losing that small amount of money now is better than potentially losing the entire pot if your opponent is lucky enough to scoop, and certainly better than to lose the amount of the rake even if you do win your half of the pot.

Also remember that if your opponents look like they have a better low hand draw than you, then you do not have a playable hand at all. It doesn't matter what your hand looks like, or how great it may be in comparison to the stringent starting standards for the hand that you have selected, because if it is obvious that your opponents have something better than the value of your hand, your hand is therefore nothing. If the cards that you need are also cards that are needed by your opponents, and on 4th street they hit their card and you don't, then your hand is a candidate for the muck because anything other than mucking it is a prescription for disaster. This is so not only because of the money that it will cost you to continue with it, but because of the inevitable result of your losing the pot by either not making your hand at all, or worse, risking making your hand only to discover that your opponent made a better one. Save your money—throw the hand away on 4th street if the card you need hits one or more of your opponents whom you also see are going for the same kind of hand as you.

In such situations, if it looks like one of your opponents is drawing to a low hand, or if you see that the majority of your opponents appear to be drawing to a low hand, it will be quite natural for you to start receiving sequences of high cards. This is simply the randomness of the draw, as well as the randomness of the shuffle. Now you can find yourself in the quite enviable position, because if your start catching such high cards, and particularly if you also started with a small pair, now playing for the high end of the pot will be to your advantage because you are facing opponents who are all competing with each other for the low end of the pot. Now is the time, especially when you know that you are likely to be the only player with a high hand, to drive the hand as much as you can. Bet, raise, and re-raise as much as possible on each round of betting, because the bigger the pot the bigger will be the high end of it, and you are virtually assured of having a lock on the high side of the pot. Try to commit all your low-drawing players into investing as much money in the pot as you can get out of them. You are now in the prime position of winning the most money by only winning half of the pot. Since in Stud/8, as well as in all high-low split games, the majority of players will always be trying for the low first, with the hope of wrapping it so that they will also catch the high, the fact remains that many such players will bust out and not achieve the qualifying low. They will probably have a mediocre high, with only one such player actually making a low, perhaps with a high that is quite unlikely to be better than your high. In this situation you can maximize the value from only one side of the pot. Usually, playing for only half the pot is not nearly as good as playing for the whole pot. It is better to relinquish low hands with a high potential that are mediocre low hands that missed the high hand draw, especially against one or more opponents who obviously have the better high end hand, or draw. As you can see from the discussion in my earlier poker book, winning half the pot isn't really winning half the pot. It is quite important that you learn that principle, and I therefore encourage you to read those chapters in that book.

When you have such a great starting hand that obviously is improving to a high while facing several opponents who are obviously drawing to a low only, you should push your high hand holdings as much as possible all way up to 5th street, and only then slow down a little bit and see what potential holdings your opponents may still be left with, or have already made. By 5th street you should have improved your high hand holdings to something which will be either the nuts already, or a hand that has a live possibility of becoming the nut high hand. Take stock of all this information, and analyze it is best as possible, and take a cheap 6th-street card at which point you take another look and make the final determination whether or not your high hand is likely to be the winning high. If it is, hammer it to the hilt. If it looks as if one of your opponents may have a low hand that can also turn into a very good high hand, and a better high hand than the one you have, take a cheap card again if you can, or simply call the bets without driving the action. If on 7th street you have hit the absolute nut high hand, such as making a very strong full house, a straight flush, the incredible quads, or anything else that looks like it will be the absolute nut high hand, then you can test the waters by either betting if it is checked to you, or raising if someone else has bet, and react accordingly. This will have the effect of not only finding out exactly how strong your opponents are, but also driving out one or more players who have still called all the action up to 7th street with the hope of a miracle only to find out now that they have missed, and therefore have no choice but to throw their hands away. By getting any one of these players to throw their hands away on 7th street prior to showdown, you increase your chances and narrow the field thereby preserving the possibility of the potential of winning your high side of the pot. Keep in mind, however, it may also be the case that your one or two remaining opponents have actually failed to make the qualifying low and are now making only a crying call to see if you may have missed your hand also. Checking if it is checked to you with no action yet to happen behind you, or merely calling bets on the river without raising, is a good play for you only if you think that your high hand is vulnerable, based upon your 5th-street and 6th-street analysis of your opponent's potential holding. However, if by this time you still have a good high hand it is never a good idea to throw it away no matter how big the action, because even if there are bets and multiple raises and re-raises at 7th street chances are that your opponents are battling for the best low, and that still preserves your high end value of the pot.

## HINTS AND TIPS FOR WINNING STUD/8

By means of a summary, and in addition to the suggestions and recommendations shown earlier (and those also provided in *Powerful Profits from Poker*), I would now like to offer you a few brief tips that in addition to these already mentioned will together provide you with a solid foundation and framework upon which to build your profitable success in playing Stud/8 in cyberspace. All of the suggestions and recommendations can be applicable to land-based real-world Stud/8 games, but they are primarily designed to help you play in Internet poker rooms.

### Don't Gamble

As soon as you start playing Stud/8, and particularly so on the Internet, you will soon realize just how many people gamble with little or nothing in the way of a reasonable hand for the action. The vast multitude of Internet poker players, and this applies to just about all poker games especially in the lower limits, and particularly so for Stud/8, continue with the erroneous perception that just because they are playing a high-low split game they can continue to chase everything with anything because they could luck into at least one-half of the pot. This is not how you should play if you want to play well and profitably. Do not gamble and do not push your hand if you're not absolutely convinced that it is the best hand, be it low, high, or both. This does not mean that if you don't think so, you should automatically fold. But it does mean that instead of raising, re-raising, or driving the action by being the opening bettor, you should instead check and simply call if someone else makes a bet. This is the safest play when you are uncertain as to the viability of your hand, and applies particularly to your low hands, especially if you are competing for the low end of the pot with a hand that is not the nuts. Most of the time you will not have hands that can be considered the absolute nuts, and many times you will have to base your assessments of the viability of your hand upon the observations of the viability of your opponents' hands because these values exhibit potential strengths and weaknesses, versus your hand. If you are certain you have the best hand, particularly the best low hand, by all means drive the action. If you're not, don't gamble. Remember this and you will be well ahead of most Internet poker players, and will assure yourself of minimizing your losses in Stud/8 and maximizing your profitability.

## Take a Calculated Gamble

Although I have just advised you not to gamble when playing Stud/8, there is a significant difference between a reckless gamble and a calculated gamble. A reckless gamble is the one that I described above, which will be the case of pushing your hand and driving the action when you are not certain it is the best hand. However, in most poker games, and particularly Stud/8, there are many circumstances and situations where a certain amount of risk is involved. Notice that I said the word "risk," and not "reckless gamble." Although taking what is called "a calculated risk" is sometimes referred to as "a calculated gamble," it is really not a gamble at all, but rather *a rational decision to commit yourself to a risk situation*. Such a decision should be made by you only in circumstances where your opportunities to make a very significant profit justify such a risk. Such situations—as these apply to Stud/8—occur significantly more often in this game than in other poker games, except perhaps for other split pot games. This is due to the nature of the game, and handling these situations is a necessary part of your profitability arsenal of skills and knowledge. Such decisions apply particularly when you have significant implied pot odds as well as a hand that not only has a good low potential, but also has at least a good potential to become the winning high hand as well. For example, your hand is suited Ace-2-3, and on 4th street you pick up the suited 5, which now gives you not only the inside straight flush but also the inside wheel draw. At the same time this gives you the nut flush draw with the potential possibility of catching another Ace. This would make a high pair, which could eventually result in you also double pairing, thereby potentially gaining a winning high hand even if you miss your low draw and all of the low possibilities that can also make a high hand. Even though this 5 is not the perfect card, suited or not, because it requires you to hit the perfect inside card—that being the 4, suited or not—it is nevertheless a good card for you because it preserves all of these listed possibilities. Under such circumstances it is appropriate for you to take what I call a "calculated gamble," which should perhaps be called a "calculated risk" as a better description. This is because it is a rational decision made by you in the assessment of not only your hand, but also the potential of the implied odds that the pot will offer you not only now, but later, particularly if you subsequently see that your opponents are drawing to a multitude of low and high hands, neither of which will beat your hand if you make it. Even if you should miss your draw on 5th street, under the conditions as I described for this example—which in reality is not that unusual because it will happen more times than you think as you play this game—you should continue past 5th street as long as your draws are still live. Naturally, if you determine that on 5th street or 6th street you are now drawing dead, it would be foolhardy to continue with the hand thereafter, unless the cards that you catch have now turned your hand from the possible nut low with a high potential into a high-only hand that looks like it will probably be the winner because the rest of the field is competing for the low side of the pot, and their exposed cards indicate they are unlikely to make a better high than you. This can also happen even if you missed the draws as described in this example. Therefore, under those circumstances, your calculated risk will still be to your advantage as long as you can make these decisions progressively and accordingly, and as accurately as possible.

### Use Aggressive Play with a Low Hand Only

If it becomes obvious on 4th street that you are the only player likely to be competing for the low side of the pot, with the remainder of the field apparently competing only for the high end of the pot, you should at this point shift into the mode of the calculated aggressor and begin to either bet if you are first to act, or raise and even re-raise any bets and/or raises made by other players in front of your turn to act. When you are correct in your assessment that you are the only one competing for the low end of the pot, you will now have several of your opponents trapped in multiple raises and re-raises competing for the high end of the pot. This is the same set of circumstances described earlier, and one to which I will also allude again a little later when the situation is reversed. It is only under this situation, and the reverse of it, that competing for only one side of the pot becomes advantageous. It is now in your interest to force your opponents to commit as much money to the pot as you can possibly get from them on this street and subsequent streets, assuming that your low hand continues to improve while your opponents' high hands also improve and not begin to look like they might in fact be hitting cards to a potential low. All circumstances being equal as stated for this example, when it is obvious that you are the only low, force your opponents to commit the most money you can into the pot, because this will increase the value of your hand since you are likely to be the only winner of that side of the pot. It is only in this circumstance that you should be so aggressive. Naturally, if you are not the only apparent low you should play more cautiously. In those circumstances you should analyze the potential value of your holdings as opposed to that of the other player who may also be competing for the low side of the pot, and if you are able to determine that your hand is likely to be better than the hand that he is hoping to make, you can then also become the aggressor and not only have the high side players pot-committed to investing the most money you can get out of them, but now you also trapped your other low-drawing opponents into committing dead money into the pot.

## Be Frugal, Not Cheap

When you are drawing to any low hand at any stage where you are yet unsure whether this hand will end up as the best low possible, your objective is to save as many bets as you can and take as many free cards as possible, or as many cheap cards as you can get. By so doing you are being frugal, and not cheap, because you are trying to minimize your exposure to potential losses and therefore diminish your risk while at the same time maximizing your opportunities to catch the cards you need. This will maximize the value that you can gain later on from the pot's implied odds after you hit your hand, when you can then trap your opponents and continue to drive the action. Learning how to be frugal with your bets and calls will not only diminish your risk exposure and costs of playing the game, but will add substantially to your sense of discipline and comfort playing this game.

## Play the High Hand

Whenever you find yourself drawing to a high only hand, be as aggressive as you possibly can on 3rd street and 4th street, but on 5th street if it doesn't look like you already have the best high hand possible, apply the frugalness principle I just mentioned, because it will also provide you with the ability to minimize your risk, and therefore diminish your exposure to the volatility of this game. Although the frugalness principle that I just described above for the low hand was intended primarily for circumstances when you have such low hand draws, it can be applied equally well to this circumstance, and particularly on 5th street and 6th street. This is because if you are the aggressor all the way up to 5th street, and now you all of a sudden check, chances are pretty good that your opponents will give you a free card. This is a very good and very valuable play, and is the epitome of frugalness as it applies to the playing of high hands only. Even if you do not get a free card on 5th street, you are highly likely to face only one bet and no raises, when otherwise you would have probably faced several bets and multiple raises and re-raises. If you catch the card that you need on 6th street to make your hand the best high hand possible, you can again become the aggressor because now you are playing for the high side of the pot and are again trying to force your opponents into committing as much money into the pot as possible. This is particularly true for those opponents who are competing for the low side of the pot only, as well as any of your opponents who might also be drawing to a high hand only, not realizing that you are now holding the best possible high hand and therefore you are forcing them to commit more and more dead money. This is how you drive profitability for yourself when faced with a high hand only draw from the very beginning.

## Try Making the Last Call

If you find yourself in a situation where you played your hand all the way to 7th street, but wound up with a hand that may or may not be the winning hand for either the low side or the high side of the pot, do not fold your hand to any bets as long as your hand still has some potential of winning either side of the pot. Naturally, if by this time it is absolutely obvious that you missed everything and therefore your hand is absolutely dead and has no value, then you should by all means fold it to any bets. However, assuming that you played a hand all the way to 7th street that had at least some potential, you should always call the bets even if you are unsure that your hand can win either side of the pot. Many times quite a few of your opponents will bet, raise, and even re-raise with a hand they themselves have failed to make precisely in order to drive out opponents such as yourself whom they perceive to have a hand that now is better than theirs. They might not be aware that it is not the best possible hand; therefore, they are trying to drive you out and force you to fold. So, if you have any hand that has such a potential for either side of the pot, never throw it away and always call just to make sure that you see the final showdown. You will win pots that you otherwise would have lost if you had thrown your hand away and discovered later that you were the victim of aggressive play by players who wanted to drive you out. Also, you have the value of the pot odds that will by this time, and especially in Stud/8, offer you more than the correct odds to make such a call. Furthermore, this also serves notice to all your opponents that you will not be bullied on 7th street, and that if you are calling you are doing so because you have something. This will have the direct effect of making your opponents fear your call if they missed their hand, and thereafter they are unlikely to try to bully you in this same manner under similar circumstances.

### Learn to Spot the Best Hand Opposing You

One of the most crucial skills that you need to acquire is the ability to spot the best opposing hand to the hand you are trying to make, or that which you are playing. In high-low split games, oftentimes your only option is to go for either the high side or the low side of the pot, but not both. In such circumstances, you should pursue your hand only if it appears that you are likely to be the only winner of that side of the pot, and that means that you will have to locate that one hand among your opponents' potential holdings that will be your most significant competitor. In high-low split games you are unlikely to face more than one such competitor, because it is unlikely that there will be more than two hands whose holdings will be such that they could closely compete for one side of the pot or the other. Therefore, paying close attention to your opponents' holdings as well as the potential value of your own hand, in addition to making sure that all of your draws are still live, is very important. Unfortunately, you usually acquire this skill only after extensive play because it is something that you cannot learn without doing it. To help you acquire this skill, remember that your focus is on that one competing hand that could potentially beat yours, assuming, of course, that you have learned to play only the best starting hands for whichever side of the pot it will eventually become obvious that hand fits best.

## Don't Fall Asleep, Don't Be Bored, Don't Take a Vacation, Always Pay Attention

Even if you are not in a hand, pay attention and don't take a vacation. The greatest mistake that many high-low split players make, and poker players in general, is to stop paying attention to what is going on in the hand in which they are not participating. In high-low split games, failing to pay attention to everything that is going on even when you are not involved is a prescription for disaster because you are now giving up a great opportunity to study your opponents and how they play, as well as what they play, in which positions, and what they do with the hand that they either draw to or hope to get, or miss, and how they play thereafter. This is particularly important in cyberspace, because in Internet poker games you have complete anonymity and therefore no one can see you study, and no one can see you make careful notes and observations. Whenever you find yourself in this premium situation of being able to observe what is going on, remember that close observation will enhance your skills in being able to make accurate reads on your opponents and their holdings. Give yourself the opportunity to improve your skills in this manner, and always pay careful attention to everything that is going on in the game, especially when you are not in the hand. Many players will relax when they are not competing for the pot because they feel they are not at risk. As a result they give up a great many opportunities to add to their arsenals of skills and knowledge, and particularly their observational skills and situational analyses. This is the school of experience, and what you learn from doing it is something that no one else can teach you. Consequently, do not give up this great opportunity and always remain acutely focused.

### Pay Attention to Dead Cards

I know I have said this before, but it bears repeating. Whenever you have a hand that is not made but a drawing hand, continue playing it only if you know that all of the cards you need to complete your hand are live. This seems like such a simple concept, but unfortunately one that is ignored by a great majority of poker players. Cyberspace players and especially players of Stud/8 ignore this, and experienced players who are at least partially able to command these skills can exploit such weaknesses among these players for substantial profitability. The potential is obvious because if you are paying attention not only to your hand but also to the hands of your opponents, and it becomes obvious that your opponents are drawing to a specific hand whose cards are dead, you no longer have to fear that opponent. You can, in fact, isolate that opponent and use that opponent's weakness not only to add value to the pot, but to drive out other players whose hands could have perhaps improved against your holdings. This is a highly specialized skill that is enormously profitable if performed correctly. The danger is, of course, that you yourself will become one of those players who are not paying attention to dead cards. Dead cards are those cards that are no longer in play—discarded by those players who have folded at the various streets—or are cards that are now falling in the hands of your opponents. If you are the one who needs these cards, and you see them so folded or falling among the cards of your opponents, then those are dead cards as far as you are concerned. To help yourself see and focus on such cards, don't bother memorizing the cards already on your screen among your active opponents, because they are clearly visible on your computer screen and you can look at them as many times as you want, and at any time while those players are still active in the hand. Therefore, all you have to remember are the dead cards that were thrown away by those players who have folded their hands as the game continues. What you are looking for are not only cards that you need, but cards that are needed by opponents who are still active in the hand. Make sure you are drawing to a hand whose draws are still live, while at the same time paying attention to the potential draws of your opponents, equally to determine whether or not their cards are still live, but more particularly to pay attention to whether or not their cards are in fact dead. Since it is the norm rather than the exception that cyberspace poker players entirely fail to notice this—or understand the importance of this concept—and therefore as a result pay little or no attention to whether or not their cards and the cards of their opponents are live, you can now exploit both sides of this powerful tool for profitability.

### Play More Low Hands Than High Hands

In high-low split games it is to your advantage to play low hands more often than high hands, usually in the 2:1 ratio. This is because a great many low hands also have the potential to make very good high hands, and as a result provide you with the opportunity to scoop the pot. High hands, on the other hand, are useful for one way only, and that is as a high hand, because such high hands can never make a low. Therefore, whenever playing Stud/8, or any high-low split game, always pay attention to the 2:1 ratio of low hands to high hands, and wherever possible focus far more on the play of low hands than on the high hands. It takes a little getting used to, particularly if you are used to playing Seven Card Stud high only. In traditional Seven Card Stud high only, the object is to make the best high hand possible, and therefore low hands are only so much garbage. In Stud/8 the precise opposite is true. In this game you should focus primarily on the kinds of hands that you throw away in traditional Seven Card Stud high only, because these hands offer you the greatest potential for profitability in Stud/8.

### Don't Steal and Bluff Too Often

One of the often-quoted pieces of advice for the play of Stud/8 is to try to steal the antes whenever possible. This is pretty good advice for land-based real-world Stud/8 poker games, but is an ill-advised recommendation for cyberspace games, particularly for the vast majority of Internet poker games. These games are mostly offered primarily in the low to middle limits. It is ill advised because in cyberspace nobody will let you steal anything. Stealing the antes in Stud/8 may indeed be a very important part of playing the game in the real world, but that advice does not translate well into cyberspace poker. In Internet poker games, including high-low split games, and perhaps particularly so for high-low split games, you will face large fields of players who are constantly willing to invest any amount of money with any kind of a hand, and for any reason, just because they might catch a hand or make something with the cards they are playing. Although this is primarily so among the low- to middle-limit games, this is a phenomenon in cyberspace poker that transcends the limits. No matter how expensive the game, there are always several players in any Internet poker game willing to invest any amount of money even if they only have one long shot that might happen once every millennium. They continue to bet, call, and invest any amount of money, often even when they have absolutely no shot. For these many reasons (and several others that I discuss elsewhere in this book as well is in my previous books), trying to play Internet poker in the same way that you would play real land-based poker games is often quite foolhardy. Although there may be situations and circumstances in which the stealing of the antes in cyberspace Stud/8 may actually work, such will be few and far between, and consequently trying to do so is far more likely to cost you a lot of money both in the short term and long run than you can ever hope to regain by being successful at doing it. Most of the time any such plays will not only generate calls from other players, who are determined to play anything, but it will also expose you to additional cards that may provide your ugly hands with some hope and thereby commit you to the pot that in the end will cost you a great deal of money, only to discover that you will either have to throw it away in subsequent streets, or wind up with the second or third best hand. There are some well-known texts that apply this play for cyberspace as well as real-world, and although I agree with this for the real world poker games, I vehemently disagree with this kind of play for the Internet. I will therefore advise you not to do so in Internet poker games, and leave it up to you to make that decision once you reach that level of expertise and skills.

Similar such situations apply to bluffing, as I have already mentioned elsewhere and often. For the same reasons that I advise you not to try to play to steal the antes in Stud/8, I also advise you not to try to bluff, at least not too often. Sometimes it is okay to bluff, primarily if you have hands that are still live and can easily turn into winning hands. Although this is more correctly called "semibluffing," because you are not actually bluffing with a hand that does not exist but with a hand that does have potential to become the winning hand, it is nevertheless a very touchy play indeed. Until you become experienced and skilled at playing this game, I advise you to stay away from trying to bluff and even semibluff. Naturally, once you gain experience and expertise and comfort at playing this game in cyberspace, you can then begin to vary your game and perhaps incorporate the occasional bluff or semibluff into your poker-playing arsenal. But until you do become so experienced and knowledgeable and comfortable at the game, avoid doing it, because it will save you money.

### Be Patient

Many aspects to your personal playing discipline contribute to your success in poker, and particularly Internet poker, and especially Stud/8, as well as any other high-low split game or Internet poker game. Having good discipline based on knowledge allows you to gain profitable experience. Lack of such discipline could mean that no matter what amount of knowledge you possess, you will not be able to make the fullest use of it. Lack of such discipline also means that you cannot acquire your playing expertise as quickly as you would otherwise, and that experience will not be as pleasurable as it could be, and definitely not as profitable. You must have patience, and remember that in Stud/8 especially stringent and strict starting hand standards are an absolute prerequisite to profitability and success. Your patience is especially required on 3rd street and 4th street, and oftentimes 5th street as well, depending on your hand and circumstances. On 3rd street especially, if you don't have three cards that can potentially make one or more of the several best possible hands for this game, save yourself the money and do not pursue a hand past this point. This will be perhaps the hardest aspect of your personal playing discipline, but it will be the most profitable not only because it will save you money at that point, and all subsequent streets, but primarily because it will keep you from becoming pot-committed with substandard hands.

### Learn Aggressiveness and Determination

Finally, remember what we have already talked about when we discussed selective aggression, and for Stud/8 also combined with a sense of determination. Assuming now that you have already learned how to discipline yourself and how to select the best starting hands, once you make these decisions and choices, then it is the time for you to be determined and not allow yourself to be swayed from your initial and continuing judgments and assessments of the hand in progress, and to be selectively aggressive based upon your observational analyses of everything that is happening at each and every street as the hand progresses. These two skills allow you to neatly wrap up the total package that has now become you, the knowledgeable and experienced and dedicated Internet Stud/8 poker player.

Let us continue with the next chapter, which will include both Omaha High only and Omaha/8.

# Omaha High and Omaha/8

This chapter illustrates a game that has lost a great deal of its popularity, primarily in the United States. It has, however, made up for it in Europe where Omaha high only is actually the preferred game of choice among poker players. The Europeans play this as a pot-limit game, as opposed to a structured-limit game or no-limit game. Why they have become so enamored with this game is anyone's guess, as are perhaps the mysterious reasons for their choice of pot limit as the preferred wagering structure. Although the game is called Omaha, it does not come from Omaha. Texans claim that the game was actually invented there, those who come from Nebraska claim that state as the origin, and Oklahoma natives claim it as their own. Actually, the game was most likely invented in Louisiana, probably as a variation on the old French game of Chemin de fer.*

*The game of Chemin de Fer is mostly credited as being the precursor to the modern game of Baccarat, and it was very popular with the French. They brought this to Louisiana, and although no one knows for sure, there is cause to believe that it was there that the game was merged with poker and became a version of the game we now call Omaha Hold'Em, or Omaha for short.

No matter the origin, it is a Texas Hold'Em–style game, and it is played identically in the manner of dealing and wagering procedures as is Texas Hold'Em. However, that's where the similarity ends. Omaha High is a game where the best high hand wins. The game consists of each player at the table being dealt four hole cards, followed by a three-card flop (just like in Texas Hold'Em), followed by a turn card, followed by the river card. Therefore, just like in Texas Hold'Em, there will be a three-card flop, followed by one card on the turn, followed by one card on the river, at which point there will now be five community cards displayed on the board for all players to use, again just like Texas Hold'Em. However, unlike Texas Hold'Em, each player in Omaha has four hole cards and not just two. But while in Texas Hold'Em a player can use either both hole cards to combine with the board for the best five-card poker hand, or only one, or in some cases none when the board plays, in Omaha each player must use two, and only two, and no more and no less of their hole cards to combine with three, and only three, cards from the board to make the best five-card poker hand. Among many other differences, this also means that a four flush on the board combined with only one flush card among your hole cards will *not* produce for you a flush, as it would in Texas Hold'Em. The same also applies to every other possible combination of straights, even full houses, and all other hands in between. In Omaha you must use *two* of your four hole cards to combine with three—and three only—cards from the board in order to make your five-card poker hand. This not only has the effect of increasing the volatility of this game, but for Texas Hold'Em players in particular it can be extremely confusing when trying to transition from knowing Texas Hold'Em into playing proper strategy for Omaha.

In Omaha, your best starting hands are those that have what I call "the double barrel potential." By that I mean hands that can make primarily straights both at the low end as well as the high end. For example, a hand such as Jack-10-9-7 offers you the potential for hitting either the low end of the straight with the flop such as 8-6-5, without exposing you to danger of being outdrawn because any 9 or any 10 will give you a higher straight. This, therefore, protects your hand in Omaha from being vulnerable to another player's higher draw with that same board, and one of the higher danger cards. On the other hand, if you have a hand that contains cards such as 8-6-7-5, you no longer have a hand that can be called the double barrel potential hand, not only because now the flop is unlikely to help you, but because even if it does any one of a number of cards can potentially hit the board and make someone else a higher straight. In the first example, you have about twenty outs, while in the second example most of those outs that will help your hand are likely to result in you receiving the second-best straight, while about half of those outs will most likely help one or more of your opponents make a higher straight. In fact, you should remember that making straights in Omaha is your preferred play, because a straight can occur more than two-thirds of the time in this game. Especially when you start with cards such as these, as well as any number of other good starting hands applicable to Omaha high only. (For more information on this I refer you to my earlier book *Powerful Profits from Poker*, in which I elaborate in much more detail about both Omaha high only and Omaha/8.)

Although Texas Hold'Em is by far the better game, and is justifiably and rightly so preferred by the majority of poker players the world over, there are nevertheless a few diehards—particularly in Europe—who swear by Omaha as the better of the two games. I do not share this opinion personally, primarily because Omaha is such a streaky and volatile game and offers far too many opportunities for people with big bankrolls to simply run over the game by dominating it just because they can, as well as players who are so financially endowed that they will call anything with everything and oftentimes absolutely destroy any sense or semblance of knowledgeable and careful play. Naturally, Omaha purists will argue with me through hell and high water that for precisely these same reasons Omaha is really and truly the game of better skill. Not so, because to my mind Omaha is a game for masochists, and this perception can be proved by the fact that it has all but died out in the United States, except for some notable exceptions in tournaments. The rails of poker rooms everywhere abound with broken and broke former Omaha players who now aimlessly wander the halls of the casinos and poker rooms muttering to themselves how in the world they could have lost everything when they played well and had the best hand all the way up to the very last card. If you are a player who enjoys such great punishment and wish to heap more of it on yourself, depleting your playing bankroll at a staggering rate by diving headlong into the poverty of the insane and feeble, then by all means venture into Omaha as your staple game of choice. For the rest of us, I advise that Omaha is a fine game to learn, and a terrific experience on the Internet, but only from the perspective of curiosity as well as providing you with yet another opportunity to add to your repertoire of game knowledge and poker expertise. If this is your approach, then bless you, because you are truly a poker adventurer and will be rewarded for the knowledge you will gain (even though it is likely to be a very expensive journey through the lowest pits of your stomach).

Omaha is a better Internet game primarily because it is much faster than its real-world cousin. As with Seven Card Stud and Stud/8, in the real world this game is notoriously slow simply because of the nature of what the game is and how it must be dealt by the human dealers. In cyberspace this is not a problem, and therefore these games, as well as the Omaha/8 games, can be played considerably faster, which significantly adds to their appeal. Once you venture into the world of Omaha on the Internet, remember never to start playing with real money. You should take advantage of the many opportunities that the Internet sites I mention in this book offer, and that is to experience all of their games for play money first, before investing any of your real money. This provides you not only with the experience of the games without costing you anything, but it will sharpen up your knowledge and show you exactly why Omaha games are so extraordinarily volatile. You should, however, remember that other players who are playing for free money will also play considerably differently in free-money games than they do in real-money games, and as a consequence you should take your experience from playing Omaha for play money cautiously. Although you can gain needed experience, quite often you garner erroneous perceptions as to how other players will act and react. Players who are playing for free money are far looser with that than they will be in real-money games, although not always. Sometimes players who learn first by playing with play money on the Internet assume that that's the way the games will be in the real-money arena as well, and consequently enter the real-money arena playing the game exactly the same way. This is very good for the knowledgeable players, because such foolish players build huge pots and provide a great deal of dead money. Therefore, your first lesson should be not to become one of those players, but instead learn the game with play money, and then log on to some of those real money tables and, without playing, simply observe how the players play and how the game unfolds. You will quickly realize that real money games are not played in the same manner as play money games, and if you are able to make that observation and determination, and are subsequently able to translate that into your own abilities to play the game for real money, then you will be well ahead of most other players and probably significantly improve your chances of not losing a whole lot.

The second thing you should remember about Omaha games, and this includes Omaha/8 (which I will discuss later on in this chapter), is that because of the popularity of Omaha in Europe just about every Internet poker site that offers Omaha games will be populated mostly by European players. This is especially so for pot-limit games, many of which will be offered in Internet poker rooms. Since European players have such a great familiarity with Omaha, and most of them have been weaned on this game as opposed to Texas Hold'Em, be wary indeed about venturing into such games for real money. Although it is difficult to gain skill and mastery of Omaha games, it is nonetheless possible to do so. It takes a great deal of time, dedication, experience, and a lot of mental and intestinal fortitude, but it is achievable. Since European players have spent the greater majority of their adult poker-playing lives playing pot-limit Omaha, as well as other Omaha derivatives, they are formidable opponents indeed for any American-based, or Texas Hold'Em, player trying out his or her mantle in the Omaha arena. Therefore, as your second piece of advice, if you do want to play Omaha games on the Internet, stay away from the pot-limit games because they are filled with European players who are far more likely to have years of knowledge and experience. Instead, stay with the structured limits because this will be more familiar if you are primarily a Texas Hold'Em player, as most Americans and most other players will most likely be.

The Internet offers structured limits from as low as a few cents to a dollar limit, all the way up to the higher structured limits, and then the pot-limit games, and even no-limit games. If you want to play pot-limit Omaha, or no-limit Omaha, I suggest that instead of playing them in the cash games where you risk losing all of your money, join some of those Omaha tournaments that can be found in both pot-limit and no-limit formats. You can buy into those tournaments for just a few dollars and receive tournament chips, and with those you can experience the thrills and pitfalls of pot-limit or no-limit Omaha. In addition, you are likely to win a pretty significant amount of money if you make it into the money rounds of the tournament, while at the same time risking only the amount of your buy-in. Any poker player in any poker game should heed this advice, especially if you are quite new to the world of poker, or at least new to the world of cyberspace poker. You should never play Omaha in pot-limit and no-limit versions as cash games, but if you must play Omaha or Omaha/8, limit yourself to the experience in the low- and middle-structured limits, and play the pot-limit and no-limit versions only in tournaments. If you play pot-limit or no-limit Omaha for cash money, you risk a great deal to win potentially very little or nothing, whereas if you play pot-limit on no-limit Omaha in tournaments you risk only the small amount of your buy-in while gaining the potential to win a great deal. To my mind this equation is simple to understand, and I will therefore leave it at that.

The third recommendation you should understand if you

are planning to venture into the arena of Omaha games is that small flushes are really not very good. While in Texas Hold'Em it is quite possible to make a mediocre, or even a small flush and still win the pot, in Omaha High this is not so. If you are drawing to a flush, it better be the nut flush or at least the second nut flush. Anything other than these is a prescription for disaster because with four hole cards it is quite likely that at least one of your opponents will have the same flush draw and, therefore, if yours is not a flush draw to the nuts or at least the second nuts, you are very likely indeed to wind up with a losing hand even when you do make that flush. You are far better off with starting cards that include a straight draw, preferably the double-barrel straight draw. If your straight draw also contains suited connectors so much the better, because now you also have the potential of making the straight flush if you get that lucky. Nevertheless, remember that a flush will beat a straight, and therefore it is better for you to have flush rather than a straight with three cards on the boards to any flush. Your straight will play much better if there are no suited cards on the boards that make a three flush and, consequently, the very strong possibility of someone already holding a flush. If all you have is a straight, and the board shows three cards to a flush, and if in particular it also shows a pair, your straight is all but dead and a candidate for the muck.

Similarly, if you are holding a flush, including the nut flush, but there is a pair on the board, chances are very significant that at least one of your opponents has already made a full house. In that case your flush is again a candidate for the muck, and that is something that you will be able to determine only after reading your opponents and making the appropriate analyses of their actions. Such observations are far more easily made in the real world, because there you can actually see your opponents and consequently are able to gain a great deal more information from their behavior. In cyberspace, unfortunately, you cannot do that, and therefore it is often very difficult to accurately determine your opponents' holdings and put them on a hand, particularly for Omaha games. Although you can practice some analysis of your opponents' actions based on past observations, the very same hints and tips and recommendations and suggestions that I offered for observational analyses of Texas Hold'Em games rarely apply to Omaha games in cyberspace. Four hole cards hold the potential for a variety of hands and holdings, so you simply cannot make those same kinds of judgments about your opponents and their potential strengths and weaknesses. Such judgments are much better made in the real world, where you can base everything on the totality of that person's behavior, not only on the cards themselves. In cyberspace all you have are the cards, and all you have are the actions by the other players, which in cyberspace will always happen in turn without any fluctuations, fumbling, indecision, or exuberance. All of those situations and tendencies are eminently observable if you are facing real-world opponents, but are all but impossible and impractical in cyberspace. Therefore, your best recommendation is to play only the best and strongest possible hands, and if your hand does not hit the nuts on the flop, or at least has a very strong possibility and potential to hit the nuts on the turn, throw it away and wait to play another day. As a general rule for Omaha high games, and cyberspace Omaha in particular, you do a great deal more throwing hands away and very little playing. Consequently, you need to have even a thicker skin than you need for Texas Hold'Em games, and even a greater sense of personal discipline and patience.

Starting with any low cards is a prescription for disaster in Omaha High, and therefore such hands should be thrown away immediately. Although in Omaha/8 these are precisely the kinds of hands that you actually want, in Omaha High they are never playable. Hands such as Ace-2-4-5 may be great hands for Omaha/8, but they are entirely garbage for Omaha High. Save yourself money by not playing them, and learn the difference between Omaha High and Omaha/8. Just like it is very important for you to learn the difference between Texas Hold'Em and Omaha games, it is even more important for you to learn the difference between Omaha High and Omaha/8. Although both games are called Omaha, and they all look very similar, they are as different as an orange is from a brick. This is another one of those areas of confusion that many cyberspace players make, especially if they are also interested in high-low split games, and have perhaps experienced both in Texas Hold'Em as a flop game and Stud/8 as a high-low split game. The similarities between games belie their complexities and differences, and that is why so many players find themselves completely befuddled when they enter into these arenas.

Sometimes when you find yourself with mediocre holdings, such as cards that are smack in the middle between those low cards (candidates for being thrown into the muck) and high cards (always playable in Omaha, especially if they are double suited), it is hard to decide whether or not to continue. Hands like 8-7-10-Jack are problematic hands for Omaha High not only because they have the potential of making a straight, but particularly if they happen to be suited, and especially if they happen to be double suited. These midrange-type hands may or may not make a hand, and they face the real danger of actually making a hand that will not be the winner. These holdings often have the potential of making a straight either to the low side or to the high side, while somebody else has made a Queen high straight to your Jack high straight if you hit your high straight, or has made a straight that is higher than the 10 high, or 8 high, or 9 high, or any one of the number of other potential straights that you can make from such holdings, depending on the flop. Furthermore, if your hand is suited, and especially so if it is double suited, you may find yourself in a situation where you make a flush only to discover that your flush is the third nuts and therefore a really bad hand. The danger here is that you actually make your hand only to discover that is not the winner. Whether or not you continue playing with such holdings largely depends not only on your analysis of the game in progress, as well as your opponents, but primarily from your observation of what happens on the flop if you actually progress with this hand that far, or with hands of this nature. If the flop absolutely hits your hand, then it is appropriate to drive the action because this not only allows you to see exactly what your opponents will do and how they will react to your aggressiveness, but also because it has the potential of adding money to the pot in the event that your hand actually turns out to be the winner. Of course, you must pay careful attention to what hits on the turn, and on the river, if the action continues that far. If the cards that hit the turn and river are blanks, inasmuch as you can make such determinations based on your holdings and your analysis of your opponents' potential holdings as well as their patterns of play, then your initial assessment is probably good and you will actually have the winner. However, with holdings such as these among your starting cards, most of the time you will have to hit the flop absolutely and convincingly and thereafter survive the turn and the river in order to preserve the playability of your hand.

The final recommendation that I can share with you for Omaha High is perhaps to practice extreme caution at all stages. Naturally, if you are a European player, then you will have a great deal more familiarity with this game and as a result it will most likely be the kind of game that you choose to play. For American players, as well as players elsewhere in the world, my recommendation will be to stick with traditional Texas Hold'Em and traditional Seven Card Stud, and avoid Omaha games altogether, including Omaha High and Omaha/8. If you absolutely must play Omaha High, then experience the game on the Internet because the Internet poker rooms that I feature in this book offer a wonderful variety of both tournaments as well as limit games in various ranges. After you have gained such experience, file it away in your arsenal of knowledge and commit it to memory, then go on to the far more lucrative games of Texas Hold'Em and traditional Seven Card Stud. If you absolutely must play games like high-low split games, by all means try Omaha/8, but after you have experienced it you will quickly realize that it is far better to play Stud/8—if indeed you must for some strange and inexplicable reason play high-low split games at all. And so this now leads me to the discussion of Omaha/8, which will now be the subject of the remainder of this chapter.

## OMAHA HIGH LOW SPLIT EIGHT OR BETTER

Omaha High-Low Split Eight or Better, more commonly referred to simply as Omaha/8, is a derivative version of Omaha. It is similar to the game of Stud/8, inasmuch as it is a high-low split game in which the best starting hands usually consist of cards that can make both the low as well as a high. Just like in Stud/8, the object of playing Omaha/8 is to scoop the pot, thereby winning both the low and high. To accomplish this, the best starting hands for Omaha/8 are precisely those hands that you would automatically throw away when playing merely Omaha High. Just like in Stud/8 where discipline and a strict adherence to proper starting-hand principles are important to your overall success and profitability, so it is with Omaha/8. This is, however, where all similarities end. Just because Omaha/8 is similar to Omaha High, and in some respects similar to Texas Hold'Em (at least in the procedures of how the game is dealt), and that Omaha/8 is somewhat similar to Stud/8 inasmuch as both are high-low split games with the eight or better qualifier, this does not mean that Omaha/8 can be played purely and only from the perspective of strategy and knowledge as such may apply to these other games. Omaha/8 requires an entirely different set of principles, skills, knowledge, experience, and their application in order to provide you not just with an entertaining but also profitable experience. Grasping the differences between Omaha High and Omaha/8 is equally as difficult as grasping the differences between Texas Hold'Em and Omaha games. What you see is not always what you will get, particularly in Omaha/8. For these as well as many other reasons, starting-hand standards for Omaha/8 are your first and most important key decision. As I have discussed earlier and in *Powerful Profits from Poker,* your best starting hands are those that contain low cards with the potential to also make a winning high hand. Therefore, your best starting hands are usually ones that contain an Ace, because the Ace card can be used both to make the low as well as a high, with the very best four card starting Omaha/8 hand being Ace-2-3-4, with the next best hand being Ace-2-3-5, preferably double suited. If your hands are double suited, you could make a flush for high or straight flush in either suit, with one being the nuts (the one containing the Ace) and the other still containing the possibility of a flush, perhaps even the nut flush if you catch an Ace on the flop. This would also pair your Ace for an even stronger high hand possibility and at the same time preserve the possible straight flush draw for either hand, as well as a variety of straights. In addition to the hands that I outlined in my earlier poker book, in the chapter on Omaha and Omaha/8, following is a listing of very good Omaha/8 hands that are particularly playable in Internet versions of this game:

**Reasonably Playable Hands**

| | |
|---|---|
| King-2-3-4 | Preferably this is double suited, with at least two cards suited. |
| King-Queen-2-3 | Preferably this is double suited, with at least two cards suited. |
| King-King-10-10 | This is preserving the possibility for a straight; however, with a hand like this you are probably going to be drawing mostly to the high hand only. This hand will be playable particularly if you can see that your opponents are probably drawing to low hands and as a result you are quite likely to be the only high hand candidate, or at least a favorite if there is only one other high hand competing against you. |
| Jack-10-9-8 | Preferably this is double suited to preserve the flush and straight flush possibilities, with at least two of the cards suited if not both. This will preserve not only the flush, the straight flush, but also the straight possibilities. Even if this hand is nonsuited it can still be |

| | |
|---|---|
| | playable as a straight only possibility for a high hand. |

**Good Starting Hands**

| | |
|---|---|
| Ace-3-5-7 | This is not as good as the very best hands, but if double suited this is a very good starting hand, and should contain at least two of those cards suited, preferably the Ace-3. |
| Ace-2-5-5 | This is a slightly better hand than the one immediately above, not only because it preserves the low with a high potential, but now you also have a pair that could possibly assure you of having a lock on the high hand in situations where you can flop a full house, or even the rarest of all rare breeds, the quads. Any time you have a pair with an Ace and a low card, such hands are also eminently playable for Omaha/8. |
| 2-3-4-5 | Any hand that does not contain an Ace but consists of all low cards below the rank of 8, preferably below the rank of 6, are very good playable hands for Omaha/8. Especially when they are double suited, with at least two of those cards suited, and preferably the suited connectors. But even in mixed suits this is still a playable hand, and is vulnerable only to a hand that also contains these same cards, but with an Ace. |
| 10-Jack-Queen-Ace | This is the kind of hand with which you are hoping to hit high cards on the flop. If this hand is double suited, which would be the preferable |

circumstance, of course, or at least two of those cards are suited, you're also looking to flop a flush, or at least the draw to nut straight or the nut flush. Hands like this are high only hands, of course, because they cannot make a low, and therefore should be played only in situations where you know you are the favorite to compete for the high side of the pot, or at least feel that you have no other opponents that could beat these hands if they also are drawing for high, or, preferably, isolate only one other opponent who may also be drawing to the high side of the pot.

**Great Starting Hands**

| | |
|---|---|
| Ace-2-3-4 | As I already mentioned, this is one of the best possible starting hands in Omaha/8, preferably double suited, or with at least two cards of the same suit, preferably with the Ace being one of them. This hand provides you not only with the potential to be able to make a scoop, but also protects you if other low cards hit the flop because you can still preserve your almost certain lock on the low hand. |
| Ace-2-3-5 | Not as good as the hand just described, but this is the next best thing. Although not necessarily the best possible starting hand, it is nonetheless a very good playable hand for this game. |
| Ace-2-3-anything | If your Omaha/8 starting hand consists of four cards where your first |

| | |
|---|---|
| | three cards are those as here listed, and your fourth card is an apparent indeterminate brick (meaning a card that cannot immediately be of help), it is still nevertheless a very playable hand for Omaha/8 because it still preserves the possibility of making a good low hand, as well as making a scooping double barrel hand. Although you would be making it with only these three cards, with the other card being an apparent brick, you can use only two of the cards to complete such a hand, which is considerably more difficult than with the above listed hands, but still quite achievable. |
| 3-4-Ace-King | If this is double suited, you not only have the opportunity for making a very good low hand, but also the potential for making a very solid high hand. This is not a hand that can scoop, however, unless, of course, you make the nut low with the 3-4 which also turns into the best high hand. |
| Ace-Ace-King-King | This is a double-barrel blockbuster where you have a virtual lock on the high side of the pot (at least prior to the flop, of course). Although this hand does not have a low potential, in the event that this is double suited you will almost always be guaranteed that you will be drawing to the high side nuts. |
| 2-3-Ace-Ace | This is preferably double suited, but if not at least one Ace suited with either the 2 or the 3. Here you not only have the potential of making a very strong |

high hand, but you also preserve the possibility of a very strong low hand, while at the same time also preserving the possibility of actually having the best low hand that turns into the best high hand as well, thereby scooping the pot.

These hands are among the most playable starting hands for Omaha/8. Although other playable hands can occur as well, you are well advised to learn these hands first, to help you reach the necessary level of discipline required to make this particular game profitable. Especially so for Internet Omaha/8, not only because this game is much faster than its real-world cousin, but because so many players do not have this knowledge and will play basically nothing more than any-four-cards-will-do strategy that is extremely vulnerable to your good starting hands—if you are able to preserve your strict discipline and stringent starting hand selection skills. As you gain more experience you can vary your hands depending on the circumstances, but that will become part of your expertise only after you have gained the necessary experience and comfort at this particular game. If you are new to Omaha/8, begin your hand selections with only these hands, as well as those that I have identified in my earlier poker book for this game.

## THE FLOP

Now that you have learned at least a very best of the starting hands for this game, it is important to figure out what exactly you want on the flop. Here is a list of the potential outcomes of what could be facing you after the flop:

## High-Card Flop

Whenever the flop hits with high cards only, or at least two high cards with rank above 8, this means that you are preferably going for the high side of the pot. If not, you should consider mucking your low draw. You should also be aware that if all three cards on the flop are ranked 8 or higher, this immediately means that no low is possible for this particular hand, and therefore all players will be competing for the pot as if this was Omaha High only.

## Flush Cards on the Flop

Although it is quite unusual for three suited cards to hit the flop, if you have played Texas Hold'Em you are eminently aware that this does happen quite often, or at least with reasonable frequency in accordance with the statistical probabilities for this event. If this happens in Omaha/8, you can safely assume that someone has already made a flush; therefore, unless you hold the same flush—and preferably the nut flush—you should now immediately forgo any possibility of a high hand unless you also have a very good low draw with perhaps a pair that could potentially make a full house if the board pairs on the turn or river, or with such a draw that your low hand can turn into a straight flush as well as the nut low.

## Two Flush Cards on the Flop

Of course, the more likely outcome on the flop is that at least two of those cards are suited. If this is the case, it is quite certain that at least one or more of your opponents are drawing to a flush, so if you do not have the draw to the nut flush, or at least the second nut flush with equally a good low potential, you now really don't have much of a hand. Of course, if you hold a pair you still have the potential of making a full house, but this will be better if you actually hold two cards that form two pair on this flop.

### Low Cards on the Flop

If three low cards of the rank of 8 or lower hit the flop, you now have to make the decision of exactly how well the holdings that you have match this particular flop. It could be that you actually flopped the nut low, in which case you are sitting pretty, especially if you also have the potential to make the nut high to your already nut low. If you do not have this miracle hand, which does not happen often immediately on the flop, what you have is probably a very good drawing hand with which you should see at least the turn, and quite possibly the river. It all will depend on exactly how well your four hole cards match this low flop.

### Pair on the Flop

Whenever any pair shows up on the flop, you immediately face the potential of being up against the mother of all hands, which is the quads. Since all players in Omaha/8, just like in Omaha high only, start with four hole cards, quads will happen far more often than in Texas Hold'Em. This is another aspect of Omaha that Texas Hold'Em players often fail to understand, and find themselves exposed to monster high hands such as quads, or at least full houses, which are eminently possible whenever a pair appears on the board in any Omaha game. You are now facing the very real possibility that unless you are the one with the quads or with at least the full house, or at the very minimum with a very powerful draw to a very strong full house, your high side of the pot hand may be all but dead. You now have to determine whether or not you have any possibility for a low draw—difficult to achieve particularly if the pair that hits the board is of the rank of eight or higher. Any time the pair on the board is of the rank of 8 or lower and the third card on the flop is also a low card (and you have started with a low draw potential, although it is now obvious that you have not immediately hit your low), you should at least have a very good low draw. If you have such a low draw, then you can compete for the low side of the pot, fully expecting someone else to already have the high side of the pot locked.

### Three Connectors on the Flop

Sometimes the three cards on the flop are connected to each other, such as, say, 3-4-5. Now there is the straight potential, and if they are suited, a flush possibility (as well as the straight flush potential and the very eminent possibility that someone has already flopped the nut low). Of course, flops like this do not have to have all low cards. Any such three sequenced cards hitting the flop usually means that either someone among the competing players has already flopped the straight, or at least has a very good draw to make a straight, and depending on the cards that will fall on the turn and the river there is equally the high probability that one or more of your opponents are likely to have draws to the highest possible straights available to be made from the cards that flopped, and then hit the turn and river. Therefore, if you are not the player that either flops the nuts, or flops the straight, or has the potential to have or make an even higher straight based upon whatever these three connectors are, your hand is now dead. If the flop of sequenced cards is of the rank of 9 or higher, then you also know that no low hand will now be possible, and that, therefore, everyone will now be competing for the high end only.

### Potential Straight Gappers

Of course, flops containing three sequenced cards will not be that common. What happens more often are cards that contain gappers—by that I mean hands such as 8-9-Jack, with the 10 being the gapper in between. Any such combination of a multitude of potential flops that contains maybe straights with gaps in between are also very dangerous, particularly if no low hand is possible, and particularly if you are not the player who actually has the possibility for making the best straight out of those hands in subsequent draws.

## AFTER THE FLOP

If you don't flop the best hand, either the low or the high or, preferably, the best low with the best high hand potential, then you should at least flop hands that can *make* either the best high hand, or the best low hand, or preferably the best low hand with the best high hand potential. If you don't flop a hand that meets this criteria, you should rarely play past the flop. Remember this simple rule: If you haven't flopped the nuts, or at least are drawing to the nuts, chances are that in Omaha/8 someone else has, or is. If all you remember from reading this section on Omaha/8 is this advice, you are far ahead of the greater majority of Omaha/8 players, and particularly the vast majority of Internet players of this game.

## STARTING WITH THE BEST LOW

As I have stated many times for high-low split games, beginning with the best potential low hand is by far the preferred situation for all your starting hand selections, primarily because low hands can also turn into high hands, while high hands can never turn into low hands. That is why you should always divide your starting hand selections into the ratio of 2:1 of low hands versus high hands. Therefore, assuming that you will pursue the starting hand requirements of mostly low hands, preferably with high hand potential as well, exactly how often are you likely to win with such holdings? Statistically, and bearing in mind that statistics are laboratory numbers designed to reflect the perfect world under ideal conditions and not necessarily the real world in the immediacy of the moment, the following are some circumstances that you are quite likely to face whenever playing Omaha/8, situations which you will particularly encounter with great frequency on the Internet:

### Starting with Two Low Cards Only

If among your starting four cards you only have two low cards, your statistical chances of making something out of it are as follows:

- Before the flop you have a 25 percent chance of winning.
- If you flop one low card you have a 16 percent chance of winning.
- If you flop two low cards you have a 60 percent chance of winning.

### Starting with Four Low Cards

If among your four hole cards you have all low cards, your statistical chances of making something out of it are as follows:

- Before the flop you have 50 percent chance of winning.
- If you flop one low card you have a 24 percent chance of winning.
- If you flop two low cards you have a 69 percent chance of winning.

### Starting with Three Low Cards and a Brick

If among your four hole cards you're starting with three low cards only and a nondescript fourth card (as I have shown earlier in one of the examples of starting hands for Omaha/8), your statistical chances of making something out of it are as follows:

- Before the flop you have a 39 percent chance of winning.
- If you flop one low card you have a 27 percent chance of winning.
- If you flop two low cards you have a 72 percent chance of winning.

All of these statistics are, of course, for the low hand only. It is quite pointless to try to do this for high hands as well, because the object in Omaha/8 is not to play this game in the same way as you will play Omaha High only, but to play it for the game it is, and that is the high-low split game, where you should almost never enter the pot unless you have very good low starting hands prior to the flop, and improving those on the flop as much as possible. Since this is the object of Omaha/8, the above statistics will provide you with a window into the likely success of your becoming a winner with the starting low hands under the circumstances as described. And that, dear friends, is about all that is required to provide for you the best possible starting framework for playing Omaha/8.

# PartyPoker.Com

I now take great pleasure in being able to bring to you a chapter in which I describe one of my favorite poker sites on the Internet—PartyPoker.com. It occurred to me that such a book as this on Internet poker should not only include information about how to play poker games in cyberspace, but also actually show readers what such poker sites look like, and how to navigate through them. I wanted to be able to not only tell you about Internet poker, but also *show* you. Yes, it is true that the pen is mightier than the sword, but it is equally as true that one picture is worth a thousand words. In all of my books, I have tried to strike a balance between describing what you will encounter and offer you the best recommendations and strategies applicable to the games, as well as showing you as many photographs and pictures of the games as I could. When writing this book on Internet poker, it soon became obvious to me that I should also show you what the experience will actually be when you begin to log on. If you are new to Internet poker, this should help you overcome many of the obstacles that new Internet poker players face as they are trying to navigate through all the various screens and menus. If you are already familiar with Internet poker, these examples can help you make the best use of all those Internet poker sites and their various menus, and in particular how it should be done when it is done correctly.

That's why I have chosen the Internet poker sites I mention in this book. If you follow all that I offer you in this chapter about PartyPoker.com, and the information that I offer elsewhere in the book, you will enjoy playing at PartyPoker.com and learn how to navigate the world of cyberspace poker in general, thereby allowing you to gain an immediate mastery of this technological phenomenon. When I first started playing Internet poker, I would have been grateful for a book such as this wherein I could find chapters that show me how all of it works and how I can get the best possible experience. But when I began playing Internet poker, nothing like this was available. Over the years as the Internet poker phenomenon blossomed and mushroomed the world over, I still could not find any books that actually described the real experience of Internet poker as it actually exists, which showed the poker sites in all of their details, including how to select tables, how to select tournaments, how to make deposits and withdrawals, and how to locate all the various specials and bonus offers. I have therefore tried to make this book precisely into such a great resource that includes all of this information. So, I now wish to invite you to enjoy a cyberspace trip with me as we explore the terrific Internet poker–playing experience that can be found at PartyPoker.com.

## PARTYPOKER.COM HISTORY

PartyPoker.com is the world's largest poker room. With more than 70,000 simultaneous players during peak traffic time every day, PartyPoker.com is larger than all of the land-based poker rooms in the world put together. Known for its highly innovative marketing strategies that attract both new and experienced poker players, PartyPoker.com is the blockbuster success story of online gaming. With the incredible upsurge in poker around the world, greatly driven by televised poker, the online poker rooms may actually be the biggest winners. While brick-and-mortar poker rooms saw a 40 to 50 percent percent increase in the number of players in 2003, the online poker industry grew 500 to 600 percent. But PartyPoker.com rocketed an astounding 1,500 percent. Through a combination of aggressive marketing and robust technology, PartyPoker.com has managed to garner more than 50 percent of the global poker market share. Players at the PartyPoker.com site have access to 10,000 tables from which to choose, plus large-scale tournaments that are held on the site all day. Currently, the weekly tournament prize pools run to more than $5 million.

A key to the company's growth has been the creation of the simplest user interface in poker, designed to be appealing to even the most technology-challenged and intimidated individuals. PartyPoker.com offers 24/7 customer care by phone, e-mail, and instant messaging. Since its launch in August 2001, Party Poker.com has been a major success. The management team takes its poker input from a panel of highly experienced consultants from the poker world. That panel includes World Poker Tour commentator Mike Sexton and the "First Lady of Poker" Linda Johnson, who is a highly respected poker player as well as successful businesswoman. In March 2002, PartyPoker.com staged its first major offline tournament, bringing together many of its leading players who had won their way into the event via satellite tournaments. The first PartyPoker.com Million tournament was held on a cruise ship and paved the way for an annual event. The inaugural tournament guaranteed a first prize of $1 million, making it larger than any other limit Hold'Em tournament in the world. The tournament was also historic, as it was the first major won by a female poker player, Kathy Liebert.

The privately held PartyPoker.com is licensed and regulated by the government of Gibraltar, and the company operates from Gibraltar in Europe. Its software is audited and certified by BMM International, a leading Australian casino software testing firm.

## PARTYPOKER.COM HOSTS

PartyPoker.com is hosted by poker expert Mike Sexton, commentators of the World Poker Tour. PartyPoker.com is a charter member of the World Poker Tour with its flagship event, the PartyPoker.com Million.

Mike Sexton is among the world's most preeminent poker experts, and long considered the "ambassador of poker." He was on board with PartyPoker.com from the very beginning, helping to develop and design its proprietary poker software and the PartyPoker.com Million tournament. He continues to advise PartyPoker.com on software issues, promotions, and tournaments.

## HOW TO START PLAYING ON PARTYPOKER.COM

To play a game at PartyPoker.com, you'll need the PartyPoker.com poker software. This is freely available for download at www.partypoker.com. When you first log on to this site from your Internet browser, the first image you will see is what is called the PartyPoker.com Welcome Screen Index Page. You can see what this actually looks like in Photo 1 (opposite).

Once you have downloaded the software, locate the PartyPoker.com icon (the poker chip on your desktop) and double-click on it. Or you may click on the Start button on the bottom left of your screen and then search for PartyPoker.com in the first menu that opens up. You should find PartyPoker in the upper half of the menu. Just click on it and that will launch the software, taking you directly to the main welcome screen where you can fund your account and start playing. When you have accessed the welcome screen of the site—known as the Lobby in the software language—you'll see a wide selection of live games (both real money and play money). You can see what the Lobby looks like in Photo 2, on page 100.

Once on this screen, the first thing you should notice is the

**Photo 1.** This is the Welcome Screen Index Page that you will see when you first log on to the PartyPoker.com website.

giant jackpot which is displayed immediately to the right of the PartyPoker.com logo. PartyPoker.com is the only site with a progressive jackpot, an innovative system for which the company has filed for a patent. The jackpot amount is visible in the lobby at the top, and the picture shown in Photo 2 shows a jackpot of over $200,000. To put that in perspective, when land-based card rooms run similar jackpots, the amounts are often less than $25,000, with some casinos in Las Vegas offering jackpots that start at $100,000—which is still only half this amount. The way that you can play on the jackpot tables at PartyPoker.com is by clicking on the Bad Beat Jackpot on the list to the left of the screen. The list of jackpot tables will open up and you can then choose the limits you want to play. The house takes a small amount from each pot in addition to the rake and this goes to the jackpot. Given the number of people plying at PartyPoker.com, these small amounts quickly add up to large amounts and the jackpot goes up by almost $50,000 every day. It routinely crosses over the $200,000 mark, giving players yet another unique reason to play at PartyPoker.com.

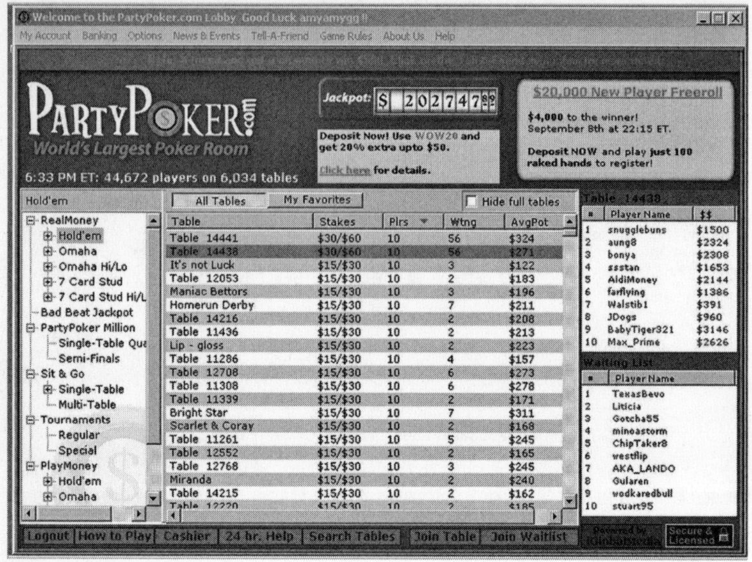

**Photo 2.** PartyPoker.com main welcome screen, known as the Lobby.

After you have investigated all about this giant jackpot, you can then search for the games and limits in the left hand menu and find the game you want to play. When you single-click it in the menu, all the available tables will appear in the main center area. You'll see how many players are playing and how many are waiting, as well as the average pot size. You can also see who is playing at each table. To get to a particular table, simply double-click on it and the software will take you there automatically. Once at the table you can either just observe the game and learn how it works, or you can just watch the game play, or you can take a seat if one is available. You can see what a typical game table looks like in Photo 3 (opposite).

**Photo 3.** A typical game table on the PartyPoker.com Internet poker site.

## PARTYPOKER.COM GAMES

From the Lobby menu, you can choose a variety of different poker games. The poker games that can be played on the Party Poker.com website are as follows:

- Texas Hold'Em
- Omaha High
- Omaha 8 or Better
- Seven Card Stud
- Stud 8 or Better

These games can be played as limit, no-limit, and pot-limit games. Thousands of tables offering a huge variety of limits are available at any time, and around the clock. All of these games are divided between the *ring games*, which are most commonly known by that name but they are games that could perhaps be known to the majority of new players as *cash games*.

There are also play money games, which are free. The cash games, which you will see identified as ring games on the on-screen menus, can be played for very low limits, all the way up to very high limits, as well as in the pot limit and no limit formats for all games available on the PartyPoker.com website. To see what the ring game lobby menu screen looks like, please see Photo 4 (below).

### Free Games

In addition to the real-money cash games, PartyPoker.com also offers all of their games for free! You can learn to play at PartyPoker.com by using the free Play Money options available from Your Account menu. You can use this to help your game, whether you're just learning to play poker, or learning to play a new game, or just want some extra practice. PartyPoker.com offers a huge variety of play money games, including play money tournaments.

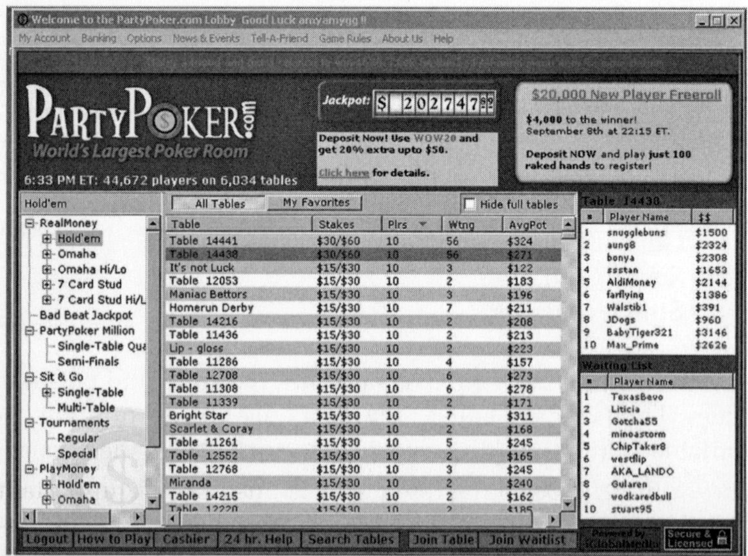


**Photo 4.** This is the PartyPoker.com Cash Game main lobby screen.

### How to Play

If you're not sure about how to play some of these games, or perhaps would like to get a refresher course that can quickly help you understand something you may have forgotten about your favorite poker game, or learn something that is new to you when you are trying to experience a new game for the first time, PartyPoker.com also offers an extensive poker rules and lessons and tips area. Whether you are brand new to poker, new to online poker, or just want to sharpen your game, PartyPoker.com provides you with a complete poker resource.

### 24/7 Live Customer Care

PartyPoker.com has a giant customer care department, always on hand to help you with any concerns you may have, from software installation, to game play, to cash outs. They are available by phone toll-free, and by e-mail, 24/7. The customer care hotline is available at the following numbers:

- +1 888-206-4659 (toll-free USA and Canada)
- +1 206-203-5004 (international toll charges apply)

In addition, there is a free 24/7 e-mail service where you can write to PartyPoker.com with any questions, comments, or suggestions. They respond to e-mails within twenty-four-hours, and you can reach them at info@partypoker.com. You can also check out the main website for an updated list of contact telephone numbers.

## PARTYPOKER.COM SECURITY

Security when playing online poker is one of those important aspects that safeguards and guarantees the integrity of your personal and private information, as well as your banking and playing security. PartyPoker.com uses 128-bit encryption, through

Thawte Security, to ensure the highest level of security and privacy of your data, and all your information is kept confidential and is not shared or sold to third parties. Their state-of-the-art player identification and controlled access login ensure maximum account safety.

The RNG (random number generator) system used by PartyPoker.com ensures that players get a fair deal each and every time. The RNG system generates innumerable permutations and combinations in the fifty-two-card deck when dealing cards that it is virtually impossible to predict. To be considered truly random, numbers must be unpredictable and not related to each other in any way. But PartyPoker also took their security system to the next level through the installation and application of a one-of-a-kind collusion prevention system, created by PartyPoker.com with the help of renowned poker experts. This collusion prevention system detects fraud patterns and identifies colluders. The system employs highly sophisticated automated tools that both detect and prevent players who try to defraud others by getting an unfair advantage over them. In addition, PartyPoker.com's dedicated and ever-vigilant investigations team is trained in using sophisticated tools to the optimum, and as a result you are guaranteed a clean and safe gaming environment.

Players are only allowed one account per player, and the PartyPoker.com security system performs random security checks and other log-file reviews to maintain system integrity and fairness at the tables. Any players found to be participating in collusion or deceptive practices have their accounts immediately closed. Such stringent security measures and dedication to player security and protection of their transaction and personal data, has allowed PartyPoker.com to become licensed and regulated by the government of Gibraltar. Their proprietary systems are subjected to ongoing testing for randomness and fairness by the world's leading tester of gaming and wagering devices, BMM International.

## PARTYPOKER.COM DEPOSIT OPTIONS

When you have learned all about how this works on the PartyPoker.com website, from the information that you have read so far, as well as from the information available from the lobby menus, as well as the About Games menu, and the various instructions under the Help tab on the main screen lobby menu, you are now ready to begin to play poker seriously for real money. Depositing real money on the PartyPoker.com website is made very easy through the cashier deposit procedures that you can quickly learn by clicking on the Cashier icon. You can deposit real money to your PartyPoker.com account using a variety of options including your credit card, direct debit to your checking account, e-wallets including NETeller, e-Passporte, Firepay, and Citadel, and popular phone cards including the Global Connect phone card. There are also money transfer and bank wire transfer options available. For details, simply click on the deposit button on the lobby and follow the easy instructions. In case you need any help, contact the PartyPoker.com friendly customer support at the numbers provided earlier, which are also available on the website at http://www.partypoker.com/. Most of the options allow you to make a deposit and start playing in less than a few minutes and are absolutely safe to use.

## PARTYPOKER.COM CASH-OUT OPTIONS

Of course, after you have won all the terrific amounts of money by playing at PartyPoker.com, either in ring games or the tournaments, you have to know how to collect your money. That procedure is the exact reverse of the deposit options that I have just shown. When you cash out, you must select options for the amount of money that you want to be sent back to you by selecting one of the payment methods that I am about to show you, below. Naturally, all cash-outs must first be approved by the PartyPoker.com internal review process for security purposes. This normally takes one or two days from the time you request your cash-out. Reduce this time by becoming a verified user. You can obtain the details about how to do this by writing to customer service through e-mail or by contacting them through the telephone or fax options I had already listed earlier in this chapter.

So, now that you are ready to cash out your winnings, you first click on the Cashier icon from the main lobby menu, and this will then take you again to the site that displays various logos. There are several options for you to cash out your winnings, depending on which part of the world you live in. You can choose to get funds sent straight to your checking account using iGM-Pay, or get funds on a debit card, which—if you choose options such as NETeller or e-Passporte—gives you instant access to your funds that can be used in stores and ATMs.

There are equally as many cash-out options as there are deposit options. Depending on your location around the world, you may choose from that withdrawal system which will provide you with the best and most inexpensive service. Personally, I use the services of NETeller because I have found them to be a very easy online wallet to transact deposits and withdrawal activities. NETeller also offers a NETeller debit card, which works exactly like your ordinary bank debit card, and which you can fund directly from your NETeller account. The fee is only $2.00, and the ATM withdrawal fee is only $1.75 per transaction. Funding your NETeller debit card takes only one hour and the funds are available instantaneously, meaning that you can withdraw them from any ATM worldwide up to the total amount available, with no restrictions. You can also use this particular NETeller debit card for point of sale purchases, such as gasoline, supermarket groceries, or any other purchases where you would ordinarily use your regular debit card. Although it is up to you to decide which of these deposit and withdrawal options are best suited to where you happen to be in the world, I would encourage you to open a NETeller account especially if you are within the United States.

## PARTYPOKER.COM TOURNAMENTS

There are a great number of tournaments going on day and night at PartyPoker.com. Such tournaments are offered not only in a variety of limits, but also in no-limit and pot-limit formats. In addition, there are also a great variety of play money tournaments where you can practice your tournament playing skills, and become familiar with how these procedures work. After that you will feel much more secure in being able to play the real money online tournaments, which are basically divided into two groups:

- Multitable tournaments, usually with a preestablished starting time
- Sit & Go tournaments, which can be either single table or multitable

Multitable tournaments are the kinds that you see on television during the WPT and WSOP tournaments, as well as that which you will see on the WPT PartyPoker.com Million championships. Multitable simply means just that, that there are many tables, as opposed to just one table. These tournaments usually have a predetermined starting date and time, and that is how you can differentiate between them and some of the multitable Sit & Go tournaments. In these traditional multitable tournaments, as players get eliminated, the tables are "broken down" and remaining players reassigned to reduced number of tables. Such tournaments consist of many players, often many hundreds of players, and in some instances many thousands of players. Buy-ins to these tournaments range from as low as a few dollars, sometimes $5+1 (with the amount after the + being the fee charged by the house), to as high as several hundred dollars for some of the major tournaments. PartyPoker.com not only offers entry into the PartyPoker.com Million championship, but also to a variety of tournaments, including some very high-paying online tournaments exclusive to PartyPoker.com. You can access all of these tournaments from

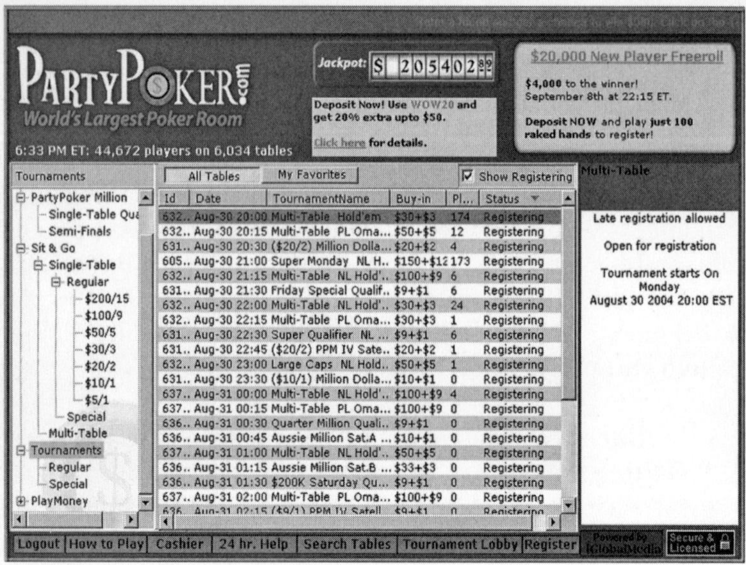


**Photo 5.** The PartyPoker.com Tournament Lobby screen.

the Tournament Lobby menu, which you can see displayed in Photo 5.

The Sit & Go tournaments simply mean that these tournaments start as soon as a preannounced number of players register for the tournament. These run around the clock, and the main advantage is that you don't have to wait too long for the tourney to get started. PartyPoker.com offers both single and multitable Sit & Go tournaments, any one of which will start immediately as the required numbers of players are seated. If such a tournament is a single-table tournament, for example, in most Texas Hold'Em tournaments of this type there will be a maximum of ten players per table. To join such a Sit & Go one-table tournament, all you have to do is select this particular option from the tournament lobby menu; select the game that you wish to play; the limits of the buy-in; whether or not you wish to play limit, pot-limit, or no-limit; and then simply double-click on that particular table of your choice. That will take you to that particular table, and there you can simply click on any available seat.

One of the great features available at PartyPoker.com is the fact that these popular Sit & Go tournaments are not limited to just single-table formats. PartyPoker.com offers a range of multitable Sit & Go tournaments, from as few as two tables, to several. The only difference between the multitable Sit & Go tournament and the single-table Sit & Go tournament version is the number of total players. For example, if you are playing in the traditional Texas Hold'Em game that has ten player positions per table, and you are playing in a Sit & Go multitable tournament with four tables, that means that there will be a total of forty players participating in this particular tournament. To join this particular tournament, you simply select that option from the tournament menu shown in Photo 5, and then relax and wait until all forty players have joined this particular tournament. When that happens, the tournament will start and proceed in accordance with a description of that particular tournament and the tournament rules as displayed on the tournament lobby screen for that specific tournament. To continue with this example, if instead of four tables this particular Texas Hold'Em tournament offered two tables only, that means that you would be participating in a Sit & Go tournament where the maximum number of participants is twenty players, ten players per table—hence this being the traditional maximum number of players per table and for this tournament. And so on, for whatever number of tables there are available for the multitable version of Sit & Go tournaments.

All such Sit & Go tournaments will start as soon as all players are present at the table. Therefore, if you're playing on a traditional Texas Hold'Em table that has ten player positions, as soon as ten players are seated at this table the tournament software will automatically begin the game. As with all tournaments, the pay structure will depend on the number of participants. The pay structure varies for multitable tournaments, but in the Sit & Go versions usually only the top three places are paid. For the actual details as they apply to the particular tournament of interest to you, simply log on to the tournament through the tournament lobby screen shown in Photo 5, and that will tell you all about that particular tournament and its rules, and how many places will be paid. Other than that, playing a tournament in the Sit & Go version is identical to those with which you may be familiar as multitable tournaments. Naturally, there is yet another option available for your tournament pleasure on PartyPoker.com, and that is the PartyPoker.com Million championships. This is the WPT tour championship as you will see on the WPT broadcast on television.

### PartyPoker.com Million

The PartyPoker.com Million tournament remains one of the very top events in world poker. Now in its fourth year, this World Poker Tour charter event takes place each year aboard a luxury cruise. Players qualify online at PartyPoker.com (the 2004 buy-in was only $32) for the live tournament, and qualifiers receive not only their seat at the Finals, but also a luxury cruise for two. The Finals package alone is valued at over $12,600 (Finals seat plus cruise for two). The 2005 prize pool was over $7 million as of the time of this writing, making this the premier poker tournament on the major poker tour. It is the PartyPoker.com's flagship event. To enter the qualifying rounds for the PartyPoker.com Million championships, all you have to do is to locate the PartyPoker.com Million championship logo and click on it, or locate these tournaments in the tournament lobby menu under tab marked Special. To see what the PartyPoker.com Million championship logo looks like, please see Photo 6 (opposite).

## PARTYPOKER.COM PROMOTIONS

PartyPoker.com offers many special sign-up bonuses and frequent deposit bonuses that will make your experience even better. Whenever you are ready to play for real money, take advantage of some of these great offers. Typical promotions include a 20 percent up to $100 bonus, or a $25 fixed bonus, and/or a PartyPoker.com Million tournament freeroll. Deposit

**Photo 6.** This shows the PartyPoker.com Million championship logo. If you want to enter this particular tournament's qualifying rounds, all you have to do is find this logo and click on it.

bonuses keep the action hot. Real money players receive emails with deposit incentives like percentage bonuses to commemorate holidays, the PartyPoker.com anniversary, and other events.

In addition, PartyPoker.com has a five-star customer care team to assist regular players, twenty-four hours, seven days a week. Regular players are assigned dedicated hosts that give great comps and bonuses plus specialized customer care. For more information about current bonuses and promotions, contact PartyPoker.com at info@partypoker.com.

## A Very Special Promotion Just for This Book

I wish to thank PartyPoker.com for providing me with all of this wonderful information, as well as the great pictures that I am able to share with you in this book. As a thank-you to my readers, PartyPoker.com has agreed to provide all of my readers with a *very special bonus* when you sign on to a new account and make your first deposit of real money. By using the special sign-up bonus code: **PARTYCODE,** all my readers will receive a deposit bonus of up to $100 at PartyPoker.com.* This is not something that you will usually find, and therefore if you wish to try PartyPoker.com it is only in your interest to take advantage of this great offer. I thank the staff and management of PartyPoker.com for being so kind to provide me not only with their wonderful information and photographs, but also for this special offer, exclusive only for my readers.

*The fine print: 20 percent bonus only on first deposit. Additional conditions apply. See www.partypoker.com/signup20-100standard.htm for details. Management reserves the right to alter or cancel promotions at its sole discretion.

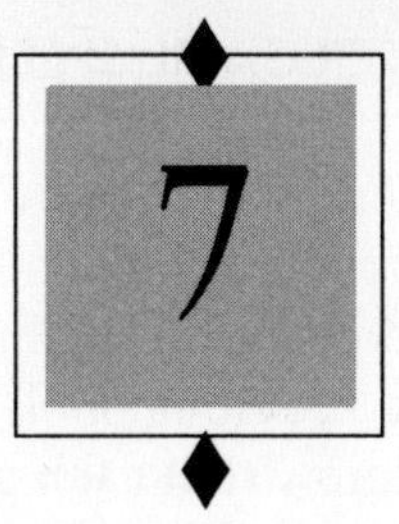

# Strategy for Internet Poker

The first and probably most important strategy tip for playing Internet poker is for you to realize that playing Internet poker is completely different from playing land-based poker in brick-and-mortar casinos or card rooms. Although there are many reasons for this, and I explore most of them in this book, there are three major differences that you must properly understand before you can ever hope to gain a consistently profitable experience playing online poker games:

- Faster game speed
- Lack of physical tells
- Few opportunities to bluff

I will get to some of the other strategy suggestions as we continue with this chapter and those that follow (as well as those that are part of other discussions elsewhere in the book). But for right now I will first briefly describe each of these three major differences between Internet poker games and real-world poker games.

## FASTER GAME SPEED

This means that not only will you play at a pace that is almost double that of the real-world casino poker rooms or card rooms, but also that you will experience exponentially higher costs per game. If you read my previous book *Powerful Profits from Poker,* then you already know that each game carries within itself an inherent expense regardless of whether or not you play a hand or participate in any pot per each hour that you sit at the table. Although all Internet poker games are currently rake based, instead of fee based, this doesn't mean that you do not experience a cost per each hour that you sit at the virtual table in an online poker room. If you're playing a game such as Seven Card Stud where there is an ante, you will experience that ante each time that you are dealt cards regardless of whether or not you choose to continue with the hand. If you are playing Texas Hold'Em games, including Hold'Em derivatives like Omaha games, then you will be faced with the blinds and, in some instances, perhaps even antes. Since you are playing in a virtual card room on a virtual poker table in cyberspace, there are far fewer distractions that traditionally tend to slow down the game in real-world brick-and-mortar casino poker rooms or card rooms. It is also an undeniable fact that the virtual dealer deals the deck and the cards a lot faster than any human dealer can possibly do in any real-world casino card room or poker room. That is why Internet poker games experience double and on some occasions even as fast as four times the number of hands that can be dealt by human dealers in real brick-and-mortar casino poker rooms or card rooms in any one hour. This has the direct effect of exposing you to not only more hands, but it directly means that your cost per game will be exponentially higher.

In a real-world casino card room or poker room, you are exposed to roughly forty hands per hour at a reasonable cost of somewhere around $90 per hour, depending, of course, on the nature of the game and the rake and/or collection that you might be facing. You can properly budget your playing bankroll and your playing time and your selection of hands accordingly. But now you find yourself in that same game in an Internet poker room, where you are suddenly playing at the rate of sixty or eighty hands per hour. For the simplicity of this example, let us assume that you are playing in a shorthanded game where you find yourself facing the speed of eighty hands per hour, which is not all that uncommon, even with up to eight players per Texas Hold'Em game. Consequently, our theoretical example of a $90 per hour cost now all of a sudden jumps to the enormous $180 per hour cost. Even though these are just examples that I am using arbitrarily here to illustrate the point, it is not that far-fetched. I have personally played in games where the cost per hour of just sitting at the game approached these exact figures. In games with higher limits and higher blinds, and perhaps even antes, this can very easily be much higher than even these examples. The effect of this is equally dramatic. When you know that you are facing the attrition of your buy-in at this hourly rate, it becomes just as important for you to plan accordingly. This not only means that you must have an appropriate bankroll for that game and its cost, but that you also must select your hands with an eye out for opportunities to steal the other players' blinds and antes and pick up smaller pots more frequently, all of which is perhaps a little bit different to what you would do in a real-world casino under similar circumstances. It means that you not only have to be more aggressive, but that you also have to be more skillful at the selection of the proper spots in which to be so aggressive. Selective aggression is, therefore, one of the most important and key ingredients in your strategy play.

Equally important is the fact that you have to be more aggressive in the selected circumstances and play a few more hands than you would normally play in a real-world brick-and-mortar casino poker room or card room under the same game circumstances. If in the real world you identify for yourself the formula of at least one decent-size pot per hour that, under your analysis of that particular game, will cover the costs of sitting at the game and provide you with commensurate profitability, now in this Internet poker game your goal will have to be at least two such pots per hour just to keep pace with the game's expense. This has the direct effect of loosening your play, and it will therefore require that you select your starting hands with a great deal more flexibility than you would in brick-and-mortar casinos. However, this should not mean that you would select your hands willy-nilly and forget all starting-hand principles that you have so carefully learned. Just because you have to win at least two decent pots per hour in order to keep pace with the costs of this game doesn't mean that you always have to do this for each hour that you are at this table. Selecting starting hands in a fashion that will cause you to have to enter pots where you do not have the best of it will not have the desired effect of keeping pace with the costs of the game, but will have the direct opposite effect of depleting your bankroll at an even faster pace by causing you to lose pots you should not have entered in the first place.

Part and parcel of your decisions to keep pace with the costs of the game are also your key decisions as to which pots you will enter and how and why. Entering pots with medium or substandard hands simply because you are running out of your two-hands-per-hour formula is counterproductive to the goal. Your object in this game is not to win the theoretical two pots per hour to keep pace with the costs of the game, but to win money. Winning pots is not equivalent to winning money (as we will discuss later in this chapter). Each game of poker, including brick-and-mortar casino poker rooms, card rooms and Internet poker games, is a process of flux. Your theoretical formula may be to win two pots per hour to keep pace with the costs of the game, but this doesn't mean that you should risk losing pots when you know that entering them may not result in the profitability you seek. Although it may be in your favor to extend your starting hand requirements to perhaps the top twenty or top forty hands, and maybe even beyond these as based on your abilities and skills and experience in playing Internet poker, or any poker game, your greatest ability to safeguard yourself against the costs of these games and attrition of your playing bankroll, as well as the losing of pots that you should not have entered, is your ability to select the position in which you will actually commit to any pot. Position selection in any kind of a poker game is important, and particularly so in online poker (as we will also discuss a little bit more later in this chapter). The point here is that just because you know that you are playing poker at a pace about twice as fast as you would experience in a real-world poker room or casino card room, and just because you are also aware this means that your costs of playing at this game can be double that rate, doesn't mean that you have to always stick to that theoretical formula of two pots per hour. Internet poker games are fast and furious, and the pots can be extremely large at times. Biding your time, selecting your proper position and starting hand, and experiencing the proper circumstances all directly influence your profitability, and overcome the commensurate costs of playing in this game. Clearly, the theoretical formula may say that you have to win about two pots per hour; however, in Internet poker it is possible to win just one pot in two hours in order to cover all of these expenses and assure you of a profit, because many times the action is so fast and so furious and the pots so large—and the players entering them so extraordinarily inexperienced—that if you are the experienced and knowledgeable professional player (and pick your hand and your position and your timing well), you will be able to pick up such monster pots often quite easily and thus assure yourself of not only covering the costs of this game but also of profitability in the end.

What is often misunderstood in strategy advice as it pertains to the costs of playing in any given game, or the costs that will be encountered by Internet poker players due to the faster speed of the game, is that most opponents in such games are generally vastly more inexperienced than you are, particularly if you have read at least something about poker—including this book—and hopefully my previous books as well, or any number of the great and excellent books that you will find about poker now available everywhere. Such opponents may have read some poker books, but this does not mean they will be able to translate that knowledge into actual experience. Many online players enter these games primarily to be entertained, and only secondarily to win some money. Naturally, as you increase in limits, these kinds of "let's shoot from the hip" tendencies of the Wild West–kind of Internet poker player become proportionately diminished, but not entirely. Like in the real-world casino poker rooms or card rooms, just because players are playing higher stakes games does not mean that they are equally as proficient in playing them as they should be. The simple truth is there are many people around the world who have a great deal of money and they simply wish to splash it around in games that will be sufficiently exciting to them based on their financial circumstances. And, of course, there are other players who perhaps are not as financially secure as these players, but who will venture into these big games because they think that they can beat them and make some money for themselves. Sometimes it is true, and sometimes it is not. What is an undeniable truth, however, is that even at these higher limits or high-limit games, you can find a great smattering of players who are simply unprepared to play poker of any kind, and even more so unprepared to play poker at these limits and levels. As a direct result, situations such as these provide for you ample opportunities to recover your costs of the game, even games that are as fast as these, and also provide you opportunities to win large pots to assure you profitability, even if you play less than the theoretical two pots per hour. Naturally, these are all examples and each and every circumstance that you may actually experience in Internet poker, as well as real-world poker rooms or card rooms, will always be somewhat different from everything you learn. This is where your flexibility comes into play, and this is where your knowledge and skills and experience are prominently required. How you are able to handle these circumstances ultimately determines exactly how many hands you have to play, and how often, in order to overcome the costs of these games. Remember: be a little more flexible, much more aggressive, and most important, *selectively aggressive* in correct and proper positions. This means playing more hands more aggressively in late positions, and very much fewer hands in early or middle positions. This simple device, as well as everything that has preceded it here, and that which follows or appears elsewhere in this book, will provide for you the necessary framework on which to build your success.

## LACK OF PHYSICAL TELLS

If you have been exposed to poker or poker knowledge, even if this comes just from watching poker on television, you most likely have heard the word *tell* referred to and spoken about many times. The famous poker book, *Mike Caro's Book of Tells*, and its accompanying video, explores this subject in great detail and great extent. It is not my intent to duplicate that work, but I simply wish to refer to it because it will provide you with much more in-depth knowledge as to exactly what a tell is. For the purposes of this book, and this chapter, we shall identify a tell as simply a mannerism exhibited by poker players which allows you to gain an insight into their potential holdings, or the strength and quality of their hands, or lack thereof. For example, if in the real-world brick-and-mortar casino poker room or card room, someone looks at his hole cards in a Texas Hold'Em, or in any poker game and suddenly looks up quickly and his eyes dart around, just exactly what does that mean? Well, in most poker games this means that that person has just picked up a monster hand, something extraordinarily wonderful, such as a big pocket pair, usually Aces or Kings in Texas Hold'Em, rolled-up trips in Seven Card Stud, or some other such big starting hand in whatever game this happens to be. If you see such a player, keep looking at them. Very often this player will look at his hole cards again, perhaps even more than once. They want to assure themselves that they did not make a mistake and that the hand is still the big hand that they thought it was. They might look around the table again just to see if anyone noticed. Usually this is not done because they think somebody has spotted a tell that they might have, but because most such players are completely oblivious that they have just experienced and shown the biggest tell of them all. Most of the time they are looking around the table as a purely animal reaction. An animal that has just made a kill in order to feed itself and its brood will always look around to see if there's any threat to that food they have just obtained. Similarly, the natural reaction of the human predator in such circumstances is to look around to see if somebody can take what they have just received. These are precisely the reactions that you can observe in real-world casino card rooms and poker rooms, because there you can actually see the players against whom you are playing. While I understand that the examples I have just given are extreme examples of someone who is obviously telegraphing such tells, the fact remains that players like this do exist in real-world casino poker rooms and card rooms, and very often just by observing how they deal with hands that are this good, or how they deal with hands that are not that good, or perhaps bad, will allow you to get an understanding as to what that player might possibly be holding, and therefore, how to play against them. None of this is possible in Internet poker rooms.

In the world of cyberspace, no one can hear you scream. You are sitting alone in front of your computer, and the action that goes on is virtual action in the virtual world that really does not exist, except for your perception of it. This is equally so for every other player, no matter where they happen to be. You might be playing in a game with players located in Europe, South Africa, Australia, Netherlands, Sweden, Canada, Mexico, or wherever else in the world anyone has access to the Internet. These are circumstances and locations that are completely foreign to you, as are any of their mannerisms. Since you can't see them, your interaction with them is only through the virtual cyberspace of this poker game. All that exists for you and them are those icons on the computer screen and the commands that the software allows players to make in order to play the game. Everything else, including the hands now being dealt and played, and even the chips you use to bet with, are all simply icons in the virtual world that do not exist for you or them. Therefore, it is impossible for you to use the same kinds of principles that you would in real-world casino poker rooms or card rooms in order to be able to assign any specific or particular tells to any such opponent you might be facing. It becomes difficult to actually use the principles of any kind of a tell recognition method to make judgment calls about what your opponents might or might not be holding. At least this is so for playing the same kinds of strategies and principles that are embodied in books and strategies for real-world poker games, where recognition of physical tells is possible.

There is, however, something which is often referred to as "online tells." Playing Internet poker will expose you to an entirely different kind of world, and entirely different kinds of poker-playing experiences as I mention many times throughout this book. In this particular situation, as it pertains to this discussion of online tells, one of the things that you quickly discover is that even in cyberspace there are patterns of behavior that you can learn, many of which may give you an insight into other players' patterns of playing and therefore a window into their likely holdings. Quite a few articles in the various poker magazines, online discussion groups, as well as books deal with this particular subject. Suffice it to say that some of it is extraordinarily insightful, but some of it is not. The most commonly offered advice for spotting an online tell is to see how quickly a player makes a bet. Usually this refers to a circumstance where the player will bet quickly when she has a hand, but if she has a marginal hand, or something that is not as good, she takes her time about making a decision. Although this may be useful in some circumstances, in the general circumstances of Internet poker this is really not so. Many players make decisions in different patterns, and the speed of a decision is not necessarily a tell. A particular player who acts fast in this hand, and has perhaps acted as quickly over the past several hands (and then all of a sudden acts slowly for the next several hands), may not have altered his decision patterns or playing selection decisions in any way whatsoever. The apparent slowness on his decisions as he is making them now may simply be to a slower connection between his computer and the server. This is a very common problem. Alternatively, any particular player may have to leave the computer momentarily. He may have to go to the bathroom in between hands, and now his hands are dealt before he is able to return and it therefore appears as if he is taking a long time to make a decision. Maybe he went to get a cup of coffee, a cup of tea, or to make a sandwich. Or, perhaps the player is a woman with a baby who has been distracting her for the last several hands, and this means that that particular player is now acting much slower than before. All of these are reasonable explanations why a player would suddenly act slower than before, and none of them have anything to do with a pattern of playing. To base your decision on something called an online tell that has to do with the speed of a decision when it comes to the players actions is usually wrong. Among all of these possibilities, the most common reasons why players act fast on some hands and slow on others is simply the problems with the connection speeds. Or with home-based distractions. That is all. It has nothing to do with the kind of patterns that they play with, or the hand that they might or might not be holding.

The only real and significant tell that is possible to be able to use to great effect in Internet poker games has nothing to do with the speed of the game or the speed of the decision of the player, but more so to do with the kinds of cards that they show, and the kind of betting and raising and calling that they are doing, and in which positions they are doing it. It doesn't matter how long it takes them to make that decision, but the *nature* of the decision—once made—is what provides you with the tell. To spot such tells from such online players, you must pay careful attention to what they do, when they do it, how they do it, and if there is a showdown, exactly what kind of hands they are showing. Many times you may notice that these players habitually raise on the button, or in very late position such as the next to the button or the second seat off the button, regardless of what kind of hands that they might have. You can spot such habitual raisers simply by taking a note of what they do, how often they do it, the positions in which they do it, and what kinds of hands they are showing at the showdown, and whether or not they actually get to the showdown. Many such Internet poker players simply raise from these positions no matter what they have because they have learned that many people respect such raises from such positions and therefore they can pick up the bets that have already been made in front of them almost without any action, or certainly on the flop or on the turn if it's checked to them and they continue betting. However, these very same players will quite often relinquish their hand if it is raised, or re-raised, or if they are simply bet into at some point. The best way to tell if that particular player does or does not have a hand is to check-raise them. Wait until you have a reasonable hand, or perhaps even no hand at all, and then do this prior to the flop, on the flop, on the turn, and even on the river, if that particular player is still there and still betting. Particularly if you have noticed that this player habitually raises from this position and then when it comes to continuing with a hand either relinquishes it habitually, or in the showdown shows what is a very small or mediocre hand, or no hand at all.

This is actually a real online tell, and it is common in all poker games, particularly Texas Hold'Em and Texas Hold'Em derivatives. I call this the TV syndrome because most of these players have learned to do this by watching the WPT and WSOP on television, and they very often see players at the final tables make huge raises in these tournaments from those positions, often with nothing at all. Erroneously, these online players translate this into something that can be explored and exploited frequently, even habitually. Such situations may work in tournaments, and particularly during final table play, but it does not work in any Internet-based limit poker game, particularly at the lower or middle limits, especially when done habitually. Unless, that is, you actually do it well and always show down what is the best hand, at least a hand that was the best at the time when you raised with it. Even if such a hand does not turn out to be the winning hand at showdown, players will notice that when you raised with it, at that moment it was the best, or at least had the potential of being the best at the time when you raised with it. But habitual position raisers, such as those I describe here, rarely do this and simply continue to raise willy-nilly no matter what they have because they think that that's what they're supposed to do in those positions. Once you can recognize such a player, and identify them as being precisely this kind of player, you have just picked up an online tell. You can now act accordingly.

Another similar online tell is by observing what players do in early situations. Some players habitually call the small blind because they consider this to be "only half the price," something again they have learned from watching television and listening to the commentators. When you are playing in an online poker room where you get about fifty to sixty hands per hour, and let us here postulate the very conservative fifty hands per hour as our base per hour hand counts for this and other examples from now on, consider the fact that you will be exposed to the small blind every ten hands in any Texas Hold'Em–type game. Therefore, you will face the small blind a lot more often then you would in a real-world casino poker room or card room. If you habitually call each and every small blind you are now almost doubling the cost of your per hour exposure to your bankroll, and significantly contributing to overall bankroll attrition. Players who habitually do this are always putting dead money into the pot. Take a careful look at the players who are playing their small blind, and how they handle it. If they always call from the small blind, then take a careful look as to what they do afterward. If they then throw their hand away if there is a raise, or if they then throw their hand away if there is a bet on the flop, or even on the turn, this is another online tell because you can now safely assume that about two-thirds of the time the small blind will call with dead money and with a hand that eventually will be relinquished, or one that will not be a winner. Playing against such random hands as the blinds is always a problem in any Texas Hold'Em–type games, but by paying careful attention to how players play their blinds, particularly the small blind, you can pick up yet another tell that you can exploit. If you know that the player habitually calls the small blind, then call that small blind from late position if all you are facing is the small blind and the big blind. Make them put their dead money into the pot, and then hammer them on the flop, the turn, or the river, if you have any kind of a hand and they are still in there with you. Most of the time you can pick up the small blind's extra bet, as well as the big blind with later bets, while raising the small blind and the big blind from the button (or in the cut-off seat); this may have provided you with only the small blind or the big blind instead of the complete bet from the small blind and perhaps an extra bet from the big blind later on.

A similar tell from a person playing the big blind is much more difficult because the big blind now has a full bet invested. That particular person may call a one unit or two unit raise from the big blind, but this does not mean nearly as much as the player doing the same thing from the small blind. You now need to pay attention as to how that big blind plays afterward. See what they do on the flop. Sometimes, the big blind always bets if the flop does not hit any paint, meaning the face cards. This big blind has learned, not only from books but primarily from watching poker on television, that most players enter the pot holding big cards, often referred to as "paint," and therefore such players are wary of flops that do not contain cards that hit them, but cards that could potentially hit any random hands such as the blinds. The small blind is much less likely to make this play, particularly if they have called a raise in addition to merely calling the half-price bet by matching the big blind. In such circumstances the small blind probably did that because they did pick up some paint, or perhaps a reasonably decent hand with which they could call such an extra bet. This also means that if the flop comes with a smattering of small cards, it is unlikely that the small blind calling such extra bets will actually have a piece of it. It is much more likely that the small blind will be in an equally desperate position as any other player that had called with paint, and it is now that the big blind seeks to exploit this particular flop.

Although sometimes the big blind will succeed, what you are looking for is a habitual player in the big blind who always does this. There may be times when they actually do hit the flop with such rags, but if you spot a big blind player habitually doing this, such is also an online tell because no such player always can match such raggedy flops from the big blind equally at all times. Internet poker allows you to make notes and keep notes anonymously about such players, and this makes it possible for you to keep a record of players who do this and identify them as such habitual players, and remind yourself that they are actually exhibiting what can easily be called online tells. It is really only in the circumstances that I have just described that you can actually identify anything that could even reasonably be called an online tell with any kind of a degree of at least workable and useful accuracy. There are other online tells that could be possible, such as betting behavior from players in middle positions, in addition to the betting behavior as I have just described for early and late positions; however, those are really much harder to determine because players in such middle positions can basically have anything. The main problem with Internet poker is that you are facing a far greater number of random hands, because many Internet poker players play with just about anything because they are hopeful of catching something, no matter how much it's going to cost them. This is especially so in the lower to medium limits, and less so in the higher limits, although it is still prevalent. To my mind, therefore, observing the pattern of behavior from habitual players from early and late positions, as I described, is a far more useful discipline than to try to pick up something called an online tell simply from the speed of the action of the player. That is not an online tell, because the speed of somebody's decision has almost nothing to do with what they are holding, but much more so to do with whatever it is that is distracting them in their home environment, or at work where they might be playing, or, which is much more common, the simple problems with the Internet connection speeds with which they are connected to that particular game server. What is often called online tells I like to call playing discipline and observation. Watch what players do in very early positions and in very late positions. What they do, how they do it, what they do it with, and how and why they continue with those hands thereafter—that is what will actually provide you with the most accurate information that you can actually use. Therefore, these are the only online tells that I think can be workably useful.

## FEW OPPORTUNITIES TO BLUFF

Bluffing is an important part of any successful poker player's arsenal of skills. It is also something of an art. Equally, it is something that can be easily explained but something that cannot equally easily be put into successful practice. Being able to bluff properly and successfully requires a multitude of skills, as well as the ability to recognize the proper and correct opportunities in which to do this. It is much easier to bluff in real-world casino poker rooms or card rooms, precisely because this is the real world and there you can actually see your opponent. Because you are able to see your opponent, many times you can pick up on tells, just like those we discussed earlier, and those that you will learn as you continue to play and gain more expertise. Successful bluffing, therefore, requires a combination of skills, opportunities, table image, and presence, as well as your ability to be able to read your opponents and recognize their tendencies as well as tells, if any. Just about none of this is possible in cyberspace. Although it is still possible to bluff in cyberspace, many of the principles used in real-world casino poker rooms or card rooms that allow players to successfully bluff on numerous occasions, and thereby add a substantial portion to their profitability portfolio as a result, is not equally as successful in Internet poker games. This is primarily due to the difference between how poker is played in the real world as opposed to how poker is played in cyberspace. Although there are many such differences, the most important differences between cyberspace poker games and real-world poker games are:

- Real-world poker games are more about *playing your opponents*, and less about playing your cards.
- Cyberspace poker games are more about *playing the cards*, and less about playing your opponents.

As you can see, these two principles are diametrical opposites. In simple terms, in the real world you can concentrate more on the study of the players who are your opponents and concentrate less on the cards that you are holding. Of course this does not mean that you entirely drop you're starting-hand requirements, or the value of the cards that your playing, or how they match up to the flop, or the remaining cards yet to be dealt, depending on which poker game you happen to be playing. But it does mean that your study of your opponents, and how they react and how they play, directly influences your ability to be able to control that game and make profits from it on a regular basis, often regardless of what the value of the hand that you are actually holding may be, and much more so vested in the value of the hand that you are *representing* as having to your opponents. This is also why bluffing is so important in real-world poker games, and so much more successful in them. If you want to learn more about real-world poker games, I refer you to my book *Powerful Profits from Poker*. In that book I discuss not only this aspect of your skills, but also the various hand rankings and selections that contribute to your ability to be able to not only establish a solid table image and reputation, but to be able to exploit it in derivative circumstances as they apply to the game in progress, and thereby being able to exploit your opponent's weaknesses for added consistent profitability.

In cyberspace Internet poker games you cannot see your opponents, and therefore you are unable to successfully and consistently determine their behavior patterns in the same manner as you could in real-world casino poker rooms or card rooms. As we have seen previously, it is nevertheless possible to be able to determine some kinds of patterns of betting behavior, something akin to what we might be able to call tells. These are borderline tells, but it is nonetheless possible to exploit them successfully, albeit cautiously. This leads us to this item and illustrates one of the most significant reasons why in cyberspace poker games playing your cards is far more important than playing your opponents. Many successful players in real-world casino card rooms or poker rooms do not understand this principle and therefore cannot play successfully on Internet poker sites. Playing Internet poker by using the principles you have learned in the real world, or from advice found in books and texts pertaining to real-world poker, or probably in the school of experience and hard knocks, will not succeed there. The world of cyberspace is much more volatile, with many greater and wider swings in your fortunes, and playing solid poker based on the kind of experience that you would have learned for play in the real world simply means that you will be exposed to a great many more bad beats. That becomes incredibly frustrating, and you might even begin to question your own abilities as a successful poker player. Conversely, players who have learned to play on the Internet find it difficult to transform and translate their play and their acquired playing principles in the real world. Cyberspace newbies, as I like to call them, are mostly young players who have experienced a great many hands in cyberspace but have not experienced equally many poker games as they are really played in the real world. Consequently, when they venture into the real-world poker games they become just as confused as real-world poker players trying out the Internet. Cyberspace poker players usually are frustrated by the apparent slow pace of real-world games, and this usually causes them to play many more hands much more aggressively. As a direct result this causes them to loosen their starting-hand requirements and play bad hands out of position simply due to the apparent frustration factor of the seemingly slow progress of these games. Cyberspace players are used to fast games, and they are definitely not used to sitting for long hours waiting for good hands to show up and circumstances becoming advantageous and applicable to them. Although eventually cyberspace players find their game to be much more easily adaptable to the real-world casino poker rooms or card rooms, as opposed to real-world players trying out the Internet, nevertheless this learning curve is likely to cost them a lot of money. This is not only due to the above-mentioned frustration factor, but also because these players are used to playing their cards more than their opponents, and this leaves them vulnerable to a great many plays that real-world poker players have in their arsenal and can now use to exploit the cyberspace newbies.

The problem is, therefore, one of diametrically opposite styles and expectations, and this leads us to the point of bluffing. Cyberspace newbies are vulnerable to a successful bluff from the real-world player when playing in the real-world casino poker rooms or card rooms, while real-world players trying out the Internet poker phenomenon are equally as vulnerable to aggressive plays by cyberspace players who have experience in cyberspace and who play aggressively, much more aggressively in those positions than real-world players would anticipate. This makes real-world players who are trying out the Internet vulnerable particularly to early position bluffs. Here, cyberspace players play aggressively into what is obviously a very strong hand held by somebody who is an experienced real-world player, and who therefore expects that their opponents have a hand that is much better than theirs and are therefore much more willing to relinquish such holdings rather than continue with the hand, only to discover to their chagrin that such a player betting into them actually had a very substandard hand and was simply pushing it to be able to bully the table. Such bullying play is a borderline bluff, although most such players in cyberspace actually don't recognize this for the skill that it is. Most of these players do it because aggression appears to be natural, and because aggression is something that they hear from all of the commentators on television. They also read about it in all the poker books now available, as well as various newsgroups, discussion groups, and cyberspace chat groups that contribute to the worldwide phenomenon of poker. Unfortunately, what many of these players forget is that aggression is qualified, or should be qualified, by the word *selective.* These players seem to forget that the entire expression consists of both words *selective aggression,* and they remember only the word *aggression.* This makes them usually strong players against someone who gives them too much respect, but also leaves them vulnerable to real-world skills of bluffing when they venture into real-world casino poker rooms or card rooms. Eventually this leaves them vulnerable to counter plays by players who learned that their aggression is nothing more than blustering aggression, and not very often backed up by hands that deserve such aggressive play.

All of these circumstances are problematic, and in cyberspace in particular almost entirely eliminate any kind of principle of bluffing that can be currently understood as applicable to poker games as they are known in the real world. As a consequence, finding good opportunities to bluff are few and far between in cyberspace poker games, although not entirely absent. I have just described one situation where blustering aggression from early position into what is obviously a better hand held by somebody in later positions can very often work by causing that player to relinquish those holdings, particularly if that player places the aggressive player on holding something that might be better than the hand that they actually have. This same bluffing principle can also be used to such effect in real-world poker games. It is, however, more effective in cyberspace particularly because of the nature of those games. Of course the direct opposite is also true. Although in the real world, bluffing from late positions, particularly when you are on the button or in the cut-off seat to the button, or in any one of the three late positions (particularly in Texas Hold'Em–type games), it is most definitely advantageous—and an important part of the profitability arsenal of any skilled poker player—doing so in cyberspace poker games usually results in your losing a lot of money. Many cyberspace poker players have learned poker first by watching television, and on television they see plays like this and hear commentators constantly say what a great bluff this was from late position, and how important it is to be able to bluff in late positions, particularly on the button, or in the cut-off seat. As a consequence, the cyberspace newbies think that everyone making a bet from late position is bluffing, and as a result they will call you down no matter what they've got and no matter how much it costs them. This has the direct effect of practically eliminating all bluffing possibilities from such positions, although not all. But the most beneficial by-product of this is that if you actually have very strong hands in those late positions, you can very easily exploit such Internet players for many additional bets that you would have never received in real-world casino poker room or card room games. It is precisely because cyberspace newbies think that anyone in late position is bluffing, particularly if they are raising or re-raising or continue to bet and call and re-raise and raise previous bets, that you can use the direct reverse psychology effect of this play and only make such plays from those positions if you actually have very strong holdings, and preferably the nuts. You can also use the reverse psychology principle by bluffing from early positions as opposed to late positions and entirely confuse the whole table of cyberspace players you might be facing. Once you have achieved such confusion among your players, you can then exploit it for a variety of plays, including strong plays with strong holdings, as well as bluffs with naked aggression. Only then will any kind of bluffing work on a semiconsistent basis, although you must be very careful not to do this too much because eventually you will start getting called down, and if you are unlucky enough to have to show your very weak hand, from that point on you will have to do a great deal more work to reestablish your position and the confusion among the remaining players before you can ever do this again. You will find in cyberspace that once you turn over weak holdings, everyone will always think that you are bluffing all the time, and you will be called down no matter how much it takes. The converse is also true, and that's where the benefits lie, because if you show strong hands on a consistent basis this will open up your avenues to bluffing, and you can do more of it as a result. But don't get married to bluffing, particularly not as something that you will do regularly and often. Before you ever consider bluffing in cyberspace poker games, first make absolutely sure that you establish not only a solid reputation in this particular game, but confuse your opponents as much as you can.

To confuse your opponents, first show down really strong hands from just about every position, and then make your plays from different positions trying to do the exact opposite to what your opponents expect you to do in those positions and with those flops, or cards. Once you have established both a solid reputation and the ability to confuse your opponents, only then can you bluff successfully in cyberspace poker games. Knowing this, becoming aware of this, and putting it into practice successfully and consistently allows you to bluff in cyberspace much more frequently than many other players are now able to do. But always be wary of doing it too much. Once shown as a bluffer, it might take you several days or even months of solid play before the rest of the cyberspace players again start believing that you actually have what you represent. And that is actually the key to almost everything in cyberspace, including just about any strategy advice applicable thereto.

You must play your cards more than your opponents before you can play your opponents regardless of the value of your cards. This is a very important lesson, so please read it again and understand what it means. In cyberspace, holding good cards and playing them well and, in particular, showing down very strong hands, is extremely important not only to your long-term profitability, but particularly to your image as a strong player. Only then will you be able to bluff successfully, because if you do *not* first do this, you will thereafter be seen as a chaser or habitual bluffer, and this means you will *not* be able to bluff successfully just about anywhere or at any time, and instead, you will be called down each time. Even your good hands will be run down by a multitude of players, causing you to experience an increasing frequency of really bad beats and suck-outs. This is not what you want, so learn to play good hands well, and learn to bluff only after first establishing yourself and your table image and strong hand selection starting skills.

# Strategy Hints and Tips

The several items of strategy advice that I have just outlined in the previous chapter, including all of their many details, are perhaps the most important to your arsenal of knowledge and skills for any cyberspace poker game. They are, however, by no means all that there is or that you should be aware of. Consequently, this chapter includes a potpourri of various other strategy advice, hints, and tips, as well as appropriate and pertinent discussions of such topics that I personally consider to be important for anyone to have success in playing cyberspace poker, both for cash or ring games, as well as tournaments. Chapter 10 continues with more general advice for Internet poker strategy. For right now, I begin by showing some of the most important differences between Internet cash games and Internet tournaments. These are important distinctions, because although both types of games may look the same and share many similarities, including procedural similarities, they most definitely are not the same.

## INTERNET RING GAMES AND TOURNAMENTS

Cash games are also known as ring games, because they are basically limited to the ring of the players at that particular table and do not extend beyond that particular ring of players in the game. Tournaments, on the other hand, are usually what's called "multitable" tournaments, and this simply means that there are many tables with many players all competing for the final prize, which in most such tournaments is a series of pays usually from the first all the way through to however many there might be scheduled for that particular tournament. You can find this information on the specific Internet poker site's tournament menu. In addition, other chapters in this book, particularly those in which I describe my favorite poker sites, also show how all of these tournaments and ring games actually work.

### Ring Games

Ring games are the cash games into which you can buy for as low as the minimum requirement for that table, and they usually play to what is called "limits." Unless this is a cash game that is either a pot-limit or no-limit game, most such games will have posted limits. These can be as low as several cents to as many as several thousand dollars. For many new players, the kinds of games they like to play are usually in the $.50 to $1 range, or perhaps in the $1–$2 range, $2–$4, or even as high as $8–$16. These kinds of limits can easily be found on many Internet poker sites, among all of their games. Because Texas Hold'Em is such a worldwide phenomenon, and such a popular game (primarily due to its exposure on television), about 90 percent of all the kinds of games that you will experience will be Texas Hold'Em games, even though other games are frequently available. To make things easier, I use Texas Hold'Em as an example—unless I say otherwise—because it is appropriate to that particular content.

Whenever you are playing in any cash game on a cyberspace poker table, perhaps the first thing that you notice—and something that you have to get used to—is that garbage sometimes wins. Sometimes it appears as if garbage is winning most of the time. This is particularly noticeable in small-limit games, but even noticeable in higher-limit games because of the quality of the opponents that you are facing. More than three-quarters of the players that you face in the small limits, and perhaps two-thirds of the players that you face even in higher limits, are what I call Internet newbies. These players are usually young, sometimes even teenagers. They are from all over the world, with access to a computer and the Internet, and they play for these very small stakes. More sophisticated and older players usually play in the higher-limit games, but even there you can face opponents who know very little or nothing about poker, and are learning as they are experiencing these games. Such opponents simply don't know that they should throw their hand away when beat, and sometimes the garbage that they are playing will turn golden as they hit miracle draws to defeat you. I have seen incredible suck-outs and one-out miracles that simply defy any concept of poker, and even the statistics that apply to them. "How in the world could you stay in there against all these bets and raises with that garbage?" is a question asked quite often by a multitude of players, perhaps including yourself when facing such horrendous bad beats and suck-outs. Although it is true that in cyberspace the language is considerably more colorful and very often peppered with profanities—the nature of which would make a sailor blush—the point is always the same: the incredulity that many players so often express when they see their good hands get absolutely clobbered by hands that such a player should have never played in the first place, and certainly not have continued with past the flop, or past the turn, especially when there are multiple raises and re-raises facing them and they require absolutely perfect hits of cards in order to even make a hand, much less a winning hand.

Learning to deal with this is a part of discipline, but it is also a part of strategy. Although it is true that in the long run good hands in poker always wind up with the money in the end, the inevitable fact remains that—in cyberspace in particular—such strong hands often get defeated, and sometimes horrendously defeated by such bad beats and suck-outs. Most of your opponents simply don't know any better, and they get lucky. If you are sitting at a ten-handed poker game, such as most Texas Hold'Em games are, and you are actually the kind of solid player that we all think you are, that means you are facing a table where 80 percent of the players are not as good as you. This also means that you might face roughly eight to nine opponents who don't know what they're doing, and are probably going to be playing just about anything. In real-world poker games, you are usually facing random hands almost always only against the blinds, and sometimes perhaps against one or two other opponents who may be poker greenhorns. But in cyberspace you can face an entire table composed of such players, particularly in the lower limits. Therefore, you now not only have to defeat opponents who actually might have something, but at the same time have to defeat a multitude of random hands held by players who can be playing just about anything. As a direct result, good starting hands—such as big pocket pairs, for example—lose a lot of their value, even if they happen to hit the flop. I have faced many situations where I have raised with pocket Aces, including doing so in prime positions, and have actually flopped a set of Aces, which under normal circumstances would be considered as an extremely good hand, particularly against random holdings by opponents. To my chagrin I was facing a table where I had five callers. Based upon my analysis of this particular game, only one of those players could possibly have held anything that could have defeated my set of Aces on the flop. I felt relieved when I bet on the turn and that player folded. This left me facing four other players, none of whom I could have put on any kind of hand other than the random hand. It did not appear from the flop, or the turn, that there would be anybody still in the hand that could actually have anything. Imagine my surprise when I was check-raised, and then the pot was raised and capped by the other players before it ever got to me. Furthermore, imagine my continuing surprise when this continued all the way through the turn and to the river. I did not make a full house, and that left me vulnerable to a variety of hands, but it didn't appear to me that there could be any hands there that could have actually made anything other than either a smaller set, or perhaps two pair. Therefore, imagine my surprise when the winning hand was a 7-3 offsuit, having flopped a 4, and then turned a 6, and then rivered what I have later learned was a 5 to make a 7-high straight. Not only was this player all but drawing dead on the flop, as well as on the turn, but in order to make anything from that garbage he not only had to have perfect running cards, not only had to avoid a pair on the board which would have given me the nut full house, but had to hit the last remaining 5 in order to make that garbage into the straight that turned out to be the winning hand.

This is an actual example of an actual hand and an actual situation that I faced, in which this happened to me exactly as I have outlined it here. What is even more incredible, this is not the only time it happened. This exact situation happened to me no less than twelve times over the six years or so that I have been playing Internet poker regularly. In addition, situations similar to this, such as someone playing deuce-trey offsuit and catching a 5 to make the wheel to beat my set, have happened hundreds of times. The more you play Internet poker, the more you are exposed to these horrendous beats and suck-outs. The point I'm making here is that such garbage sometimes wins, and often appears to you in the short term to be winning far too often and far too much. In order to overcome this, you must have strong discipline to not let that sway you, put you on tilt, or force you into the maelstrom of a trap in which you start playing exactly those kinds of cards hoping to catch exactly those kinds of miracles. This is the problem that is faced by the majority of cyberspace poker players; they see the garbage winning so often they begin to think that's the way they should play, then quickly disregard all of their discipline or poker-playing knowledge and skills and try to shoot it out with everybody on every hand. This is self-destruction at its highest point, and such a player is on super-tilt. If this is you, you'd better remember what it is that you started out to do and try to regain your sense and sensibility and discipline, or you will spiral down the maelstrom into a pit from which you will never recover. Don't become such a victim. Remember that in cyberspace garbage wins, and it appears to win much more often than you would expect, even statistically. Equally remember that this is a *perception*, made even more visible by the simple fact that in cyberspace you play usually at about twice as many hands per hour as you would in any real-world casino poker room or card room. As a result you see many more hands, and this means you see many more beats, and you face that many more beats and suck-outs yourself. You will observe many more such garbage hands winning against other opponents, even if you are not involved in the hand. This has the effect of reinforcing your perception that this is happening far too often, and that as a result you have to play that way in order to be able to win in cyberspace. This is not so, it is only your perception, and it is a human vulnerability because we are more likely to remember these bad occurrences than those in which the hands we expect to win actually do win and are not so defeated by such garbage so frequently. Additionally, you must also remember that you are facing a multitude of random hands because many of your opponents simply will not know what they are doing, and certainly not recognize that they should have never entered the pot in the first place with such substandard holdings, and not know that they should throw the hand away because they are drawing all but dead. Unfortunately, the sad reality of cyberspace poker is that many times these fools are reinforced in that erroneous opinion because they actually catch such miracle hands and cards once in a while. To overcome this perception, you must take all that you have in your arsenal of discipline and knowledge and recognize that these are situations and circumstances that only *appear* to be as they are, and that over the long haul, playing good hands well will prevail. However, in the short term it nevertheless will hurt, but that is part of the Internet poker experience. Learn it, realize it, be aware of it, understand it, and deal with it. By doing this, you learn and acquire perhaps the most important aspect of cyberspace poker discipline, and that is a serious piece of very good strategy advice.

## CHAT WINDOW

Every Internet poker site and every Internet poker table, including tournament poker tables, have what is called a "chat window." This is an area of the computer screen and graphic design where you can type messages to send to other players that are on the same table with you, and basically serves the function of community chitchat. If you're sitting at a real-world poker table you would be able to see the other players and talk with them. Unless you are playing in Europe, where talking at the poker table is generally frowned upon, most poker games involve quite a bit of discussion, and in the United States in particular quite animated discussion. Like in the real world, where you can very often pick up a physical tell from one more of your opponents, not only depending on how they are behaving and how they are playing, but also how they are talking, that is also possible on the Internet. Use the chat box to monitor the chitchat between other players, regardless of whether or not you participate in that discussion. As a means of a strategy provision, I encourage you to monitor those discussions, but do not participate in them. Even if you are specifically selected by someone who wants to chat with you, such as a player who wishes to tell you "nice hand," or something like that, it is usually better to ignore it because if you do not you can very easily become embroiled in a chitchat with that player, or other players on that table. This can be very distracting on the computer, because you cannot simply speak what you wish to say, but you actually have to type it in and then hit "enter" on your keyboard in order to post a message, all the while keeping track of what is going on at the table. Some players can compose messages easily, not only because they can type very well, but because some of them may also use voice-recognition software to allow them to make such chats without actually having to type anything; they simply speak it into a microphone. Although such voice-recognition software it is not yet universally available, nor would always work with every Internet poker site, nevertheless should it be available to such a player this would almost be the same situation as that you would encounter in the real-world poker room, where anything you have to say to your opponents you can simply say without being distracted from what's going on in the game. However, if you do not have such voice-recognition software or the computer capability to make use of it, or if it doesn't work with the poker site where you are playing, your only alternative is to use the keyboard and that can be time consuming and distracting. In fact, many poker sites automatically lock you out of chat when it is your turn to act, because it has been the experience of many players on the Internet that those who wish to chat are often very slow in actually posting their chats, and thereby delaying the action while they are trying to type what it is that they wish to say. Personally, I very rarely chat with anyone, primarily because it distracts me from observing what is going on in the game, and who's doing what, how, why, when, and all of these other observations that are possible in Internet poker rooms that provide you with a multitude of information about those players' playing tendencies. These situations combined are cumulative observations that collectively can be called "combined tells." Although individual tells are very hard to obtain and make accurate use of, as I had described earlier, a combination of these factors can together form a very powerful combined tell.

Keeping track of what is happening in the chat box can often provide additional valuable information into the mindset of the players who are so chatting. Combine this with their playing tendencies as you are observing them and you might be able to add an additional small factor to your overall concepts of those players' combined tells. The kinds of tendencies you are looking for are either expressions of frustration, or bravado, lack of knowledge, lack of experience in playing poker, expressions of a long losing streak, discussion of hands and how they were played, expressions of a long and protracted winning streak, expressions of home-based distractions, people chatting to make friends and therefore not paying attention to the game, as well as an entire variety of different psychological perspectives all of which can be glimpsed from monitoring such chatting in the chat box window. Although some players use this effectively precisely to combat this kind of perception, by doing exactly the opposite to what they are saying, those players are very few and far between and therefore I don't think you should worry about them. In most Internet poker games, and particularly so in the lower limits and small entry fee tournaments, people usually say exactly what they are thinking, and may also represent exactly the kinds of holdings that you might think they have. If someone says that they are tired because they have been playing for twenty-four hours without any sleep, you can pretty much assume that that is a true statement. If someone says that they have been late making action because they've got kids playing in the room, then that is exactly what's happening in their home-based distractions. If somebody says something like, "Sorry I was late but I had to stir the soup," then you know that this player is cooking something and only partially paying attention to the poker game. Same with players with the distractions from their kids, or whatever such stated distractions may be. Basically, this allows you to see whether players are actually committed to the playing of poker for profit, or simply using this as a distraction for something to do while they are dealing with boring or mundane things, no matter how distracting that might be in their own home environments. This same kind of psychological mind-set is also a window on exactly what they are playing. If you see such a player checking, and checking, or calling, and then suddenly on the turn, or the river, coming out betting when a flush card hits, you can usually bet your bottom dollar that more than 90 percent of the time that player did so because they actually made a flush. This applies to any kind of a hand, including pairs, straights, sets, two pairs, or whatever number or variety of possible holdings these players might have. Again, although there are some players who will actually do the exact opposite to what you think they might be doing based on this information, such as coming out betting when that flush card hints, or whatever "danger card" they might think it was, those players are not all that common. As a general rule, players who represent what could be their potential holdings as per your observation of the exposed cards and their subsequent actions, or inactions, almost always have exactly what you actually think they have. Yes it is true that about 10 percent of the time these players do not have what you think they have, or have something much better, or do not have anything at all but are instead trying to make a play on you, you are far better advised to give them credit for having what they are representing, particularly if they suddenly come out firing when a potential danger card hits, as that card is relative to what you have. This is yet another situation where you can gain valuable information by monitoring the chat box. Perhaps after this hand has concluded that player will say something like, "I finally hit my second pair," or "Phew, I thought I would never hit that straight!" or "Glad I stayed with those overcards"—all of this provides you with valuable information as to how they are playing, and what they were hoping to get. It also simply tells you that these are those kinds of players who only come out gunning when they actually hit a hand, or have a hand. You can, therefore, play them accordingly not only in these situations but in other situations where their actions will lead you to believe that they either have a hand, or have just made one.

As you continue to monitor the chitchat that goes on in these chat boxes in Internet poker rooms, you will soon become familiar with these distinct patterns of talk and how they apply to the manner in which the players chatting played their game. It also allows you to see how other players who are not chatting played against these players, and this provides you with additional information as to how to handle them. Generally, keeping your opinions to yourself as they may apply to whatever is being said, or as they may apply to the game, or as they may apply to any questions that you might be asked from other chatting players during the progress of this game, can help you remain more focused and less distracted. Don't share information with other players, and in particular don't try to educate stupid players who have lucked out or made stupid plays that worked out. The less information you provide to other players about yourself and how you play, or how much you know, the better are your results. Additionally, the less education you provide for other players in the game, also the better your results. If someone makes a stupid play against you and they succeed because they catch a miracle card on the turn or the river, say nothing. Simply let it go, practice your own personal self-discipline and understanding of exactly what happened, and go on with your game. It doesn't matter what kind of a flurry of discussion may occur in the chat box of that particular game after such an event, or a series of such events. It doesn't matter at all, as far as your participation in such discussions is concerned, but you should instead carefully monitor what is being said, by whom, and why, and what information is being exchanged and by whom. Internet poker allows you to remain completely anonymous, except for your screen name, and that is a distinct advantage if you know how to take advantage of it. Many players get sucked into participating in these discussions and it costs them. As much as you might be steaming, and as much as you might want to jump in and say something, learn to practice self-discipline and don't do it. Instead, use the window of opportunity that these chat boxes provide for you to view information provided by others, while you stay behind the plate glass window and not let anyone see in. The less you talk, the more mysterious you are to your opponents, and therefore the more money you will win from them.

Also be aware that in many of these Internet poker sites some of the comments that are being exchanged in the chat boxes have almost nothing to do with poker, or the game in progress. This is also important to note, because this tells you that these players are distracted and are more interested in making social contact than in playing the game. Sometimes players use the opportunity to do this to try to make friends; to set up dates; or to talk about football, baseball, basketball, hockey, sports in general, or any of a variety of subjects—none of which have anything to do with poker or the game in progress. This is again something that provides you with valuable information, and you should make use of it as much as you can. However, perhaps the biggest problem with these online chat boxes is that many players use them to express statements of crude profanity. Some players seem to find it important to belittle anyone else who wins a pot against them, and often to do so in language so raunchy and raw that a boat full of sailors would blush and plug their ears. Most of the time these players are only teenagers. Since the Internet and the world of instant communication offer them the possibility and opportunity to be able to talk to just about anyone anywhere, and particularly so in Internet poker games, many of them express their anger, or whatever problems they might personally be experiencing, in extraordinarily foul language in the chat boxes at Internet poker games. If you plan to play on the Internet you should immediately develop thick skin and recognize and understand that the human being is not only a social animal, but one that is linguistically skilled, and that the real world of human communication in the twenty-first century does not necessarily revolve around the pristine language that is permitted by the American FCC for broadcast standards. Words that are banned in public, or frowned on, are freely thrown about and exchanged in Internet poker chat rooms. Be aware of this, and be able to deal with it. Fortunately, every Internet poker site that now exists has strict standards against profanity. If they find a player expressing themselves in such profane language, they immediately remove that player's chat privilege for at least a month, and if such a player persists in such profanity, or player abuse, then that player is entirely removed from their poker site and placed on the Internet players' blacklist. If you want to know what such an Internet players' blacklist is, I refer you to my book *Powerful Profits from Internet Gambling.*

If you find yourself offended by some such actions by another player, or yourself spotted a player or players expressing themselves profanely, the best thing you can do is to either immediately telephone that Internet poker site's customer service, if a telephone link is provided, and while still at the game tell the customer service operators which players are committing these acts of profanity. Make a note of the hand number displayed in the upper left-hand corner, or perhaps somewhere else on that particular poker table, or in the chat box, and tell the customer service operators who these players are and point to the hand in question. Or if the poker site where you are playing does not have twenty-four-hour telephone support, which most of them actually do, you can always take note of that offending player's screen name and immediately e-mail customer service and support and tell them the same information, including the hand number if possible, the name of the table where you were playing, the time when you were playing if you can, and especially the player's screen name. Community policing of this nature quickly weeds out those that would misuse this chatting option for purposes of profanity. Every Internet poker room that I mention in this book has made great strides in keeping such players out of their poker rooms, as well as monitoring and policing the exchange of information as best as that can be done. I applaud this, and I compliment them, because it is extremely difficult to do, particularly when such players may be frequent losers. Nevertheless, the Internet poker rooms I mention in my book have gone to great lengths to protect not only the integrity of their game, and the enjoyable experience of their players, but they make absolutely certain that misuses of this wonderful window of communication are not permitted on their sites. Of course, you can help them do a better job, because no one can know everything or everyone at every time, particularly since all of these Internet poker sites have many thousands of players playing at the same time, and new players joining practically every minute. Help yourself and help them by monitoring abusive players, and report them as quickly as you can. Nevertheless, you should be aware that if you join any Internet poker room you might run into such a situation, and you should be able to handle it appropriately, and not let yourself be disturbed by it. On the contrary, use this as an opportunity to exploit such a player, because they are obviously demonstrating gross stupidity, and to tell the poker site that this player has conducted himself or herself in such an unpleasant and unacceptable manner. Today, and especially on the poker sites I mention in my book, these kinds of occurrences are becoming increasingly more rare, but you should be aware that you might become exposed to them inadvertently, and therefore allow yourself to be equipped with enough discipline not to be distracted by such situations and occurrences, and also possess enough foresight and determination to report it immediately to that site's customer service representatives.

## DECISION PATTERNS

Another important part of your strategy discipline is to observe the decision patterns among your opponents. I have already discussed this in the section on tells, but here we focus more on your own decision patterns rather than those of your opponents. While it is true that you may not always be able to tell whether or not your opponents act slowly at one time and quickly another time because they either have a good or bad hand, or vice versa, because such observations may be entirely due to situations completely irrelevant to the holdings of cards, such as perhaps connection problems, what you can control instead is how *you* behave. This is good advice for real-world casino poker rooms or card rooms, and you can apply it equally well to Internet poker games. If you always do the same thing the same way, no matter where you play, your opponents will quickly pick up on it and play you accordingly. If you're playing in a real-world casino poker room or card room and you look at your hole cards in Texas Hold'Em–type games, and you spot a really big pocket pair, or a really big starting hand, and immediately thereafter you snap your cards down to the table and your eyes go up and dart around the table, this is about as obvious a tell as there can be in a live poker game. To everyone around the table this immediately tells them two things: first, that you are an inexperienced player, and second, that you have a visible tell. Everyone will thereafter play you accordingly. Of course, if you become aware of this, you can turn the tables on them by doing the exact opposite when you actually have nothing, and that can help you with your bluffs. But that is something that you can do only if you are very sophisticated and if you are able to pick up on the fact that others have picked up the tell on you, and you actually know what that tell is and when you do it. You can do something similar as part of your playing discipline on the Internet.

On the Internet it is not possible to act out of turn, because your action buttons do not allow you to make that action until it's your turn to act. Although you can use the pre-action buttons—the raise, call, or fold buttons—prior to it being your turn to act, that action will actually not happen until it becomes your turn to make that action. This prevents you from making a spontaneous or out of turn bet, or raise, or any kind of an action, something which is very possible and often done by inexperienced players in real world casino poker rooms, particularly if they spot such a nice hand and can't wait to simply act on it. You may find this on Internet poker sites, but to a much lesser extent because there you simply cannot pick up on any such possible tell because the players' action is always in turn, no matter how quickly they want to act on whatever it is that they might be holding, or represent as holding. Therefore, the best thing you can do with this particular piece of advice is to teach yourself not to fall into any such patterns that others may be able to recognize. Don't always do the same thing the same way. By that I mean to vary your play and your decision style. Sometimes when you have a good hand, you can click the "raise any" button and comfortably sit back until the action comes to you and the software will automatically raise whatever bets have been made before it becomes your turn to act. At other times when you want to do the same thing, don't do anything until the action bar appears with its accompanying chime, and then perhaps wait a few seconds before you make that very same raise. Similarly so for any other action that you may want to do, no matter what that may be. Don't always raise quickly when you have a raising hand, don't always call quickly when you have a calling hand, don't always fold quickly when folding a hand, and basically try to vary your game and decisions as much as you can without any kind of protracted lingering or excessive waiting to make the decision.

As you become more experienced in Internet poker, and perhaps poker in general, you will quickly discover that every poker game has its own peculiar heartbeat. Each game paces itself differently from any other, and as players join the game and others leave the pace changes, often quite quickly and perhaps many times during even a single round. Keeping tabs on the pace of the game gives you an indication of the kind of timing that is appropriate for the variations of your decisions, and you can thereafter clock yourself accordingly. Maintaining an equivalent pace while at the same time varying your game is not something that comes easily, but it is something that can help your profitability. Exactly how well you do this will depend on you and your mastery of Internet poker, as well as your knowledge of the game and your ability to be able to observe the pace and conditions of the game in which you are playing. None of this is always the same, not only in different games on different tables but in each and every hand that you receive while playing in that particular game. Although it is not possible for you to accurately predict such patterns in your opponents, because of the various circumstances of exactly what Internet poker is, you are after all in control of yourself and therefore should be able to make these decisions as part of your own playing discipline.

You can also help yourself by observing the way that the combination of factors that I have already described apply to your particular game. Make the decisions that allow you to determine whether this is a loose game, passive game, chatty game, or silent game, and if a Hold'Em game, whether it is an aggressive game, a loose passive game, an action-packed but passive game, or any of the many possible combinations thereof. One other thing you can do to help yourself is to make the decision to never just call a hand if you are in position, but to always raise with it. Making the decision to always either raise or fold is something that will help your poker game, but it has to be qualified with knowledge and experience. As with any patterns, particularly those we are discussing now, falling into this pattern all the time can be counterproductive. As a general rule of thumb, you should always try to either raise with a hand or fold it. But that is a general rule only, and not something that should be considered as a hard and fast requirement. There are many circumstances that mitigate this particular strategy advice, and how this might apply to your particular hand in progress depends not only on the game itself, but on a myriad of circumstances that surround the play of this hand, including the hand that you have and the position in which you hold it. Although the rule of always raise or fold is good to learn and to appreciate and to practice, the problem is that becoming married to it can cause you to become transparent as a player. You will find this in Internet poker rooms just about everywhere, because there will always be a bunch of players who never do anything other than raise with the hand or throw it away. You can quickly spot these kinds of players and therefore be able to play against them accordingly. If they raise in early or middle positions, it is obvious that they have something. If they raise in late positions, they either have something or they are trying the positional raise play. Either way they quickly become transparent and then you know how to deal with them. The problem we are trying to overcome here, as it pertains to you, is for you to avoid falling into exactly these kinds of patterns. Remember the general rule, but also adapt it to best fit the circumstances. Sometimes do the exact opposite to what the other players might expect you to do, and even if you don't win the pot you will serve notice that you are capable and able to vary your play and this will instantly throw your opponents into confusion which you can then exploit later. This goes hand-in-hand with the earlier advice, and simply will help you to avoid patterns in your behavior while at the same time keeping to the tried-and-true principles of playing poker profitably, and exploiting your hand values and position accordingly.

## SOME THOUGHTS ON TOURNAMENTS

Perhaps the best piece of advice I can give you in regard to tournaments is to remember that playing in tournaments is substantially different from playing in Internet cash games. Playing online tournaments is also substantially different from playing land-based tournaments, not only because of the number of players that you most likely will have to face, but primarily because of the medium in which these tournaments take place. It is not uncommon for Internet tournaments to have upwards of 600 players, and to be concluded in less than four hours. In land-based tournaments with 600 players, it would probably take two days to play it. Or, if it does not take two days to play, it may certainly take at least twelve hours, or perhaps more. That's why most of the land-based tournaments—with the possible exception of the big buy-in tournaments or the WPT and WSOP events—usually have less than 600 players. Although this is likely to change significantly as poker becomes more and more popular, and indeed is already doing so as more and more players enter land-based tournaments, you can gain valuable experience in being able to handle the situations by playing such tournaments online. This contributes to your overall tournament discipline and experience and skill and provides you with a window on your ability to handle that many opponents and develop your skills of being able to play long enough to reach at least into the money. You can best gain this experience by entering some of the small buy-in tournaments, such as $5+1 (with the amount following the + being the juice to the house), or perhaps $10+1, $20+2, and higher thereafter. But it is these lower buy-in tournaments that offer you the greatest exposure to such huge fields of players and thus provide for you the best training ground. You can also experience this in the various freerolls being offered by all of the poker sites that I have mentioned in my books. These are usually incentive-based player reward tournaments, entry to which is free of cash buy-in, but usually require accumulation of player points as incentives. Some poker sites allow you entry into these freerolls simply by joining them, as a reward, or perhaps as a reward for depositing additional funds, or for depositing original funds. Such freeroll tournaments usually have many more players in the regular buy-in tournaments, even the smallest buy-in tournaments. These freerolls have anywhere from 1,000 upwards of 4,000 players. Clearly, you will have a very large field to compete against, and you should be prepared to spend many hours playing, particularly if you want to make it into the money. Many of these tournaments last for several hours, and the tournaments exceeding 3,000 players often last anywhere from twelve to twenty-four hours of consecutive play. This is a lot of stamina and a lot of dedication. Many of the poker sites on the Internet, including those I mention in this book, have started to limit their free-roll tournaments to no more than 1,500 players because of this. Even then it is a lot of players against whom to compete, and it will take time. Be prepared for this and also remember that if you want to play any comparable tournaments such as this in the land-based events, with that many players it usually takes three days. Although twelve hours at the computer can be more exhausting than three days in the land-based tournament, where you will get frequent dinner breaks that last at least an hour, as well as having nights to sleep and rest in between continuing the tournament, something which you do not get with Internet poker tournaments, you can still enjoy this and play well because you are playing in your own home where, presumably, you have all the creature comforts at your disposal to help you last all these hours.

When playing any Internet tournament, the advice that you always hear—usually from various articles posted on the Internet or published in various poker magazines—is that you should never use the Limit bet button to make a bet or raise. The general consensus of this advice is that because you are playing in a no-limit tournament, you should always make use of the varying bet structure, either with the on-screen slide bar, or by entering the amount on your keyboard and then pressing the bet or the raise button. The simple fact remains that this advice is only general in its applicability, and should not be used as a rule of law, much in the same way as with the item we have just discussed above pertaining to your pattern of betting behavior. You first need to study the composition of your particular table, and then clock the game and make a determination as to exactly what kind of a makeup of players you are facing in this particular situation. In tournaments you will be moved from table to table as the requirements dictate and as players are eliminated; you frequently have to make these decisions and calculations again and again, and often in very different positions relative to where you were seated at your initial table. You have to take into account a multitude of changing circumstances, and be able to make proper judgments based upon them. Sometimes, if the circumstances so dictate, it may be cheaper and more profitable for you to simply use the Limit button to make your bets or raises, and save the variety of other raises for other circumstances. There are two situations in particular in which this can be used to great effect.

First, early on in the tournament where the blind structure is relatively small. Here if you have a marginal hand, you may wish to simply bet the smallest amount, raise the smallest amount only, or simply call the smallest amount wagered by someone in front of you in the turn of action. This allows you to see a cheap flop, or to make a cheap raise, both of which allow you to gain an equally cheap exit if it turns out that you must relinquish your hand. The small raise like this may also indicate strength to the other players, and you may get several of them to drop out, something which you may not often be able to do if you take the advice mentioned earlier, and always raise more than would be the case by using this Limit button bet. Many Internet poker players, particularly tournament players in the lower buy-in tournaments, are wary of players making large raises, even if that raise is the standard three times the big blind, which is the amount often quoted in just about every poker book and poker article related thereto. Although this is a great general advice, and a terrific rule of thumb, once again it is something that should not be considered as a law. Becoming married to it will defeat the purpose for which it was intended.

You must be able to modify this betting behavior as it suits the situations that are particular to your table, and even more particular to just that hand in progress.

Second, later in the tournament when the blind structure increases exponentially, resulting in several of the short-stacked players becoming exposed to too much expense to allow them to last for much longer. In circumstances such as this raising more than the simple limit raise amount allowed for by the game software may cause such short-stacked players to suspect a bluff and consequently force them into an all-in decision. Unless you actually *want* to force your opponents into such an all-in decision, it is far better for you to make the minimum button raise. (I don't mean the button in Texas Hold'Em, meaning the latest of positions in the game, but rather by this here I mean the "onscreen icon button bet" that causes such an action bet to be made without the use of the all-in slide bar.) By making such a minimum bet, or such a minimal raise, you save yourself from exposing your hand to an all-in re-raise and provide yourself with a cheap exit in the event that you must relinquish your hand thereafter. You also allow yourself the opportunity of forcing your short-stacked opponents to make a small call with what is probably an inferior hand, and thereafter be able to get them to fold their hand when you subsequently make a very large bet, far in excess of what the minimum bet or raise would be, as based upon the limits as posted by the bet limits. The strategy here is that you first make a small bet or a small raise without using the variable bet slide bar, and then see what everyone else does. If you have a strong hand, you may be able to exploit several additional bets from other players yet to act behind you, which you otherwise would not have received if you had made a larger bet, such as the often recommended three times the big blind, or three times the next bet limit amount bet. This offers you opportunities to be able to gain additional bets, as well as additional value from your short-stacked opponents who might just be willing to call anything at this stage as long as it doesn't cost them too much, and therefore be able to get more and more money into your pots when you have a strong hand. But such a bet also allows you to relinquish your hand without additional costs if the flop does not hit you, or if the turn card, river card, or whatever combination of cards yet to come in whatever game you happen to be playing makes it obvious, or at least possible, that your good hand now appears to face a significant likelihood of losing.

By being able to so vary your betting structure you will save money in situations where a large bet would be faced with a comeback over the top re-raise, while at the same time providing you a cheap exit if you have to relinquish the hand, as well as adding substantially more value to the pot in the event that your hand remains the best and will eventually win. This may thus provide you with the opportunity to make a large raise or a large bet later on, at that time with a bet many times your original bet. This setup allows you to play your hand in a much more flexible manner and opens up for you the possibility of being able to make much larger wagers later on if it certainly appears that your hand is still good, or had improved. Therefore, to my mind, suggesting that you play any hand in any poker game, including tournaments, particularly no-limit tournaments, where you would be advised never to use the Limit buttons for your bets and raises in minimal amounts, is inappropriate because it exposes you to more volatility and more losses, while preventing you from gaining the kind of profitability that you would have if you are able to use it circumstantially by applying your variance to your experience and knowledge and observational analysis of the game and hand in progress. This goes hand-in-hand with betting patterns and behaviors, and just like in cash games, playing the same way all the time in tournaments is counterproductive in the short term, as well as in the long run. The reasons I have just outlined are only two that relate to this item, but they are by far the most important. Everything else will become second nature to you as you continue to play and gain expertise in Internet tournaments, and the more you play and the more you experience exactly these kinds of situations, the more you can vary these playing principles accordingly. If you are playing in any such tournament and you simply cannot remember these two points, as well as perhaps none of the advice provided earlier, then at least memorize this: Never do the same thing exactly the same way again. If this is the only piece of advice you remember from this entire poker book, you will be light-years ahead of the majority of Internet poker players.

## Collusion

Finally, a few short words about collusion. In case you're not aware of it, it is an inevitable fact of existence in the poker world that there are often one or more players who are playing the same game together and play by agreement against the remaining players. This is what is called "team play," and it happens everywhere. There are many real-world midrange poker games in which you will find several such players who may be playing as a team. It is difficult to make that determination exactly, unless you know these players intimately and they confess this is what they are doing. Casino poker rooms and card rooms frown upon this practice because it is borderline cheating. Although technically these players are not cheating, because they are playing the game in accordance with its rules, it is not uncommon for two or three such players to sit in the game together and keep raising the pot until only they remain, and thereafter fold their hands giving the pot to the other. By doing this, all the other players who have invested money in that pot with hands that were perhaps better than those played by such team players have now contributed pretty much dead money to this pot. They were forced out of it by the collusion of players who raised the amounts so high it appears to the other players that one or more of them really had a hand that was much better than those of the other players still in the hand up to those points. Team play such as this does not require any of the team participants to actually have any kind of a hand at all. All that is required is that these three players, or however many there may be in the team on that table, simply raise and re-raise each other until they drive out everybody except themselves. Then one of them wins the pot, and this goes on for the remainder of the game. In the end, however many there were cash out and meet up later to divide their winnings.

You may have heard of such teams playing blackjack, but the difference is that blackjack teams are playing as a team against the casinos, and not against the other players. Playing blackjack against the casinos by utilizing knowledge and experience—often referred to as card counting—or any of the other playing principles that can be mastered by intelligent and sophisticated players, is not illegal, does not defraud, and it is *not* collusion. Unfortunately, the same cannot be applied to such practices when they happen against other players in poker games, ten-handed for Texas Hold'Em, or nine-handed for Seven Card Stud games, or at whichever poker game this may be happening. When such a team is present at a poker table, they are directly exploiting the other players and no one else. The casino still gets its rake, or its participation, and therefore the victims are only the other players. Every casino poker room or card room definitely frowns upon this, and if any such players are detected in any such poker game they are treated harshly indeed, and you can take my word for it without any further colorful illustrations. Suffice it to say that if such poker teams are detected in any poker room or casino card room, they are unlikely to ever try this again after they are dealt with.

In cyberspace, however, there is no such peace and no such police. Internet poker games are very open to a multitude of such practices, not only between players, but with only one player. Although most Internet poker sites, and particularly those that I mention in my books, allow only one live account for real money, there are occasions where one player can register with several different screen names. This is not possible on the sites that I show here in my book, but it may be possible on some others. I am, therefore, mentioning it here only for you to be aware of it. On such sites a player may be able to sit at the same table with two or more screen names and perform that very same kind of collusion team play that would take two or three players to do in the real world. Although this has not been prevalent, with most single players choosing rather to play more than one table at a time instead of trying to usurp the Internet poker sites' security protocols by attempting to sign on with more than one live screen name, it is nevertheless possible. However, what is more common, and something that the Internet poker sites cannot possibly hope to combat, is collusion among players who all have a single sign-up account, but who are all playing on the same table using telephones to communicate to each other. It is extremely easy for one player to call his two friends no matter where they may be in the world, and for all three of them to sit at the same table and have a live conference call on entirely separate telephone lines, where they let each other know exactly what kind of a hand they have. In this way they can communicate to each other and practice collusion in the same manner I described for that which is possible, but not very common, in the real-world casino poker rooms and card rooms. Something like this is much more easily practiced on the Internet, and although it is not common because the Internet sites are careful to monitor this kind of betting behavior, it is nevertheless extraordinarily difficult for anyone to police because you just don't know, and can't make assumptions just because you suspect something like this is happening. To be fair, you are extremely unlikely to encounter this kind of play, particularly in the majority of the kinds of games in which most people play on the Internet, but you should watch for it and know that it may happen. It is hard to combat, not only for the Internet poker room, but for the players playing in that game. However, there are ways that you can detect this, and if you do I would certainly recommend that you instantly contact that poker site's customer service and let them know that you think this is happening. If they can confirm this, they will quickly eliminate the players who are guilty of it and blacklist them.

One way that you can spot such collusion among two or more players is to see how they behave in their betting behavior and patterns of action, and exactly what kinds of cards they show if indeed there's a showdown. The best telltale sign of collusion among two or more players is if you suddenly see them habitually raise and re-raise everything, and then as soon as it is down to only them they suddenly stop, or one makes the bet and the others fold immediately. Playing with such collusionary tactics usually is done to avoid a showdown. These players don't want to show the hand with which they have played. Any kind of a showdown is a telltale sign, especially if the aggressors turn over hands that are obviously not the kind of hands that any player would play precisely in that manner. Although it is true that sometimes novice or newbie players may appear to play exactly in this reckless manner, you can quickly spot such a newbie by the recurring patterns of this behavior, and by the fact that he or she tends to showdown hands that are very weak. Collusionary players do not want to showdown hands, and want to eliminate all opponents before it comes to showdown, so that one can make the final bet and the others will fold to relinquish the win to that player. If you suspect that this is what is happening in the game in which you happen to be, your best defense against this is to simply call everybody and *force them into showdowns*. Although this may cost you a few bets, the benefit to you, that poker game, and that poker site will be enormously higher. If there are any such collusionary players in that game, they will quickly leave because they understand almost as instantly as you that they probably have been spotted and that you will not allow them to get away with it. This works even better if you happen to get lucky against them, or hit a streak of good cards, or even if you have really bad cards and by forcing showdowns make it obvious that you will not allow them to do this. Although I understand that these situations are *very infrequent* indeed, and also that it will take a great deal of sophistication on your part to be able to actually do what I have just described, once you reach that level of experience and sophistication playing Internet poker, this provides you yet another important piece of strategy advice that permits you to continuously increase your profitability while minimizing your exposure to costs and risks.

Finally, remember that the poker sites I mention in this book are the best that there now exists, and that therefore you very likely will *not* experience this on any of their games. But if you venture outside of my recommended poker sites, you may find yourself in such situations, and if you do what I have just outlined, that is your best defense against it. Don't take this too much to heart because it is such a rare occurrence that you may be able to spend your entire lifetime playing on all of the poker sites available and never once face it. But it is possible, and therefore it is important for you to have a strategy defense against it in the very unlikely circumstance you will actually be exposed to it and have to deal with it. This much said, remember that Internet poker is a wonderful experience, and that no matter what is bad among human beings and among humanity in general, there is always beauty, wonderment, and on Internet poker sites especially a wonderful profitability.

# PokerStars.com

I now take great pleasure in being able to tell you about one of my favorite Internet poker sites, known the world over as the home of the world champions of poker. In 2003 and 2004, both WSOP champions have won their entry into that championship by playing at PokerStars.com. As a result, PokerStars.com has become the preeminent Internet poker site for a variety of poker tournaments. There is a tournament for everyone at PokerStars.com, and for every budget. You can play for as low as a few dollars to as high as several hundred dollars, and sometimes even more. The range of buy-ins for these tournaments varies, but you can easily locate all of these tournaments simply by clicking on the tournaments lobby menu, which I show you a little bit later on in this chapter in the discussion about PokerStars.com tournaments. To begin your experience at PokerStars.com, you first need to log on to their website: www.PokerStars.com. There you will find a prompt that asks you to download the software. Click on that icon, and the system will automatically download the PokerStars.com software to your computer. Follow the on-screen instructions and install the software. A PokerStars.com icon will be placed on your computer's desktop, as well as in the program lineup under the Start menu. Simply double-click on the desktop icon, or click on the PokerStars.com program name in the Start menu, and this instantly launches the program. You will now be taken directly to the PokerStars.com Main Lobby, which you can see in Photo 7.

This is your launching site to all the various gaming options available at PokerStars. com. After that, you are ready to play. Before we get to some of those playing options, here is a short history of exactly who PokerStars.com are, and how they came to be known as the Internet poker room of champions.

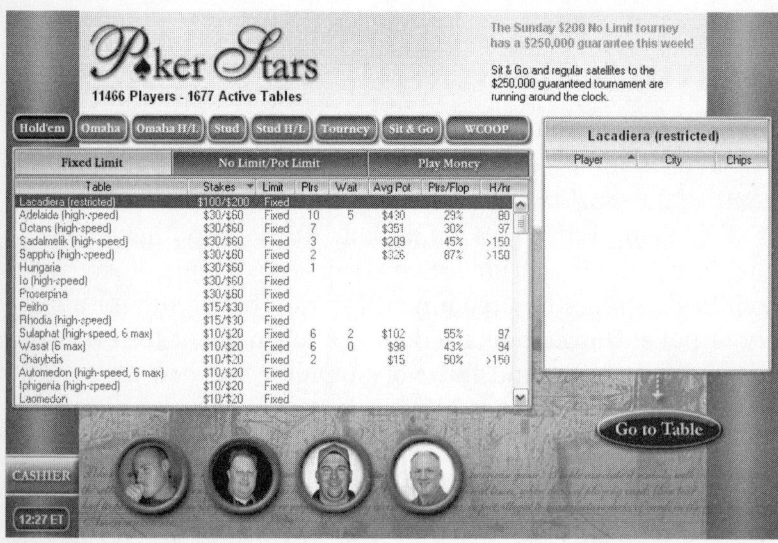


**Photo 7.** This is the PokerStars.com lobby, which you will see immediately after logging on to PokerStars.com.

## POKERSTARS.COM HISTORY

Dealing its first hand in September 2001 and never looking back, PokerStars has become one of the industry leaders and player favorites for both ring games and tournaments. While the single table games stay buzzing 24/7, PokerStars has become famous for their contribution to the recent worldwide interest in poker tournaments. From the beginning, PokerStars recognized that poker tournaments were going to be the major force in Internet poker, and something that most definitely would interest the vast majority of poker players. Spurned on again by the excitement of the World Series of Poker and World Poker Tour, this obsession with big money and globally recognized tournaments has driven PokerStars to become the world's leading online poker tournament site.

Each year PokerStars sends hundreds of players to compete on the world's biggest poker stages for millions in prize money. Through thousands of satellites and qualifying tournaments, PokerStars has made it possible for any player, no matter their bankroll, to get in the game and possibly become the next world champion. This dream was fulfilled in 2003 when PokerStars regular Chris Moneymaker took a $39 satellite buy-in and turned it into a $2.5 million World Series of Poker championship. Chris was not a professional poker player at the time of his victory. He played recreationally and dreamed of one day winning the big one. Thanks to a little luck and a PokerStars satellite, his dream came true.

Once this remarkable story became known throughout the world, the phenomenon of Internet poker snowballed. PokerStars—and Chris Moneymaker—were now equally as famous, and neither of them would ever be the same. Players flocked to Internet poker sites by the thousands to take their shot at poker immortality, and PokerStars was there to meet the demand. PokerStars.com not only offered more satellites and more free chances to play in the World Series, but because of their dedication to online poker tournaments from the very beginning, they were in the unique position to send more qualifying PokerStars players to the WSOP, and other major world tournaments, than any other poker site operating on the Internet at the time. Little did they know, however, that an even more improbable story was about to happen, and that lightning was about to strike in the same spot yet again.

In the 2004 World Series of Poker, the unimaginable happened again. A PokerStars player, Greg Raymer (one of 316 players PokerStars sent to the WSOP that year), entered a qualifying satellite in the $160 buy-in shoot-out format, and turned that qualifying seat into a record-setting $5 million WSOP championship. Back-to-back World Series victories have since earned PokerStars the moniker: "Where poker players become world champions." In addition to the winner, PokerStars players also claimed second, seventh, and ninth places, and overall took home almost $11 million of the $24 million prize pool.

PokerStars.com continues to do everything in their power to keep the streak alive. In addition to sending even more players to the World Series of Poker in the coming years, PokerStars has positioned itself perfectly to remain the "place where poker players become world champions." Relationships with the widely popular World Poker Tour and European Poker Tour have kept the championships coming. Other plans also include a focus on developing bigger and better online based tournaments, giving even more players the chance to win big with PokerStars, such as the recent record-setting World Championships of Online Poker, known as the WCOOP. The 2004 WCOOP attracted a whopping $6 million prize pool, putting it in the same category as the world's largest live tournaments.

## POKERSTARS.COM GAMES

Okay, now that we have learned something about the history of PokerStars.com, it is time for us to explore the great games and tournaments that are offered on this terrific Internet poker site. The Poker Stars Internet poker room offers the most popular casino poker games in the world. No matter what game you decide to play, you will always be playing against real people. Your fellow players may live down the street or halfway around the world, but they are playing on their own behalf.

You are never playing against the house. The games offered are as follows:

- Texas Hold'Em
- Omaha
- Omaha High-Low
- Seven Card Stud
- Seven Card Stud High-Low
- Tournaments for all game varieties

You can select any of these games simply by clicking on the game from the ring games menu, shown in Photo 8. If there's an empty seat, you can simply click on the seat and you will be in the game immediately. If a game is full, you can request to be put on the waiting list. You can play any of these games either as cash games, which are known as "ring games," or as tournaments. To play any game as a cash game, simply click on your game of choice from the PokerStars lobby, where you will see a list of available games. Photo 8 also shows the lobby.

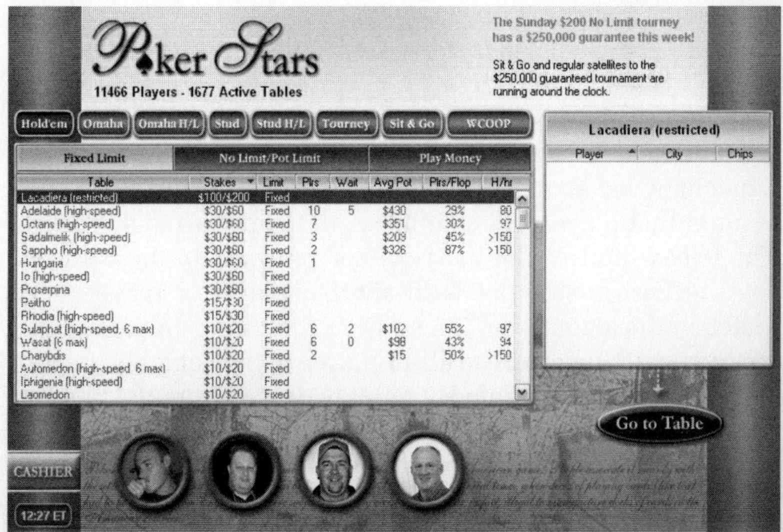


**Photo 8.** This is the PokerStars.com ring games selection main lobby menu.

## Game Limits

All the games that you find in the lobby are available at limits from as low as $0.50–$1.00 to $100–200, plus pot-limit and no-limit games.

In addition, PokerStars has play-money games that are absolutely free. I will show you how you can play for free by using play money a little later on in this chapter, when I provide you with a listing of the most frequently asked questions from players on Internet poker sites, and in particular those that will help you play and enjoy your games at PokerStars.com.

## Minimum Buy-In

The minimum buy-in at any table is ten times the amount of the bet on the lower betting rounds. For example, the minimum buy-in for a $10–$20 game is $100. Minimum buy-ins for pot-limit and no-limit games vary, and are displayed before you take your seat.

## All-In Protection Tables

When a player puts the last of their chips into a pot, that player is said to be all-in. An all-in player is not eligible to win any money bet above their final bet, cumulative up to the total amount that player had committed to the pot up to that point. The excess part of the bet is either returned to the bettor or used to form a side pot with another player or players who matched the amount bet. There is no limitation on the number of side pots. However, the all-in player will be eligible only for the main pot, and therefore cannot be forced from the hand.

Sometimes a player has enough chips to continue betting or calling but has been disconnected and unable to respond. In this case the player is also deemed to be "all-in" for all the amount of chips he has bet on this particular hand, but *not* for the rest of all the money that he has currently available as his table stakes. Therefore, such a player is said to be "protected" from being forced to put all of his money in when his connection has failed. If this happens to you repeatedly, it probably means your Internet connection is poor. It is therefore recommended that you stop playing for a while, and wait until your Internet connection improves. If a player fails to act within the allotted time (usually thirty seconds) while being connected, the hand is folded and a corresponding message sent to a player by email explaining the system action.

### No All-In Protection Tables

These tables are identified by the words "no all-in" in parentheses after a table name. These tables do not provide the all-in protection described above. If you disconnect from a no all-in table, you are given extra time to reconnect. But if you are unable to respond after that extra time, *your hand will be folded.* If you have a poor or unreliable Internet connection, it is recommended that you don't play at the no all-in tables. But this rule is not only about bad connections—it's also about people abusing all-in privileges to avoid calling huge bets on the turn or river. That's why it is very important for you to check and see exactly at which games and tables you are about to play, as well as why such rules are so made.

### High Speed Tables

These tables are identified by the words "high speed" in parentheses after a table name. These special tables are designed for those players who want to keep the game moving at a faster pace than a standard table. The following is the list of differences available on a high speed table:

- You receive only 15 seconds to act in a limit game, instead of 25.
- You receive only 20 seconds to act in a NL/PL game, instead of 35.

**Photo 9.** This is the typical PokerStars.com game table.

- You only have 1 second to show or muck, instead of 3 seconds.
- The pot is pushed to the winner faster.
- The showdown is over faster, in 2 seconds instead of 4.

In addition, "auto-posting" of blinds is required at a high-speed table and cannot be turned off. When you sit down, you're automatically in "wait for the blind" mode, and will post at your first normally scheduled big blind. Once you have learned all this, it will become easy for you to navigate through all the various table options. To take a look at the typical PokerStars.com poker table, please see Photo 9 (above).

## POKERSTARS.COM DEPOSIT OPTIONS

Once you are ready to play for real money at PokerStars.com, making a deposit is always fast and easy. PokerStars.com currently accepts the following deposit methods:

- NETeller
- CentralCoin
- FirePay
- Visa
- MasterCard
- Western Union
- Cashier's checks and money orders

To make a deposit, you first have to access the screen identified as Cashier. You can see what the cashier lobby looks like in Photo 10.

Once you have accessed this screen in the cashier main lobby, the first thing you should do is to verify your information, including your screen name, your name, your registered e-mail address, and your mailing address of record. After that, you can now buy your chips through the following procedure:

1. Click Buy Chips.
2. Click payment method—You will see a screen with the

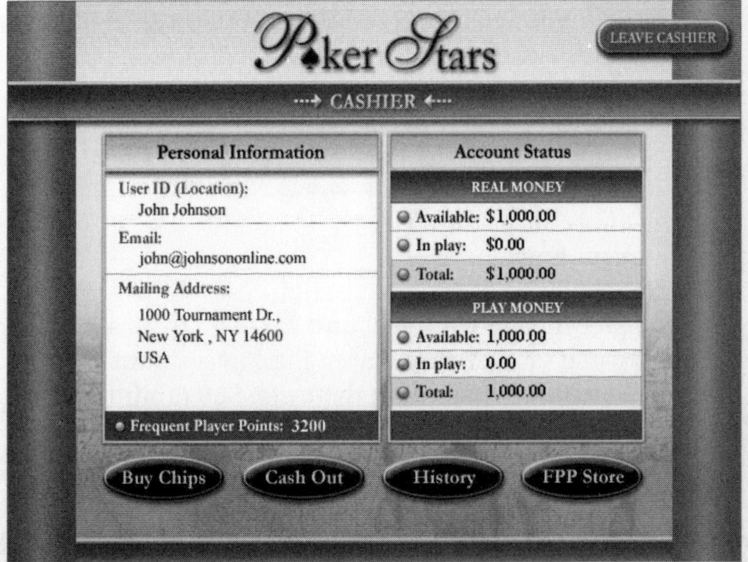


**Photo 10.** This is the PokerStars.com main cashier lobby screen.

various logos representing the available funding options as shown on these two pages. Select the one you want by clicking on it. There will be other logos as well (not shown in this chapter), but the procedures are the same. Simply select the one you wish to use.

3. Enter deposit amount and other information as prompted.

- **Payment Type:** NETeller
- **Fees:** None
- **Transfer time to your account:** Takes 10 to 20 seconds to approve if you already have a NETeller account
- **Minimum and maximum deposits:** $50 minimum, maximum depends on player status
- **Comments:** Fund your NETeller account by credit card or electronic funds transfer from your checking account
- The way you select this funding option is to click on the NETeller logo, shown above.

- **Payment type:** FirePay
- **Fees:** None
- **Transfer time to your account:** Takes 10 to 20 seconds to approve if you already have a FirePay account.
- **Minimum and maximum deposits:** $50 minimum, maximum depends on player status
- **Comments:** Setting up a FirePay account takes about 15 to 30 minutes
- The way you select this funding option is to click on the FirePay logo, shown above.

- **Payment type:** Visa, MasterCard, Diners Club International
- **Fees:** None
- **Transfer time to your account:** Takes 10 to 20 seconds to approve if your credit card is in good standing and your bank accepts e-gaming transactions
- **Minimum and maximum deposits:** $50 minimum, maximum depends on player status
- The way you select this funding option is to click on either of the two logos shown above.

Once you have selected the funding option, the cashier system will then ask you for the coded account information that is private only to you. For example, if you use NETeller—which is my own personal preferred method—you will be asked for your NETeller account number, then the security code, and finally your password. All of these are private to you only, and none of this information is shared or transmitted anywhere other than between you and your NETeller account (or whichever funding account option you choose and establish).

If you have any questions concerning these deposit methods, you can contact the PokerStars.com support team by e-mailing support@pokerstars.com. Customer service is available to answer any banking questions twenty-four hours a day.

### Deposit Security

PokerStars uses two processors—GFSL and SureFire—to process credit card transactions and deposits. GFSL transactions are identified as PStars-ECash on your credit card statement and SureFire transactions as PStars-IFUND in all such deposit communications.

## POKERSTARS.COM CASH-OUT OPTIONS

Cash-outs are credited back to any and all of the following methods that you have used to make your deposit: FirePay, CentralCoin, or NETeller. Cash-outs are processed back in the same amounts as your original purchases, from the oldest purchase to the newest. Due to changes concerning MasterCard's and Visa's policies, PokerStars.com can no longer credit cash-outs back to MasterCard and Visa accounts.

To cash out, click on the Cashier button in the lobby and then on the Cash-Out button. You will then be prompted for a cash-out amount. Simply enter the amount and click Submit. You will then be prompted to choose the method by which you wish to receive your winnings. Your five options will be NETeller, FirePay, CentralCoin, Check (in U.S. dollars) and Check in Pounds Sterling. Select the method you wish by simply clicking on the icon representing these options, and click Submit. It takes several minutes for the transaction to appear on your FirePay and CentralCoin online accounts for cash-outs below the amount purchased, and about fifteen business days for your check delivery. NETeller, FirePay, and CentralCoin credits above the amount purchased will be applied within seventy-two hours. Please allow forty-eight hours from your last deposit before requesting to cash out. In special cases, additional information may be required for a cash-out to be processed.

## POKERSTARS.COM SPECIAL PROMOTIONS AND TOURNAMENTS

The PokerStars.com promotional model is based on a system of rewarding players for their play at PokerStars. They do this in the form of FPP, known as the frequent player points. Players receive 1 FPP point for every raked hand they play, or 5 points for each dollar in tournament fees they pay. These points have a wide variety of uses. Players can choose to use their FPP points to buy merchandise from the PokerStars store, or they can use the points to enter special FPP tournaments where they can win anything from cash to a seat in the World Series of Poker.

PokerStars works continually to ensure they are providing the world's largest number of qualifying events to all major tournaments. Currently, they send hundreds of players per year to the World Series of Poker and the World Poker Tour, and they recently added the European Poker Tour. In addition to working with respected poker organizations, they also hold their own major tournaments. The World Championship of Online Poker and World Cup of Poker are unique PokerStars events that draw thousands of players annually.

In addition, their ongoing weekly and monthly tournament schedule is also the largest of its kind. PokerStars.com often sets new prize pool records with their weekly $250,000 and their monthly $500,000 guaranteed No-Limit Hold'Em tournaments. Furthermore, there are also many Sit & Go one-table, two-table, four-player, and heads-up tournaments, as well as hundreds of multitable tournaments played weekly at PokerStars.com, making them the leading online-poker tournament website.

## Multitable Tournaments

PokerStars has top-notch tournament software that provides great tournament poker action with features to keep you coming back again and again. From satellites to re-buy tournaments to freeze-outs, PokerStars is excited to host the best multitable tournaments and satellites anywhere on the Internet. Poker tournaments are played until one player has all the chips. Prizes are distributed based on the number of entrants.

## Playing in a PokerStars Tournament

Before you start playing any of the actual tournaments, particularly those for real money, look at some of the tournament details and information available from the PokerStars.com website, from the main tournament menu under the section About Tournaments. There you will find information about the following:

- PokerStars WPT events
- PokerStars European Poker Tour (EPT) events
- Daily tournaments schedule
- Weekly Round-2 tournaments
- Tournament Leader Board

To enter any PokerStars tournament, select the Tourney tab from the main lobby screen. If you select any tournament from this tab, you will see information about it in the information box on the right-hand side. Under the State column, look for a tournament which has a state of Registering. The particulars of the tournament (game, structure, and buy-in) are listed beside the state. Double-click on a tournament in Registering state or click on the Tournament Lobby button and this opens the tournament lobby. You can see what this tournament lobby screen looks like in Photo 11. Click the Register button, and log-in if you have not already done so. The software will confirm your registration. You may take your seat by selecting the Take Your Seat button. Check the tournament lobby for registration and seat times.

Note that for all tournaments and multitable satellites, players are all assigned random seats to start the tournament. This is a countermeasure designed to prevent collusion. As is customary in poker tournaments, seat changes are not allowed. The button in Hold'Em and Omaha tournaments will be assigned to seat 1.

As in a regular poker game, when it is your turn to act, you may check, bet, raise, call, or fold (where applicable). You will

**Photo 11.** The PokerStars.com tournament lobby screen.

notice another button called Time Bank when it is your turn to act, shown after you receive a time warning in the chat window. The time bank allows players extra time to decide on a course of action during a tournament, and will slowly deplete as it is used throughout the tournament.

Another way in which the PokerStars tournament interface varies from the side-game interface is the tab marked Info on the chat box. This tab gives your current position in the tournament, as well as the highest, lowest, and average stacks for remaining players. The info tab also tells you how much time is left in your time bank. The tab marked Stats provides statistical information about your play during the current tournament.

At any point during the tournament, players can check the tournament lobby for information about the tournament's progress. The lobby shows the current limit level for the tournament, information about players' stack sizes, and the breakdown of the prize pool. Also in the tournament lobby is a player search function. The tournament lobby lists all players, and double-clicking on any player's user ID (nickname), or clicking on the button marked Player Info will give the current tournament information for that player.

After the tournament is over, the winners receive an e-mail that provides comprehensive information about the tournament. Anyone can request a tournament history at any time after the tournament's conclusion by going to the main lobby and selecting Tournament History from the Request menu. Final tournament information for this tournament will remain in the tournament lobby for a while, usually a few hours after the tournament's conclusion. Specific prize money breakdown will be shown after the registration is closed.

## Viewing a Tournament

Any player in a tournament can observe any other table by double-clicking on that table in the tournament lobby's table list, or clicking the button marked Observe Table. Players who are not participants may also observe any table of a tournament.

## Tournament Dollars (T$)

As the world's largest online tournament site, PokerStars also offers a unique "tournament dollar" system. When you qualify to any event through a satellite, you have the option to unregister from the target event and receive tournament dollars. These tournament dollars can be used to register in any other PokerStars tournament, including Sit & Go's, and satellites. If you win multiple seats to the same target event, the value of these seats will be automatically credited to your tournament dollar account.

Many events will not allow you to unregister until one hour prior to the event. In that case, you may e-mail the customer service support department to have them unregister you immediately. To do so, please include your user ID and the tournament number from which you wish to be unregistered. To check your tournament dollar balance at any time, simply visit the cashier window through the lobby.

## W Dollars (W$)

In addition to the tournament dollars, PokerStars also offers special W$. W$ can be used to register into any qualifying special PokerStars event. Special events include:

- PokerStars Caribbean Adventure (PCA)
- European Poker Tour (EPT)
- PokerStars World Championship of Online Poker (WCOOP)

The W$ system works exactly the same as the tournament dollar system (see above for details). To check your W$ balance at any time, just visit the cashier window through the lobby. Tournament dollars can be used to register into regular and special events, while W$ can only be used for special events.

## Player Images

At PokerStars you have the option of selecting a personalized image to represent you at the virtual tables. The image can be of anything you want: Your pet, your favorite movie star or, of course, you. When you open your PokerStars account, you'll have the option of supplying your own picture, or not providing an image at all. Have you put on your poker face? Here's how to upload your image and see your competitors face to face. The first time you sign up for your PokerStars account, you will be given the option to select an image to be displayed to other players at the table. Here's what you do:

1. Click Select Image.
2. Find a suitable picture from a directory on your hard drive.
3. Click on that file, then click Open.
4. Please wait while the selected image is uploaded to the PokerStars server.
5. Now you need to drag the selection box over the area of the image you wish to display. The smaller window at right shows you what image will appear at the table.
6. Once you are satisfied with the image in the smaller window, click OK.
7. Continue with the rest of your registration. Once your image has been screened for suitability, it will show up along with your user ID (nickname) at the tables.

If you are not satisfied with the image you selected during registration and wish to change it (or if you did not select an image during registration), you can do so by clicking Select/Change Image from the account menu. Select Change Image, and follow the steps outlined above. Click Save when you are finished. A player's image is similar to his user ID (nickname) and it is used to identify him to other players at the table. If you are unhappy with your current image and decide to change it, simply choose your new image, but please do so carefully. PokerStars.com does not allow for an image to be changed more than once, except in special circumstances. And that's all there is to putting your face in the game.

## PLAYER STATISTICS

Have you ever wondered exactly how you are doing when playing Internet poker? Serious poker players find such information invaluable. Answers to questions such as:

- Am I seeing the flop too often?
- How many hands did I fold on 6th street?
- Am I playing too tight in the big blind?

And similar such questions are all very important to know. These are all questions we ask ourselves at the table, but finding answers can be a tedious process, as it is to actually figure out the answers. At PokerStars, they take on the task of tracking various statistical data for you. Any time you want this data, they will simply e-mail it right to your inbox. You can also view statistics accumulated during your current session right at the table. Your statistical data is available to you and you alone. But please note that that they do not archive play money or free-roll tournament hand histories, and therefore this information is unavailable for those games. For real money games, and real money buy-in tournaments, the simplest way to check on your statistics is through the chat box in the bottom-left corner of the table screen. When you click on Stats, you will be given:

- The number of times you have been dealt in
- The number of times you played your hand in various positions

- The number of pots you won at the showdown, and
- The number of times you have been to the showdown

To refresh the statistics, click Refresh. You can also get your statistics sent to your e-mail address. From the main lobby, under the Requests menu, select Statistics. You have the option of getting statistics for all hands played on PokerStars, or just a certain number of recent hands. Statistics are broken down in the following manner:

- First, statistics are separated by game type (Hold'Em, Omaha, Omaha High-Low, Seven Card Stud, and Seven Card Stud High-Low).
- One-on-one statistics are separated from statistics for multiplayer games.

Tournament players are also able to request a tournament history via e-mail. The tournament history gives information about the tournament results, as well as statistics on your own play in the tournament (where applicable). Note that tournament statistics are not included when you check your regular statistics.

## Hand Histories

You can also request a hand history for a specific game number, a full tournament, or up to a full transcript of your last 200 hands by clicking on the dealer tray and selecting Request Hand History. A hand history will show all the action during the hand, as well as the cards of anyone who did not fold during the hand. But note that you will not be able to see uncalled hands unless you were dealt in on the hand in question, and that these hand histories are not archived for play money or freeroll tournament hand histories. You should also be aware that you can *never* see *uncalled* hands. You can only see *called* hands that were exposed at showdown if you were dealt into the hand.

## Opponent Notes

As the old adage goes, poker is not a game of cards, it's a game of people. PokerStars allows you to keep a profile on your opponents by giving you a window to jot down notes about their play. Your notes are saved on your computer and ready to be accessed the next time you square off against an old opponent. It's easy to keep track of other players' tendencies and playing styles when you play at PokerStars. When you are at any PokerStars table, select the tab Notes from the chat box in the bottom-left corner of the screen. Now double-click on the image, or label, of any of the other players at the table. The player's name will appear in the top line of the chat box. Now simply type your observations in the space below the name. You can also select a player by clicking on the arrow at the top right of the chat box. This will drop down a list of all the players at the table. Next time you are at a table with the same player, all you need to do is select Notes, double-click on the player, and all your previous observations will be shown right in the dialog box. These notes are stored only on your computer, so no one else can have access to them. The notes will be available to you every time you play this opponent.

## No-Limit and Pot-Limit Play Money Side Games

Whether you want to try No Limit Texas Hold'Em, the Cadillac of poker, or prefer the strategic intricacies of Pot-Limit Omaha High, you'll get a great chance to hone your big-bet poker skills at the PokerStars popular no-limit and pot-limit play money games. By learning to play these games through the play-money options, you will be able to gain the experience necessary to try them for real. This is yet another one of those great advantages when you sign up for a PokerStars.com account, because it allows you to practice before you dive into the ocean of real money games.

## FREQUENTLY ASKED QUESTIONS

When I first began playing on the Internet, I found it difficult to learn about how everything works, and what I have to do in order to gain the best possible experience. At that time, very early in the evolution of Internet poker, there was little help offered. Internet poker rooms had the games, and although at that time most of them were only for play money, even after real money play was introduced many poker sites were slow in providing information about how to actually play on them. Fortunately, this was never the case at PokerStars.com. Therefore, I felt it was important for this book—and this chapter in particular—to help you overcome some of those problems and difficulties that you may encounter if you are new to Internet poker, or perhaps answer for you some questions that you may not have had answered previously, or perhaps have not thought of, or may not have known where to find out.

With the help of the great folks at PokerStars.com, following is a short list of some of the most common questions asked by Internet poker players. Although these are questions that were asked primarily by PokerStars.com players, they apply universally to all of your Internet poker–playing experiences. Knowing them will also help you to better navigate the PokerStars.com Internet poker website, and, most important, help you take advantage of the terrific Internet poker–playing experience that you will find at PokerStars.com.

### Your PokerStars.com Guide

I want to thank PokerStars.com for providing me with this information, so that I can share it with you, and as a result give you a heads-up as you begin your poker playing experience on the Internet, and as you explore the various opportunities that can be found at PokerStars.com. The following, therefore, represent a cross-section of the most frequently asked questions by Internet poker players:

*I've downloaded the PokerStarsInstall.exe file but now I can't find it.*

On a Windows-based system, click the Start menu, select Find, and then click Files or Folders. In the Named box, type *PokerStarsInstall.exe.* It will take your computer a few moments to find the file. When it does, double-click the file and the installation process will begin.

*I would like to play under different names, can I have more than one account?*

No. Each player is only allowed one account.

*I forgot or lost my password.*

You can reset your password manually by going to the main client window and clicking on Lobby and then on Login and then on Forgot Password. Enter your information and a new password will be e-mailed to your registered PokerStars e-mail address. If you do so, and receive an error message, then simply e-mail the customer support department with your full name and address, as well as your PokerStars user ID, and they will help you get back in the game.

*What happens if I am disconnected in the middle of a hand?*

It sometimes occurs that due to reasons beyond your control, you are unable to act on your hand in time. At PokerStars, if a player has invested money in a hand and becomes disconnected, he or she will be placed "all-in." A player who is placed "all-in" is treated as though he or she does not have any chips remaining to carry out the hand. The player is still eligible for the portion of the pot to which the player would normally be entitled. All further betting takes place in a side pot, to be contested by the remaining active players. A player is allotted twenty-five seconds to act in fixed-limit games and thirty-five seconds in big bet games. A warning message is displayed in the chat box when there are fifteen seconds left to act. If there was a disconnect and a player returned before the timeout, he or she receives at least ten seconds to act. If a player failed to act within the allotted time while being connected, the hand is folded by the system.

*The game I wish to join is full. What should I do?*

If a game is full, you can put your name on the waiting list for that game. When a seat in the game becomes available, the first person on the waiting list will have the first right of refusal for that seat. The other option you have is to take a seat at an empty table of that limit and game. Often, empty tables fill up quickly once a player takes a seat.

*What is a "rake"? How much is the PokerStars rake?*

PokerStars is an Internet poker room, not a casino. That means you never play against the house, only other players. PokerStars receives compensation by taking a "rake," a small amount from each pot. This rake from the pot never exceeds $3. At the lower limits, PokerStars takes a smaller rake. There is no rake in play money games or micro-limit games ($0.01–0.02 and $0.02–0.04).

*How do I know how much money is in the pot?*

At any PokerStars table the full amount of the pot, including all current bets, is always displayed numerically above the dealer's tray. Also, at the end of every betting round, all bets are collected in the middle of the table and converted into higher denomination chips so you can easily see the pot's total value.

*Does the software allow me to muck the winning hand?*

No, it doesn't. If you play your hand to the showdown and you hold the winning hand, it will be always automatically shown. This feature protects you from accidentally mucking a winner.

*How do I request a hand history? How many hand histories can I request?*

Click on the dealer tray and select Request Hand History.

You can request up to your last 200 hands, your hand histories for a period of time, all the hands you played in a tournament, or any specific single hand. Note however that PokerStars does not archive play money or freeroll tournament hand histories, and as such, these hands are not available to be requested. You can also request a hand history from the PokerStars lobby. From the Request menu, choose Hand History (for more details, see what I have written just immediately preceding this section).

*How do I request my play statistics?*

Click on the dealer tray and select Request Statistics. You can request statistics for any number of your most recent hands, or even the all-time statistics for your account. You can also request statistics from the PokerStars lobby. From the Request menu, choose Statistics.

*What are FPPs? How can I use them?*

Frequent player points are points you earn by playing raked hands at PokerStars.com. They are used in conjunction with their many promotions. In the past these have included the World Series of Poker Millionaire's Quest, and the World Championship of Online Poker.

*I see a little "N" underneath some players' images . . . what is this?*

This indicates that you have made a note about this player in the past, and it is stored for your viewing.

*What are the chat rules?*

PokerStars does not permit profane, vulgar, or abusive/insulting chat in their chat windows. They have a feature by which certain profane words are asterisked out.

*What should I do if someone is abusing the chat feature?*

PokerStars does not tolerate abusive or obscene language at the tables. Players are encouraged to report any offensive chat to *support@pokerstars.com*. Although they monitor the tables as much as possible, the cooperation of players is a critical part of making PokerStars a fun experience for all. You can also block an individual player's messages from coming to you by right-clicking on the player's icon and selecting Block Chat.

*Can I use language other than English when chatting at the table?*

The staff at PokerStars are aware that their players are from around the world, and that for many of them English is not the first language. However, in order to best serve the world community at large, at this time it is their policy to only allow English to be spoken at the tables.

*How do I make an image for myself?*

From the account menu of the PokerStars lobby, select Select/Change Image. Click on Select Image, and pick an image for use from your hard drive. For more information about images, and to find out how to take a picture from the Internet to use as your PokerStars image, visit the image pages on the PokerStars.com website, or read again the information that I offered you earlier.

*I find the images at the table distracting. How do I turn them off?*

From the Options menu of the PokerStars lobby, select Images. This will turn off images the next time you join or watch a game. You can turn images back on at any time by selecting Images again and ensuring that a check mark is placed beside *Images.* You can also block an individual player's image from coming to you by right-clicking on the player's icon and selecting Block Image.

*I don't like my chosen image anymore. Can I change it?*

Yes, you may change your image by selecting Select/ Change Image from the Account menu. However, you can only change your image once, so remember what I had written about this earlier.

*Does PokerStars use props or shills?*

PokerStars does not use any house players or robots. They do not hire any individuals to play on their site as house players.

*Are PokerStars employees allowed to play on your site?*

PokerStars employees, consultants, or anyone else who has access to inside information (for example, complete hand histories, playing histories, money transaction histories, and similar) are not allowed to play in money games or tournaments. This is to prevent any potential abuse of inside information at the tables.

*Where can I view upcoming tournaments?*

You may view upcoming tournaments by selecting Tourney in the PokerStars main lobby. You will see all tournaments in progress, recently completed tournaments, and tournaments which begin soon. For more information, highlight any tournament by clicking on it, then select Tournament Lobby.

*How do I register for a tournament?*

If a tournament is in the "registering" state, highlight that tournament by clicking on it, then click on Tournament Lobby. Once the tournament lobby screen opens, click on Register. You will need to log-in if you have not already done so for this session.

*Can I play a side game and a tournament at the same time?*

Yes, you are welcome to play a side game and a tournament simultaneously. In the interest of fairness to all players, you must act promptly when it is your turn in either game.

*I played a tournament several days ago, and the information is no longer displayed in the lobby. How do I retrieve it?*

From the Request menu in the PokerStars lobby, choose Tournament History. You may select any number of recent tournaments in which you participated, or any specific tournament.

*If I am faced with a difficult decision in a tournament, may I "request time"?*

All tournament players are given a "time bank" at the beginning of the tournament. If a player needs a longer than normal time to decide on an action, the player can withdraw from the time bank, which depletes as the player uses it. To use the time bank you should click on the TIME button, which appears after you receive the first time warning in the chat window.

*What happens if the system crashes in the middle of a tournament?*

In the event of a server crash, the hands in progress at every table will be restored by rolling back these hands. Each player's chip count will be reset to the amount at the beginning of the hand. In special circumstances, when a tournament needs to be canceled because of a crash or some other reason, players will be compensated according to the PokerStars' tournament cancellation policy, the details of which can be found at the PokerStars.com website under the appropriate link in the help section of the website, accessible through the tournament lobby.

*I qualified for an event that I can no longer play in . . . what do I do?*

You have the option of transferring your seat to another user. If it is a Weekly Round 2 free-roll event, you also are free to move it to a future week by e-mailing support. If it is a real-money buy-in event, you can unregister and receive tournament dollars instead, which are credits for use to buy in to other PokerStars events.

*How many play money chips do I start with? What if I run out of chips?*

You will be given 1,000 play money chips to start. However, if at any time you are below 100 chips, simply click the dealer tray and select Add More Chips. This "rebuy" feature is intended to replenish the stack of a player who has legitimately lost their entire stack in play. The new 1,000 chips are for the use of that player only. Re-buys acquired for purposes other than this are subject to forfeiture.

*How do I recognize the play money tables?*

The play money tables can be identified by the tables beginning with the word *Fun.* They are at the bottom of the tables list. If you do not see them, double-check to ensure that you have your client set to show play money tables. To do so, simply click on Options in your main client window, and ensure that the Show Play Money Tables option is selected.

*Why is my card being declined and what can I do?*

Many banks are adopting a policy against gambling, considering it too high risk. Even though poker (as well as Internet poker) is a game of skill that does not belong under the general heading of "gambling," that distinction is lost upon the world financial community, and many other various bodies. To help you overcome this, you should contact your bank regarding their policies on these matters. You may also consider opening a NETeller or FirePay account. As I mentioned earlier, I personally use NETeller and find that to be the best online wallet currently available.

*Can I transfer money to another user, or receive a transfer?*

Yes, you can. To transfer real money on PokerStars, click on Requests-and-Transfer Funds in the main client window.

## GENERAL INTEGRITY AND SITE SECURITY

There has been much talk among the various media, as well as many discussions posted in the various Internet chat rooms and poker forums, concerning the general integrity and site security of Internet poker rooms and casinos. At PokerStars.com you will find some of the industry's most stringent security measures and policies designed to protect the integrity of your personal information, financial transactions, and all of your data. This is important not only for your sense of security, but for the preservation of the safe and secure experience that you will find at PokerStars.com. To help you better understand that, I again wish to thank PokerStars.com for providing me with the following information that clearly shows and illustrates the extraordinary measures that PokerStars have undertaken to provide you with such a safe and secure Internet poker playing experience.

## Data Privacy

> When the stakes are high, it pays to go to great lengths to ensure that software is implemented with proper considerations for security and safety.
>
> —*Matt Schmid, Cigital, Inc.*

All communications between PokerStars' client software running on client computers and their servers is encrypted. That is why PokerStars have spent a lot of effort designing their security system and policies.

## Software Download

The first point at which security becomes an important factor is when the client software is downloaded from the PokerStars site. PokerStars first ensures that the client software is downloaded unmodified. To address this requirement, they built the following features into the download process:

- For Internet Explorer the validity of downloaded executable is verified by the browser using their key and Thawte certificate.
- For other browsers they use 1024-bit RSA key and a

Thawte server certificate to protect their HTTPS web server and download.

- Their client software uses the certificates issued by their own Certificate Authority (CA) to authenticate their servers.
- Their CA certificate key is 1024-bit length.
- Their client software uses the industry standard SSLv3 protocol. It is configured to use RSA for authentication and key generation and triple-DES (EDE3, in outer-CBC mode) for encryption. Currently they are using 512-bit RSA key, which is sufficient for short- and medium-term (up to several years) secrets. Since they update server private keys every three months, they are secure with a good safety margin. The use of Triple-DES EDE3 for session encryption is considered even safer.
- No private data, such as pocket cards, is ever transferred to other players.

## Collusion

Collusion is a form of cheating in which two or more players signal their holdings, or otherwise form a cheating partnership to the detriment of the other players at the same table. While on one hand it is easier to pass information between colluding players in online poker than it is in brick-and-mortar rooms, it is much more difficult to avoid eventual detection as the cards for all players can be examined after the play. No matter how sophisticated the collusion is, it must involve a play of a hand that would not be played that way without collusion. PokerStars' detection methods will catch unusual play patterns and warn the security personnel, who will then make a thorough manual investigation. PokerStars will also investigate all players' reports about suspected collusion. If any player is found to be participating in any form of collusion, his or her account may be permanently closed.

## Shuffle

> Anyone who considers arithmetic methods of producing random digits is, of course, in a state of sin.
>
> —*John von Neumann, 1951*

PokerStars understands that a use of a fair and unpredictable shuffle algorithm is critical to their software. To ensure this and avoid major problems, they are using two independent sources of truly random data:

- User input, including summary of mouse movements and events timing, collected from client software
- True hardware random number generator developed by Intel, which uses thermal noise as an entropy source

Each of these sources itself generates enough entropy to ensure a fair and unpredictable shuffle.

## Shuffle Highlights

- A deck of 52 cards can be shuffled in 52! ways. 52! is about 2225. PokerStars uses 249 random bits from both entropy sources (user input and thermal noise) to achieve an even and unpredictable statistical distribution.
- Furthermore, they apply conservative rules to enforce the required degree of randomness; for instance, if user input does not generate required amount of entropy, they do not start the next hand until they obtain the required amount of entropy from Intel RNG.
- They also use the SHA-1 cryptographic hash algorithm to mix the entropy gathered from both sources to provide an extra level of security.
- They also maintain as SHA-1-based pseudo-random generator to provide even more security and protection from user data attacks.

- To convert random bit stream to random numbers within a required range without bias, they use a simple and reliable algorithm. For example, if they need a random number in the range 0 to 25:
    - First, they take 5 random bits and convert them to a random number 0–31.
    - If this number is greater than 25, they just discard all 5 bits and repeat the process.
- This method is not affected by biases related to modulus operation for generation of random numbers that are not 2n, n = 1,2, . . .
- To perform an actual shuffle, PokerStars uses another simple and reliable algorithm:
    - First, they draw a random card from the original deck (1 of 52) and place it in a new deck—now the original deck contains 51 cards and the new deck contains 1 card.
    - Second, they then draw another random card from the original deck (1 of 51) and place it on top of the new deck—now the original deck contains 50 cards and the new deck contains 2 cards.
    - Third, they then repeat the process until all cards have moved from the original deck to the new deck.
- This algorithm does not suffer from the "bad distribution of shuffles" principle.

## PokerStars Shuffle Verified by Cigital and BMM International

In May 2003, PokerStars submitted extensive information about the PokerStars random number generator (RNG) to two independent organizations. They asked these two trusted resources to perform an in-depth analysis of the randomness of the output of the RNG and its implementation in the shuffling of the cards on PokerStars. Both independent companies were given full access to the source code and confirmed the randomness and security of their shuffle. To find out more about this, and read the details of these reports, you can click on the related links on the PokerStars.com website, under the Help icon in the main screen menus.

For those readers interested in more information about the statistical distribution of random number generators, I invite you to look at my earlier book *Powerful Profits from Slots* (Chapter 10), in which I demonstrate some of the principles of mathematical algorithms that contribute to combine what is commonly known as the RNG, and the various factors of computing that go into creating something that is so known. Similar such principles apply to the shuffle of random cards for Internet poker, and although in that book those calculations and principles shown were intended primarily for modern slot machines, the methods by which such calculations are computed are interesting, inasmuch as they can be used for illustration purposes to show exactly how this is accomplished for the shuffle of a clearly defined fifty-two-card deck for Internet poker.

And so, dear friends, this now brings us to the end of this very entertaining and informative chapter in which I was able to show you not only why I happen to like PokerStars.com, or why they are known as the home of world champions, but also a great deal of information that will enhance your Internet poker playing experience on many levels. As you begin your journey into the world of Internet poker, and as you specifically investigate all of the various features and tournaments and games that are offered at PokerStars.com, you can learn all of this information here, instead of needing to look for it elsewhere. As mentioned earlier, if I had an opportunity to know this when I first began to play Internet poker, I would have been able to jump into the world of real-money Internet poker play much sooner than I did, primarily because I did not have the availability of this information and therefore had to find it all out for myself. Now, here in this book, and with the help of the great folks at PokerStars.com, I was able to make the journey for you much shorter, and greatly more informative. Now that this has been achieved, it is time for us to continue with the discussion of the playing aspects of the poker games, beginning in the next chapter with some general strategy hints and tips.

# General Strategy for Internet Poker

Now it's time for some general strategy suggestions and recommendations, those that will complement all that I have written in earlier strategy chapters (as well as elsewhere in this book). These are suggestions more general in nature, but they apply universally to all poker games, and particularly to Internet poker games due to their volatility and speed. I will not go into a great many details concerning these suggestions and recommendations, primarily because many of them are already part of what you should know about poker, and also the fact that they are quite well covered in many poker books (including my earlier book *Powerful Profits from Poker)*. Nevertheless, they are important aspects of your overall poker expertise and acumen, and contribute significantly to every aspect of your skills.

## POSITION

Being in position on your other opponents means to be in the power position. In simplest terms, particularly as this applies to Texas Hold'Em–type games, this means you can see what everyone else will do before you have to do anything. This provides you with an abundance of information and in particular allows you to make much more accurate judgments as to the potential holdings of your opponents; it allows you to appraise your hands in much greater detail and to play a greater variety of hands with equivalently greater success rates. Late position in Texas Hold'Em games means to be either on the button, in the cut-off seat (which is the seat immediately next to the button), or in the second or third cut-off seat, which means the next to the next seat to the right of the button, and the other seat one over. Simply put, being in late position in Texas Hold'Em–type games means to be either last (on the button), next to last, (in the cut-off seat), or in the third or fourth position relative to the button to the right. On any poker table, this means the last four positions. If you are playing Seven Card Stud, then late position means to be immediately to the right of the bring-in, or the next three positions to the right of the bring-in. Of course, in Seven Card Stud games position will change as the next cards are dealt, because the order of the cards and their values as they are exposed on 3rd, and 4th, 5th, and 6th streets determines who will be first to act, and consequently who will be last to act. But since your first decision in Seven Card Stud should concern the play of your hand from that point on, assuming that you have a hand with which you wish to play, being to the right of the bring-in is equivalent to being on the button in Texas Hold'Em games.

All of this is what is meant by being "in late position." Playing in late position allows for a multitude of opportunities, the best of which is to be able to play hands that otherwise you might muck, and to be able to exploit weaknesses in your opponents to the fullest potential. For more information on such details of play in late position, I refer you to many of the excellent books on poker that are now available, as well as refer you to the help sections of the various poker sites that I feature in this book. (I have also written more extensively on this in my earlier book *Powerful Profits from Poker*.) All of these resources provide you with a multitude of knowledge and information about exactly how to play in late positions, and the hands which play the best. In this brief section, suffice it to say that if all you remember is the simple fact that acting last, or near last, provides you with the opportunity to see what everyone else does before you have to do anything, then you will be a long way ahead of many other Internet poker players who play anything from many positions, seemingly completely oblivious to the power of late position play.

## WIN MONEY, NOT POTS

Many poker players (particularly those so new to poker) erroneously think that the object of the game is to win as many pots as possible. This is akin to the similar misperception in blackjack players (new blackjack players or those unfamiliar with playing blackjack), where such players think that the object of blackjack is to get as close to 21 without going over. Of course, that is not so. The object of blackjack is to win money, and that means to beat the dealer, not necessarily go as close to 21 as you can. In blackjack, if you know how to play, you can easily choose to stand on a 13, 14, 15, or 16 hand, depending what the dealer's up card is, and even more so depending on what the count may be if you are skilled at counting cards, and then wait for the dealer to bust, thereby making your hand into a winner. As you can see from this example, which happens very often in blackjack games, the object of blackjack is not to get as close to 21 as possible, but to win money. To win money in blackjack, it is not necessary to have the best hand. All that is necessary is that the dealer busts, thereby making your garbage hand into a winner. This is similar to poker, where to be a consistent winner you do not necessarily have to have the best hand all the time, but merely the *winning* hand. You can have the winning hand either by having a hand that cannot be beaten by the players who are still with you to showdown, or you can have the winning hand by forcing your opponents to relinquish their holdings thereby avoiding a showdown and still winning the pot. Although such playing principles—some of which are bluffs or borderline bluffs—are part of the skills and expertise and experience the professional and skilled poker players can employ successfully most of the time, even novice and new poker players can provide for themselves an edge if they realize that the object of playing winning poker is not to win the most pots, but the most value of money.

If you sit in a poker game and you win twenty pots in the first hour, but the value in each pot is merely the blinds or maybe one or two bets, what exactly have you won? Well, you have won a lot of pots, but you did not even make enough money to keep abreast of the cost of the game. Not only that, you have left yourself vulnerable because you have just showed your opponents naked aggression and a complete lack of understanding of the value of pot odds and, especially, the value of maximizing your money profitability. You have also exposed yourself to other players by showing them your variety of hands and playing styles, all of which they will now be able to use against you. In a situation such as this, which I understand can be easily considered as an extreme example but it is a valuable example nonetheless, you can easily play just one pot from that point on and lose. That one loss will more than wipe out all of that little profitability that you got from winning all those many little pots, as well as take a deep chunk from the remaining bankroll that you have with you at that particular game. Therefore, if you learn nothing more from this particular strategy recommendation other than to recognize that the principal goal of poker is not the winning of the most pots but the most *money*, then you have also exceeded the knowledge of the greater majority of Internet poker players.

Most Internet poker players have little or no knowledge about these aspects of the game of poker; they continue to think that accruing the most money means winning the most pots. Trying to win the most pots means they have to play a great many hands. So, their standards for starting hands is obviously compromised. This provides all of their opponents, particularly those who know something about poker—and especially this specific advice and recommendation, as well as the myriad of other valuable information about how they play—with details about how to play against them. If you are such a player, or have such tendencies, do yourself a big favor and remember this always: The object of winning poker is to win the most money, not the most pots. After you have learned this, and have developed enough discipline to be able to remember it when you are actually playing, you can also add the following adage to it: Since the object of poker is to win the most money and not the most pots, be aware of the value of the pot odds. That is, keep track of the pot's value relative to the cost of your investment to continue with a hand, as well as the relative additional value of money that can be invested in the pots by your opponents. Consider also any additional bets you can get out of them by playing smartly in the event that you have a lock on that particular hand, or at least perceive that to be so, including the possibilities of being able to get away from a hand should the circumstances call for such action at later stages. All of this combined can signify the value of the money with which you are playing, relative to the value that the pot is offering you for the investment. In simple terms, if we are playing in a \$10–\$20 Hold'Em game, and the pot already contains \$100, and it is now your turn to act and you are considering investing \$20 in this pot, by looking at what is already in the pot you can gauge that the pot is offering you 5:1 on your money. There is five times as much money in the pot already as the amount of money it will cost you to make the investment. If this is early in the round, as this example suggests would be the case, you can also assume that additional investments occur in later rounds, and even in this round if there are still players left to act behind you, because they will also contribute to the value that the pot is offering you. If on subsequent rounds several players put in a few more bets, before it becomes your turn to act for another \$20 investment, the pot can now easily contain \$300 or more. Although the pot now also contains some of your own money, in real terms you can consider that the pot is providing you 15:1 on your money, at least relatively so given the loose nature of this example. Even though I use this example for illustration purposes only, the point of the example is obvious.

If you are conscious of your money, and conscious of the

value you can gain from the investment of your money into that pot, then you can make more accurate decisions in the moment, as these may apply to this particular game, and as a direct result learn to maximize the yield from the pot you expect to win. This is what it means to win money in poker, as opposed to the winning of pots. How many pots you can win during your session is irrelevant. What is relevant is how much money you win. What is also relevant is how much money you don't lose. These situations are important in your strategy arsenal, and learning how to manage your money along with these skills and discipline and observational analysis of the games in progress allows you to win pots with money value as opposed to just winning pots for the sake of winning pots. This is incredibly important, particularly for Internet poker, because there you are facing what is largely a shoot-out when facing so many opponents who constantly remind you by their actions that their entire demeanor and makeup is focused on winning the most pots, completely ignorant of these principles that we have just outlined. You can now use this information against them, and profit even more handsomely.

## STARTING HANDS

Hand-in-hand with the above recommendation is this important suggestion, and that has to do with the selection of the best starting hands. Regardless of which game you might be playing, whether it is Texas Hold'Em, Texas Hold'Em–type games, Seven Card Stud, or any of the myriad and multitude of other games that you can find on the various Internet poker sites, and particularly those that I mention in this book, your best friend in all strategy play is your own discipline to select only the best of the starting hands that are applicable to the game chosen. By this I don't mean that you should limit yourself to only the top ten starting hands, which is something often mentioned in various magazines and articles and discussion groups, because that would be counterproductive. The best starting hands, like everything else in poker, are not something that can be cast in iron all the time, nor should they be. In my earlier book, *Powerful Profits from Poker*, I have outlined what I consider not only the top ten best starting hands of Texas Hold'Em, but also the top 40 hands for your selections. Additionally, I have also discussed Seven Card Stud, as well as Omaha High only, Omaha/8, and Stud/8, and shown the best starting hands for those games. I have also continued this practice in this book, for some of these games in their own chapters. If you stick to just those hands alone, perhaps the top 40 hands as I described them, this will provide you with a very solid foundation for continued profitability in Internet poker play, for cash games as well as tournaments.

Nevertheless, remember that everything in poker has infinite flexibility. Just because you don't have something in the top 40 best starting hands for that particular poker game doesn't mean that the hand is unplayable. As I have discussed elsewhere in this book (including in this chapter), playing your position is equally as important as playing the right cards. But because in Internet poker games you often have to play and showdown the best hands possible, because on the Internet you most of the time have to play the cards instead of the players—the direct opposite of the strategy recommendations and profitable play principles as embodied and recommended for live poker games in real-world casino poker rooms and card rooms—it is even more important that you start your poker education and your poker expertise with the best starting hands possible for that particular game. Although this may not be very much fun, it will be profitable. Sometimes it appears as if all you do is just sit there and post the blinds and antes and then have to throw away hand after hand for what seems like a long time. In Internet poker games, a few minutes can seem like an eternity because you are sitting at home and staring at your computer, as opposed to being in a casino poker room or card room with real live people, music, conversation, and the general ambience and atmosphere the casino poker rooms and card rooms provide. In Internet card rooms and poker rooms the action is between only you and your computer. Everything else happens in cyberspace, in a computer server located many miles away. The action between players is represented only by their icons while the players themselves are seated in vastly different portions of the world. You may face the unenviable task of disciplining yourself so stringently so you can sit at that computer for perhaps hours before you get a playable hand. Even though this may not be much fun, remember that this is a *process* whereby you are gaining discipline that will eventually allow you to profit on a consistent basis. Above all, do not fall into the trap of loosening up your starting-hand requirements when it seems like a long time before you find anything you can play. Even then sometimes you will lose with it, and sometimes you will have to throw it away, adding more and more aggravation and frustration to this equation. This frustration may lead you down the path of "let's have some fun," because you will see other players doing just that.

Most Internet poker games are composed of precisely these players, players who are there to have fun and who therefore will play anything, and probably will play every hand dealt to them, or at least the vast majority of them. Of all the many possible starting hands in poker, only those very few that I have listed can be considered to be among the best starting hands. This also means that you can easily fall into the trap of entertaining yourself during the poker game, and loosening up your starting requirements in order to join the fun exhibited by the other players in the game. There is absolutely nothing wrong with that, as long as you realize that you are now paying for that form of entertainment, which can be closely tied to the enjoyment that you might get from playing a video game—either on your computer or at an arcade. Entertaining yourself by playing such a video game will result in two things—first, you will be entertained, and second, you will pay for it without ever getting an opportunity to get that money back. This is not the way to play poker. Poker is *not* a video game, not even on the Internet. It is a serious game for serious money, and while it is possible to enjoy it, I assure you that enjoying the profitability from winning value pots is far greater than the enjoyment from entering many pots with substandard hands only to see your money dwindling away to some other players who gregariously play anything and everything, and happen to get lucky to win some great pots. This is not how you should play, at least not if you want to make Internet poker profitable for yourself. Therefore, at least at the very beginning, before you gain the necessary expertise to be able to vary your hands and thereby play more starting hands depending on the composition and analysis of the game and its players, as well as your position, and all of these other factors and skills that come into making you into a professional, semiprofessional, or at least knowledgeable poker player, then you should always remember to begin only with the best top 40 starting hands as I have listed them. If that is all you remember from this particular section of this chapter on strategy, then you will also be many times ahead of the knowledge and experience and abilities of the vast majority of your opponents, especially so on the Internet.

## IMPORTANCE OF STUDYING

Take advantage of the fact that you are not playing in a real-world casino poker room or card room where everyone can see you. In cyberspace you have a cloak of anonymity and are therefore able to hide anything and everything from your opponents except the actions that you choose to take. As I mentioned earlier, do not participate in chatting or discussion groups while playing any poker table, regardless of the gregarious nature and well-meaning comments made by your opponents, or the other players at the table, be it in a cash game or in a tournament. Instead, observe them, and don't let them observe you. This provides you with the opportunity to be able to take notes. Every Internet poker site that I mention in this book provides you with the opportunity to be able to click on any player, which opens a window on your computer screen into which you can make notes about that particular player's playing styles and hand selections. You can consequently create profiles of your opponents, which is something that is extraordinarily important, particularly if you are playing in games where you will meet up with those opponents on a regular basis, or at least a semiregular basis. Although it is true that in Internet poker rooms you are far more likely to encounter new players each time you sit in a new game, even if you actually play in only one particular type of poker game, you will eventually begin to encounter the same players who will also have the desire to play in those kinds of games that you have chosen. Most of the time such players will be very few in number, but if you begin to notice that you are seeing the same kinds of players playing in the kinds of games that you choose on a regular and frequent basis, making notes about them and their play using the windows available at the Internet poker sites is an invaluable information resource.

This is something you cannot so easily do playing in real-world poker rooms or casino card rooms, because there if you were to take out a notepad and starts scribbling notes about your opponents, you will not only look ridiculous, but what is even worse is that you might give away the perception that you are somebody who is a serious student of the game and is trying to improve himself. Or, and this is perhaps far more likely, you will give the impression of being an absolute novice. Neither of these situations will bode well for your profitability in those games, and in some poker rooms and card rooms you might even be asked not to do so. No one can tell you this in Internet poker rooms, and no one can stop you from doing it, because nobody can see you doing it. That is the wonderful advantage of anonymity—a distinct advantage for Internet poker play. Use these opportunities to carefully study your opponents and consequently give yourself as much of a resultant edge as such understanding and observation will bring you. Naturally, how well you act upon this information, and how well you are able to obtain such useful information, is something that is largely up to you and something that cannot be taught. It depends on your abilities, knowledge, skills, willingness to do so, and above all, personal discipline.

## MANY DECISIONS

When playing any kind of poker game, particularly Internet poker, you constantly face a barrage of decisions. From the decision to play, and the decision of the choice of the game, to the choice of the table, the choice of the limits, the choice of your position and seat at that table, and so on. As soon as you make the first decision to play poker, you are forever faced with continuing and constant and evolving series of decisions. Chief among these is the decision to defend your blinds, particularly your small blind, in Texas Hold'Em–type games, or your forced bring-in in Seven Card Stud games, or perhaps the antes in some other games, whatever such costs may be. Using the example of Texas Hold'Em, if you are playing in a game that has \$1–\$2 blinds, and you always defend your small blind by wagering that additional dollar regardless of your appraisal of the value of the hand you are holding, you're basically throwing out \$10 every round. Although some of the time you get a hand that wins, and some of the time you have to throw the hand away, on the average always defending your small blind in a game of this example will cost you about \$5 per round. If you are playing in a game whose stakes are higher, that expense will be commensurate with those limits. Similarly, if you are playing in games with limits that are smaller, the same will apply, because the cost is constant.

The same also applies to the big blind, when that big blind is raised. If your big blind is not raised, and you do not wish to raise the pot, you get a free ride. Simply check and see what happens on the flop, because sometimes the flop will hit you. Most of the time, however, the random hand that you get in your blinds will not be worth defending to those levels of expense. Remember what I said in my earlier book, and that is this strategy hint: It's okay to fold. Folding is a principle that appears to be entirely foreign to the majority of Internet poker players. It appears as if every Internet poker player has to defend his blinds every time, no matter what they have. This adds to the overall volatility of the game, because now you are facing many random hands, the value of which you cannot easily gauge. Combine this with the fact that in most Internet poker games you are facing players who actually play an undecipherable series of random starting hands, and this simply means that in addition to the blinds in most such games you will play against at least two or three other players whose holdings often can be no better than the blinds. This applies to other poker games as well, but since we are using the most popular game of all—Texas Hold'Em—as an example, and because about 90 percent of all games that you will find on the Internet will be Texas Hold'Em games, or at least Texas Hold'Em–type derivatives, these examples are extraordinarily important to keep in mind. This goes hand-in-hand with the discipline advice I provided for you earlier, and it simply means that you do not forget the value of your starting hands just because you have already been forced to invest your small blind, or your big blind.

Whatever the cost of the investment that you have to make, remember that by *not* continuing with the hand and relinquishing this small investment up front most of the time translates into substantial savings thereafter. It will prevent you from continuing with the hand in such circumstances where you may perhaps flop a possibility, and thereafter have to invest several more bets, including many more bets on subsequent streets, only to discover that your hand—which appeared to have such great potential earlier and up to this point—simply didn't get there, and now, instead of losing just the blinds, you have instead lost a substantial portion of your stack. Saving money is just as important as winning money, and remembering that will contribute significantly to your overall profitability. And in this instance, it will directly translate into the decision to consider the value of your cards before making the decision of defending the small blind, or continuing with a raised big blind. Always defending the blinds, or the bring-ins, is a mistake made by many Internet poker players, and it is by far the most common error committed by Internet poker players everywhere. If you learn to avoid that, you will save yourself the money that you would have invested in defending those blinds or bring-ins, and more important, such personal discipline will save you the money that you would have had to invest in subsequent streets in the event that the flop actually hit you, but only partially. Such situations are in reality nothing more than pure gambling, and poker is not a gambling game. Poker is a game of skill and opportunity, and in order to establish such skills and maximize the opportunities you must do so with knowledge and discipline and apply it correctly to the circumstances at hand in that particular moment. By all means do defend your blinds every now and then, even if only to confuse your opponents, as I have mentioned elsewhere. But if you do so, do it consciously for a purpose, and not habitually. Habitually defending your blinds or bring-ins simply adds to the cost of your time at this game, and can easily result in the draining of your bankroll. Naturally, if you actually find a great hand in the blind, then use the deception value that being in such early position with such monster hands provides for you. Slow-play it, and then hammer them later. Or, come out blazing and thoroughly confuse your opponents. This is also a situation where you can maximize the pot value and your profitability yields, because your opponents will not put you on anything significant, because you're in the blinds, or the bring-in. But if you habitually defend your blind, regardless of the consideration of the actual playability of that hand, your opponents get to know that pattern, and subsequently exploit it accordingly. Don't habitually and always defend your blinds or bring-ins. Again, if you remember nothing from this section other than this simple advice, then you will once again be substantially ahead of the vast majority of your Internet poker opponents.

## COSTLY DECISIONS

Just as it is important to make the correct decisions, it is also important to avoid bad decisions. Correct and bad decisions are not necessarily the direct opposite of each other. A bad decision may be correct, but it is nonetheless bad. A correct decision may be the right thing to do, but it may also be bad at the same time. It all depends on the circumstances at hand, and under which conditions such a decision is reached. The greatest mistake most poker players make, and this includes land-based poker players as well as Internet poker players, is to fold a hand to a final bet. Usually this is done on the river, or on the last card in whatever poker game you might be playing. In such a situation it may appear to the player that his opponent who is making such a bet has made a better hand, and as a result this player now folds his hand to just one more bet. Although this may be the correct move to do, particularly if the pot odds are not in your favor, it is not always the best course of action. The primary reason for this is that you will get to see your opponent's hand for just one more bet, particularly if you know that there is no one yet to act behind you who can raise that wager. Consequently, you do not need the pot to offer you great odds in order to justify such a call. Although in some of the smaller Internet poker games you can find many players who habitually call any bet with any holdings in any position, completely disregarding any kind of consideration about the pot odds or the likely strength of the hand that their opponents may be holding, in the higher-limit games and Internet poker, and in particular in poker tournaments, you often face this decision. As a general rule, you only need to be right one time in about every ten situations in order to make the call worth the while.

Although sometimes your opponent will indeed make a better hand and therefore cause you to lose the pot and this additional bet, it is important for you not to consider the money that you have already invested in the pot, but only consider the value of this additional call to see if your original assessment was correct. If you are in a situation where there is no danger of the bet being raised by someone yet to act behind you, in which case your decision would be almost automatically to fold, you are now assured to be able to force your opponent into a showdown without risking the possibility of having additional bets made behind you. Therefore, this play provides you with the knowledge of the quality of your assessment of your opponent's holdings, and the knowledge of exactly what she did have because you are forcing her into a showdown. It is surprising how many times players try to make this move on the river just to see if they can pick up the pot right then and there, by forcing you to fold your hand to that bet. These players have learned from experience to make this play regardless of whether or not they actually have the hand that they represent, because they also realize that they equally have to be right only about once in every ten tries in order to make this play a profitable one for them. Unfortunately, by getting into this habit they make this play far too often and likely are called by their opponents. So, while you only have to make this play against one opponent, or even against more opponents as long as you are the last to act and therefore do not risk being re-raised by someone yet to act behind you, they in turn have to make this play against a multitude of opponents. As a result, once they are identified as players who make this play habitually, they quickly become exploited by other knowledgeable players who continue to call them. Therefore, although theoretically they face only the same kind of odds as you do, namely needing to be right only about one time in every ten in order to make this play profitable, sadly for them this is now diminished considerably by the fact that they are not calculating this against one opponent, but will very soon have to calculate this play against many opponents. As a result, instead of only one opponent calling them, now most likely many opponents will call, and often. Even though they may have one of those opponents beat, or perhaps even two or three opponents, if they suddenly start to face fields of three, four, five, or even more callers at this stage, the entire value of their play has now disappeared. Such players quickly find themselves wondering where their chips have gone, and it may take them a considerably longer time to recover not only their losses but their confidence and image at their games.

The counterplay to this, however, is far more profitable. Not only because you are likely to face only opponents few in number, but because you will make this play only if you know that you are the last person to make this call. If you are not the last person to make this call, and there are yet other players to act behind you, even if it is only one player, you cannot make this play with an equal amount of certainty in success. If you have one player yet to act behind you, in order to make such a call you must have an extraordinarily perceptive read on that player. If you do not know for certain, or at least are very confident in your read of this opponent, that he will not raise, then you risk the danger of not only putting in one more bet, but potentially having to face the decision of calling an additional bet, or perhaps even a raise, and then have to fold your hand anyway, but this time having invested that additional bet. On the other hand, if you are absolutely certain that the opponent yet to act behind you will absolutely fold his hand, perhaps because of your accurate read of that opponent or the fact that he looks like he's ready to fold, which is something that you will find readily evident in real-world games but less so in cyberspace games, then you can still make that play. But if you see that you have more than one opponent yet to act behind you, then this play cannot be made. The only exception to this would be if the pot odds are incredibly in your favor, such as offering you at least in excess of 8:1. Under normal circumstances, if you see that you have players yet to act behind you, you will not only have to have what I consider to be at least a reasonably strong hand to make such a call, but you also have to realize that you potentially will have to put in additional bets even after that. If this is the situation, your pot odds will have to be extraordinarily favorable and at least a minimum of 8:1.

Making a call like this with more than one player yet to act behind you is extremely dangerous, and instead of resulting in a profitable play, over time it can often have the direct opposite effect. Just as we are here discussing the mistake of not making the call on the river to just one bet, we should also point out that it is equally a mistake to make such calls in situations like this, where it is quite likely that you will have to commit more bets, or throw away your hand. Unless you are sure that your hand still has a very significant chance of actually being the good hand that you thought it was all along, and the pot odds are considerably in your favor, including the potential costs of additional bets, it is a more prudent course of action not to make such a call. Fold the hand instead. Although in some circumstances you may find that you actually folded a winner, keep in mind the number of times when you do this and eventually realize that you saved additional bets because the players yet to act behind you raised, and then they were re-raised, until such time as the betting was capped, if this was a limit game, or until such time as all players were all-in in either a pot-limit or a limit game, only to discover that your hand would have actually lost. You quickly realize and learn the value of throwing away your hand to just this one apparent bet, when the potential exists that other players yet to act behind you will make additional bets necessary.

Therefore, the best advice to offer in this section is first, do not be timid and make that call on the river when facing a sudden bet into you by another opponent whom you have previously thought held an inferior hand, if you know that you are the last to act and therefore do not face the danger of someone else acting behind you. Now you have the situation fully grasped, and you know that you can force your opponent, or opponents, into a showdown without additional cost involved. You will find that you only need to be right about one time out of every ten in order to make this profitable overall. This is particularly important for Internet poker games because many players are making such plays because they have discovered for themselves, largely through the inexperience of their opponents, that oftentimes they can get away with it without actually holding the hand that they are representing. Most of the time this is merely a gut reaction to something they have observed and learned playing on the Internet, and really nothing that is actually part of a conscious process or a consciously applied strategy to that game. Most of the players whom you are likely to face in Internet poker games play in a manner that was profitable for them in the past and therefore they continue to do so, likely oblivious to the fact that many players quickly learn to spot this and will begin to habitually call them. You should not wait for such knowledge, but should instead make the conscious decision to recognize the value of your position, the value of the pot odds offered to you, and the value of forcing your opponents into such a showdown.

Second, remember that even if there is so much as only one player yet to act behind you, this play loses much of its value and profitability. Any time the danger exists that someone else will raise this bet, and therefore open the possibility to a re-raise and consequently the additional possibility of more raises still before it gets back to you to act, is a sign of danger that almost always invalidates this play. Not all the time, but almost always. Whether or not you can actually make this play knowing that there is one player yet to act behind you depends on the circumstances and your read on those opponents. But because we are now playing in cyberspace, where being able to observe any physical tells from your opponent is almost impossible, and therefore making judgments as to what your opponent will do—even if there is only one more opponent yet to act behind you—is difficult to predict, it is my advice never to make this play unless you are absolutely in the last position and do not risk any action behind you. Only in that situation, particularly in cyberspace poker, does this prove to be equally as profitable as the advice usually provided as a strategy play for land-based poker games. I have often discovered that much of the advice offered for Internet poker tends to be provided from the perspective of those who have gained experience in land-based poker games, and therefore such recommendations for strategy plays sometime fail to take into consideration that many of the situations so proposed are either all but impossible in cyberspace poker, or can easily be invalidated by the fact that you cannot actually observe your opponents. Consequently, although it is dangerous to be timid and to automatically throw your hand away just because there is yet one more bet to call, it is equally foolhardy to always do so, or to do so when you know that there are opponents yet to act behind you.

## IMPORTANT DECISIONS

Since we are now talking about decisions in general, you must consider which decisions in cyberspace poker are perhaps the most important. There are two kinds of important decisions in poker, and they apply just about universally. We have already discussed the importance of decisions in late position, but decisions made in early position are equally as important, if not more so. Early decisions are important because they commit you to the rest of the action for the duration of that hand, as well as determine the cost factor that you will endure throughout this hand, and the potential profitability that you might be able to gain from this pot. The earliest of all decisions, of course, is whether or not to play this hand. It is a decision that is even more important if you are in an early position in any poker game, particularly Hold'Em games.

Choose your starting hands carefully, especially in early position. Remember that hands that are eminently playable in middle or late positions are often hands that are to be thrown away in early positions. Similarly, hands that may be very playable as raising hands in late positions may be worth only a call from early positions, and perhaps only what is usually known as the crying call. Conversely, hands that you would probably throw away in middle positions are the kind with which you may even raise in very early position, such as the small or big blinds. You can make all these playing decisions in early position, and they are extraordinarily important to the cost factor and profitability of that particular hand, and have a myriad of consequences later on. Early decisions, therefore, directly influence not only your costs of the game, but also your profitability, and even more important, the remainder of your game and your table image and position and perception by other players of what you play and how. Such decisions have a profound impact on how you play other games, and indeed on how you play poker in general, no matter in which game or at which table you find yourself. If you fall into the habit of making poor decisions from early positions, that habit will follow you wherever you go, and you will quickly be exploited for having it. You must carefully learn and study the best starting hands for your particular poker game of choice and play only the top selection of these in early position.

## STAY CONFIDENT AND STAY LUCKY

Okay, we now agree that you have reached a level of knowledge and experience that allows you to consider yourself to be a good, solid poker player. Particularly, you have learned how to play cyberspace poker and to expect everything from all that you have learned so far in this chapter, and elsewhere in this book. You are now confident that you can beat this game and that you can play your best while overcoming adversities. Everything has worked fine so far. But now you find yourself mired in a protracted series of losing sessions. You have entered tournaments that you have previously won, and in which you regularly place in the money. But now you are getting knocked out in early stages. Even worse, you suddenly find yourself getting just knocked out of the money. More so, you are playing in cash games that you regularly beat for profit but now find yourself losing disproportionate amounts of money to what you obviously appraise as inferior players. What is even worse is that you find yourself in this situation for a very extended period of time, let's say two or more months. Now what do you do? Your carefully accumulated playing bankroll and profitability is disappearing faster than water down a drain. You suddenly begin to question everything about your arsenal of knowledge, experience, dedication, discipline, and ability to play poker. I can testify to this from personal experience, because this has happened to me, and it will happen to you, particularly in cyberspace poker. Anyone who plays cyberspace poker on a regular basis eventually experiences this, and because in cyberspace everything moves at cyberspeed, situations like this happen more quickly and more often. They also happen in the real-world poker rooms and to real-world poker players, but because the real world is a much slower-paced situation, it does not happen frequently. Nevertheless, there are many examples of hugely protracted series of such consecutive losses. Some players have spent decades facing such enormous fluctuations over what is commonly known as the long haul. Eventually, as statistics would actually indicate, such players' fortunes turned equivalent in a short period of time and eventually overcame all of their negative outcomes, resulting in a sequence of profitability equally as protracted. This happens in cyberspace, too, but whether or not it will happen to you depends on how you handle these adverse circumstances.

When you find yourself in circumstances like this, which are usually described as long losing streaks, remember that statistical equivalency is never a single line, but is instead the heartbeat of the game. With every beat there is a peak and a valley. When you are on the up curve you are rising in profitability and success, and are consequently feeling good about yourself and your game. This is the time when your confidence is high and you are becoming even more convinced that your hard work in acquiring knowledge and skill and experience is finally paying off. On the other hand, when you are on the down curve you suddenly begin to notice this quickly as you see your carefully earned bankroll suddenly diminish. You now start to question your knowledge, your experience, your profitability, your confidence, and everything else that you have learned about poker, and all of it will start to deplete as your bankroll is depleting. Now you are starting the down spiral of confidence that inevitably leads to you questioning yourself and everything about you when you play. It is only at this point that most players will find it necessary to reexamine themselves and how they are playing. Sometimes you will find that in the up curve you have started to play with a lot more confidence and that has resulted in relaxing some of your standards. In any protracted situation of wins, these are due to your skills and to a certain amount of luck. It is often easy to dismiss the luck, thinking that because you are now playing so well you deserve it. It is also easy to fall into the misperception that just because you are playing this well such luck will always be in your favor and will always occur when you need it.

This is due to the perception that you deserve such luck because it is the result of your hard work. No such thing. Luck is fleeting, and it has absolutely no perception of your abilities or experience or skill or the amount of hard work that you have put into your success. It is true that successful poker players make their own luck, at least to the level in which their skills are able to make such situations possible on a more frequent basis; however, reliance on the expectation that your good luck will always be there for you is equally as foolhardy as relaxing your standards just because you are in a protracted situation of wins—unless you are making such variances consciously because you are recognizing that you are in a situation where luck is actually favoring you, commonly known as being in the "hot streak." Being able to discover this and act upon it is something that you will experience many times as you play poker, but actually being able to recognize it and successfully exploit it is a skill that only a few experienced players will ever have.

To give you an example of such a player, just look at Gus Hanson. Although I recognize the fact that he has made a great success in real-world poker, and not in cyberspace, nevertheless this example is a good one for this particular discussion. Gus is an incredible player who is not only extraordinarily skilled in the poker games of his choice, but who is uncannily able to exploit lucky streaks in his favor. This is a classic example of a skilled poker player who can manufacture his own luck by the application of his extraordinary skills in the game and intuitively and consciously identify even the shortest streaks of luck and completely and fully exploit them to his advantage. Even his professional peers are amazed at what he can accomplish. This is the level of expertise and skill to which we all aspire, but in which many of us fall short. There is nothing to be ashamed of in this particular situation, because not all of us can be Gus Hanson, or hope to be that good. But some of us will reach a level that is close to that, and perhaps you are such a player. If so, remember that spotting such situations of protracted luck is a skill that you can exploit for profitability, as long as you recognize that such luck is indeed fleeting and you therefore must be able to return to your solid game afterward. Many players fail to recognize this when they are in the lucky up curve, and equally fail to take it into consideration when the converse happens and they are now in the down curve.

Recognizing the balance between your skills and the luck made by your skills—and the protracted series of lucky situations and events called "the lucky hot streak"—is what will differentiate you from the many players who play instinctively as opposed to rationally. Although there is such a thing as "rational instinctiveness," or even "instinctive rationality," such are abilities and concepts that players like Gus Hanson can exploit, but most of us can't. Just as some of us can run the 100-m dash in under ten seconds, most of us can't. Although we would like to, and many of us will train and work very hard to achieve it, the majority of us may turn into excellent runners but not become 100-m champions. This analogy is very useful to poker, and particularly to this discussion. When facing a downturn in your game, you should first question how you are playing and discover whether indeed you have suddenly relaxed your standards because you are running lucky. If you find this, you have just discovered a hole in your game. Once you identify such a hole, you can fix it. But if you don't know that you have this problem, you can't fix it. Therefore, whenever you are starting to run bad on a protracted basis, the first thing you should do is to investigate your game. If you discover such holes, do whatever you can to plug them. After investigation, if you find that you are still playing as well as you possibly can, then the problem becomes not with your game but with the inevitable down curve. Now the problems become more personal. If you continue to question your game and your confidence and abilities in the game, you may fall into the trap of overanalyzing yourself. If you find yourself overanalyzing your game and still losing, perhaps the problem is not with your game, but purely with the fact that you are in an inevitable protracted losing streak that has absolutely nothing to do with your skills, your experience, or your knowledge and expertise in the game. It is, however, at this point that many players lose their confidence, or start to see that confidence erode substantially. This becomes a problem only if you fail to recognize that the erosion of your confidence is due only to your *perception* of somehow having failed. What you did not realize and recognize is not that it is you who have failed, but that you have simply fallen into a situation where no matter what you do you will not achieve the results which you had become used to. If you do not recognize this perception, you may fall even further into the trap of negativity, which inevitably will lead you to loosen up your game, such as trying to play just like all those fools who are playing bad cards and getting lucky with them, or are drawing out on you, or hit miracle one-outs on the river. I have seen this happen many times to players who are good but have failed to recognize that the problem is not with them, but merely with the world at large and its inevitable statistical equivalency. This has happened to me. At one point I experienced a streak of online poker games where for almost six months no matter what I did I could not win. Although I did have winning sessions, and although I did win my fair share of hands, the overall analysis of the profitability for the period was negative. I also found myself drifting into self-doubt, even to the point where I relinquished my playing standards and played equally as foolhardy as my opponents. This quickly depleted my bankroll even further, to a point where I started to question my abilities as a player altogether. So what was the remedy?

The remedy to that problem, and the remedy to all of these problems, is the final advice I will provide for you in this section of this chapter. This advice is simple, but one that took me a while to realize and recognize. Over these many decades I have reached a point where I have seen just about everything and experienced just about everything, and therefore this provides me with the ability to be able to react to situations and circumstances, then analyze them and take appropriate corrective measures. I am able to express this to you as well because I'm speaking theoretically as well as practically, and from personal direct experiences. The remedy that I took is the one that I will advise you to take in these situations, and one that is very simple but also one that was very hard to conceive and arrive at. That simple advice is this: Slow down.

Although this may appear to be a simple idea and concept, it is hard to determine at the particular moment when you are running bad, and even harder to arrive at as a solution to those problems. If after you have analyzed your game and found no holes in it, or have found holes and plugged them, but find that you are still continuing to lose, and you have done everything else that you can possibly think of to improve your results to the level that they used to be, then you find yourself in a situation in which this advice is most useful. Slowing down your game means you must establish for yourself a different kind of discipline. It is more Spartan and a more strict discipline, and it requires you to do things a little differently and perhaps much more boringly. Playing poker in such a down curve is no fun. It is hard to overcome, and it can often become boring and tedious. How you handle these adverse circumstances determines your level of expertise thereafter, as well as your overall profitability and acumen for the game. The first time you experience this will be the most crucial time for you, because how well you handle it this first time will determine everything else thereafter. If you overcome this adversity well the first time, then you are assured you can be secure in your confidence, because you will never have to face this adversity in this equally traumatic fashion. To help you slow down, consider the following hints and tips:

- Take a break from poker altogether.
- Don't play as often as you used to when you return to playing.
- Stay away from mediocre or troublesome hands.
- Don't give your opponents cheap outs—make them pay for it.
- Play only the top five starting hands from early position.
- Play only the top ten starting hands from middle position.

- Play only the top twenty best starting hands in late position.
- Play with confidence—don't play weak.

Finally, if all else fails, don't play at all. Take an extended break from the game, and come back only after you feel confident and secure in the decision. If you have watched some of the WPT events on TV, you probably have noticed that several players featured in those telecasts confessed that they have taken an extended break from poker, sometimes for a decade or more. One player who comes to mind in most recent times is Hoyt Corkins. He won the WPT championship and has made an appearance at several final tables since, after taking more than a decade's absence from poker. He did not state his reasons; they are incidental to this discussion because they are particular only to him. It is the example of what he did that is appropriate for this discussion. He took time off altogether, and when he came back he did so with confidence and success. I offer you this same advice in the event that you find yourself in a protracted situation of losses from which you cannot recover, and none of the remedies that are offered for you here, or those that you may find elsewhere, appear to be working. If you find yourself in a life-altering down curve from which you are apparently unable to recover, instead of losing your confidence as a poker player, as well as your bankroll and financial resources, as your final decision to help yourself when slowing down does not work—quit.

This is an extreme decision indeed, especially if you're fond of poker as much as I am, and as much as most of the players who play this game. It is perhaps the hardest decision you will have to face as part of your discipline in poker. But it may be necessary, and if this is the case, then take advantage of this opportunity to learn it and do it. When this happened to me in cyberspace poker, as I described earlier, I decided that it was time to take some time off. I took off three months and worked on analyzing my game and everything that had happened. This gave me a chance to get away from looking at the computer screen, and I did other things. When I finally came back to playing, I felt relaxed, dedicated, and committed, and I was no longer upset at horrendous suck-outs. I was willing to play my game no matter what—no matter what anyone else thought or said. In simple words, I began to play again as I had begun to play in the first place. I proceeded to win three online tournaments, to place in the top twenty almost every time I entered a tournament, and to exploit cash game weaknesses in other players. In addition, I rebuilt my bankroll. I offer this as an example from my own life because it may be useful to you if you find yourself in situations where the slow-down principle simply doesn't work. Taking a hiatus from your game under such circumstances is not defeatism or escapism, but rather an exercise in your own discipline. Taking time off allows you to analyze your game and to reflect on it and yourself and your own mental state, and even if you don't find anything wrong, it nonetheless provides you with the ability to get away from something that had become a familiar occurrence to you. Familiarity often breeds circumstances of automation, and this sometimes results in playing on "autopilot." Experienced and knowledgeable players often fall into this trap, and many times unknowingly. They begin to feel as if they know everything, and are able to anticipate every circumstance and opportunity. Therefore these players think they are able to avoid every adversity, and as a result they tend to play without focus and concentration, merely coasting along. The direct by-product of this mind-set is that such players will begin to play in easily identifiable patterns. We have already discussed pattern play earlier, and how easy it is to fall into such patterns of decisions, and how easily it is for others to exploit them. We have discussed how profitable it can be to exploit such patterns in other players, as long as you are the one doing the exploiting instead of being the one being exploited. Finding yourself on autopilot in any poker game simply means that you have fallen into the trap of pattern play, perhaps without realizing it. When the game is no longer exciting enough for you to be able to focus all the time, on each and every hand, and analyze each and every situation appropriately, then it is time to either slow down or step away entirely. Playing on autopilot results in your being quickly identified by your opponents as a pattern player, and they will exploit *you*, instead of you exploiting *them*. Falling into this chasm on your down curve will further deplete your bankroll, and deplete your confidence in yourself and your game. When this happens, and the slowdown suggestion expressed earlier does not work for you, take a little step away from the game entirely to refresh youself and allow yourself to come back with the same zeal, directiveness, goal, and confidence that you used to have. You can then return to an even greater and better up curve and profitability. For anyone experiencing a losing streak, these suggestions are invaluable advice, and at least becoming aware of them will provide you with a greater arsenal of opportunities and decisions from which to choose to overcome it.

# Improving Internet Poker

This chapter focuses on some of those items about the Internet poker–playing experience that, in my own personal opinion, could stand improvement universally across the board. Although these are largely my own personal preferences from many years of playing on the Internet at various poker sites, it has come to my attention from discussions with other poker players, including other Internet poker players, that the issues I have personally identified as those that I think need improvement are also shared by many colleagues and other players.

## CONSTRUCTIVE CRITICISM

This criticism is not intended for any specific Internet poker site. Rather, these are what I consider to be suggestions that I think will help Internet poker universally, and will certainly help any Internet poker sites that choose to adopt them.

I think that the first situation that should be addressed is the fact that Internet poker is not land-based poker. Therefore the experience of playing online poker is not, and should not be considered, as something akin or similar to what players will experience in actual brick-and-mortar casinos. Internet poker is a distinctly individual and personal experience because the interaction is between the user of the computer and the computer screen and everything happens in the virtual landscape, and not a real environment. While it is true that the action goes on between real players all over the world, the fact nevertheless remains that the interaction is between the computer user and his computer. Consequently, everything that can be done to make the computer-using experience pleasantly efficient and easy is the sort of recommendation that will be much appreciated by the person who has to actually use the computer to be able to play on the software provided by the server that contains the gaming software and plays Internet poker at any one particular site. In my own personal research, and in my own personal opinion, I have come to the conclusion that many Internet poker sites tend to largely overlook what the actual experience is for the players who participate in their games. To be sure, all of the poker sites that I have mentioned in this book have taken extraordinary steps to overcome these issues. However, in my own personal opinion, some of the issues I am about to mention have simply not been raised before, or at least have not been raised in a sufficiently public forum for all operators of Internet poker sites to take note of them. It is for this reason that I have presented them here in this chapter. There is no particular order of importance, because I personally consider them to be all equally as important to the user's experience of Internet poker.

### Can't Change Seats

This is a big problem. In a real brick-and-mortar poker room or card room whenever I'm seated at any open seat, especially when that happens to be the only open seat available in a particular game at that particular table, sometimes that seat is not to my liking. As every poker player knows, regardless of the skills of the game and the statistics and probabilities, the fact remains that in a short term some seats are plain unlucky. Naturally by this I do not mean to indicate that luck is the preeminent and overriding force in any form of poker. On the contrary. Poker is, and has always been, primarily a game of skill. But this does not mean that people who play poker are not somehow personally superstitious, or in my case, conscious of the flow of the game in the very short term. I also find it uncomfortable if I'm seated at specific seats around any poker table. In particular I do not like the very short corner seats with limited space. Here your chips and other accoutrements that you place on the gaming table are very crowded. Oftentimes I find I am squeezed in between two large players as well. There are other considerations, of course, but the point here is that in any land-based brick-and-mortar real casino poker room or card room I can change seats whenever one becomes available, and even call for such a seat change in advance by asking the dealer, "First seat change please." Today, at least as far as I have been able to experience, this is not possible on Internet poker sites.

To date I have been unable to find a method and means by which to change seats or to request a seat change. In order to accomplish such a seat change, the only way appears to be to exit the table and then log on to that table again and then click on the seat to which you wish to move. However, the problems with this are manyfold. First, whenever you exit the table and then log back on again you are considered by the table to be a new player entering the game and are therefore charged blinds. Even if you have just posted the blinds you are now charged them again, or you have to sit there and wait for the entire round to go by before you are forced to post the big blind, thereby missing out on all of the action up to that point. Second, and this is probably the biggest problem, is that most of the good games on any Internet poker site have waiting lists. So, as soon as you log off the table the next person on the waiting list is automatically assigned your seat, or automatically assigned into the seat to which you wish to move. Therefore, by being forced to first log off that table and then log back on, most of the time you lose the seat that you occupied as well as the seat to which you wish to move. You are now forced to have to sign on to the waiting list at the very bottom, and this costs you money. Especially if you play for profit, and especially if you patiently waited to hunt down the best possible game and then worked to establish a specific image at that table.

Many other reasons applicable to this issue are equally as damaging and are particular only to Internet poker, and not land-based real-world and brick-and-mortar casinos. But the one that I just mentioned is probably the most important one to consider. The solution to this is incredibly simple, and I wonder why it has not yet been included. Any player at the table should be given the opportunity to move seats. To accomplish this, either allow the player to be able to click on the available seat and click an on-screen icon that says something like: "Reserve this seat, I wish to move there." Or, alternatively, add an icon or button anywhere on the screen among the on-screen commands that are already available, whereby this icon will simply say the words: "First seat change." Just like with the waiting lists, any player clicking on this would have his screen name automatically placed into that particular box, and whenever a seat became available that player would then be given the choice to change seats and move into that available open seat before any waiting players are seated there. If the player wished to decline that particular seat he could do so, and then move himself to the bottom of that particular seat change list, or be asked whether he wants to move from that list entirely. This is the exact same and identical procedure already available on all Internet poker sites using the button marked Waiting List. The program algorithm that would make this possible already exists because it is the same one that is used for that for joining and clicking the waiting list button. All that would be required would be to write an HTML command to the graphic interface to display the words *First Seat Change* instead of the words *Waiting List.* Now every player at any table would have the opportunity to be able to move seats and everything would be done very easily. Why this has not been adopted on Internet poker sites puzzles me. This is a very significant problem and one that's universally considered by experienced players as something that substantially detracts from the ability to make profits on Internet poker sites, especially if you play cash games at the higher limits. It is a problem that should be addressed, and one that can be fixed very easily and quickly.

### Can't Buy in Between Blinds

This is something that goes hand-in-hand with the above item. While it is true that most experienced and expert poker players usually wish to wait for their big blind before committing themselves to the game, sometimes it becomes important and even profitable to buy your way in. This becomes advantageous primarily for two reasons, one of which is moving seats in the existing game. In real-world casino poker rooms or card rooms, if a particular player wishes to make a seat change, sometimes he's forced into a seat that is between the blinds. Often this player has already posted one of the blinds, but now would be denied the opportunity to be able to post the second blind and then acquired the button in that seat. Now I understand that some of these situations are highly dependent on the particular rules at that particular casino poker room or card room, and let's face it many such rules can be substantially different from casino to casino or card room to card room. But the point remains that if the player happens to change seats into one that happens to be in between the blinds, that player should be able to buy in immediately and pay the blinds, thus being able to buy the button. At the same time, any new player entering the game, who may have observed this to be a game to his liking, may actually want to buy in between the blinds. This is often called "buying the button." If you choose not to do so, or choose to sit out for whatever number of rounds that may be, you will then have to enter the game only after the button had passed. In real-world casino poker rooms or card rooms this is usually not a problem, especially since once you do enter the game most of the time you will not be asked to put up a makeup blind, often called "dead blind." On the Internet, however, any player entering the game is not allowed to buy in between the blinds, and therefore not permitted to "buy the button," and therefore then forced to wait several rounds for the button to pass. Only after the button has passed is he asked to post a blind and that enters him into the game.

This is a terrible thing to do to a new player, by charging him a blind immediately, and particularly if he is coming in from behind a blind having not yet played any hands. In any real-world casino poker room or card room, any new player coming into the game and having waited for the blinds and the button to pass him is now not asked to post any dead blinds and is allowed to sit and enter the game and begin to play without any such forced bets. This is not so on the Internet, where every player joining every table is automatically forced to put up a blind. This becomes an even more acute problem if you are a player who just moved from one seat to another at the same game, provided you are allowed to do so and don't lose your seat or the game entirely by the procedure I just described. In such circumstances, such a player doing this is automatically prevented from buying in between the blinds, and even worse, he is then forced to relinquish the button and then required to post a dead blind behind the button. In this way such a player moving seats at the same game is penalized three times for having done nothing more than change seats. Even a new player coming in for whom the process of buying the button may be advantageous is not permitted to do so, and then is required to post a blind immediately even though she has not yet played a hand. Most of these situations are bad for the players, and what is most unfortunate is that it is teaching a lot of Internet poker players rules and methods of playing poker not found in the real-world casino poker rooms and card rooms. Consequently, online poker rooms should give any new player coming into a game the option to buy in between blinds in the event that the situation of that player joining the game so makes possible. At the same time, a new player joining the game should also not be forced to post blinds out of turn. The new player should be allowed to join the game immediately without having to wait for the big blind, or without having to post a big blind in order to enter the game before the big blind. Similarly, players moving seats on the same table should not be forced to post another blind, should not be forced to relinquish the button if it was theirs in the first place, should be permitted to post the blind that they missed in the other seat, should be able to buy the button if they so choose, and should not be forced to post a blind behind the button if the button passes them. Naturally, all that I have just said applies to Texas Hold'Em games. In games other than Texas Hold'Em, the same situation usually applies with the posting of antes, but since everybody has to post an ante anyway this point is largely moot for all games other than Texas Hold'Em–type games. Of course, the changing of the seat situation applies to any kind of game, regardless whether it is a Texas Hold'Em game or any other kind of poker game available on Internet poker sites.

## Military Time

Because all of the Internet poker sites are currently located outside of the United States of America, the biggest problem facing players wishing to join games, and in particular tournaments, is to recognize exactly what time those tournaments are. Since about 80 percent of all online poker players come from the United States, poker sites have come to use U.S. East Coast standard time as the standard by which to schedule all such events. This is not such a bad idea, but the problem is that most poker sites display those times in military time. I personally find this a problem, especially when I'm trying to figure out what exactly 1630 means when I happen to be on the West Coast of the United States on Pacific standard daylight savings time, and not on East Coast standard time. Although I know that the difference is three hours, even allowing for the daylight savings time option that some western states observe and others do not, the problem of having it listed in military time becomes an exercise in mental gymnastics. At least it does so for me, because I have for some peculiar reason always had problems translating military time into real time. Although I know that 1630 means 4:30 in the afternoon U.S. East Coast time, it always takes a little effort to figure that out. Now I have to figure out whether that is daylight time, or whether that is not daylight time, and then I have to figure out exactly what time it is going to be where I am, which happens to be in Las Vegas, Nevada, which happens to be on Pacific standard daylight time. Once after I finally figured all of this out, it turned out that this particular tournament was starting at 1:30 my time. Unfortunately, if you happen to be in Arizona, which does not observe daylight savings time, you then have to try to figure out exactly what time it is for you. It happens to be 12:30 your time, but that means that you have to make more calculations. Then, of course, if you happen to be in Colorado, you have to figure out what mountain time is relative to all of this. And if you happen to be in the plains states, then you are on central time and have to figure out what all that means for you. The point is that all this takes a lot of calculating and is very confusing for a great many people and causes a lot of extra work and a lot of extra headaches for players, and it is unnecessary.

The simplest solution for all poker sites is to list everything either on East Coast time, period, or, which is infinitely preferable, to do something that every Internet weather service already does, and that is to provide for the person to be able to choose the location in which they happen to be, and to select a time frame that applies to them. On my Internet service provider, which happens to be AOL, there are very simple buttons to click to identify your location. All I have to do is click on the button that says Las Vegas and I'm automatically updated for the time frame that applies to my particular place in this world. This is such an extraordinarily simple solution to this complicated and complex problem that it mystifies me why Internet poker sites have not adopted it. They don't even have to create the program themselves; they can simply purchase the software from a number of manufacturers that create such software programs that can identify an individual location anywhere on the face of this planet and apply that particular location's time frame reference to whatever the person happens to be doing.

But what is even more confusing is that many poker sites use GMT, which stands for Greenwich mean time, and that is even worse. I seriously doubt that many people would even know where Greenwich is, or even what GMT means or stands for. Those who happen to live in New York City would think that Greenwich means Greenwich Village, but that's about as far as any kind of understanding from the vast majority of players on the Internet will go.

Confusing Internet poker players is not a good idea. It is difficult to navigate through all the masses of information and tournament schedules in order to be able to find a tournament in which to play and to figure out exactly when that tournament starts or is played. Even more problematic is the fact that many poker sites on the Internet do not use the same kind of means of doing this, and many of them are very different from each other. So, as soon as I get used to calculating military time on one site, that may not be exactly identical to anything else that happens to be done on some other site. The problem is that there are no standards, and while we understand that the world of Internet poker, and Internet gambling in general, is a wide-open new frontier, I think that in the same spirit that Internet poker sites have voluntarily joined regulatory bodies for the purpose of security, they should also all get together and start listing their tournaments in something that is very easily understood by the majority of their players, which happen to be coming from the United States. It really doesn't matter to me how it's done, as long as it is done the same way everywhere. Pick a time. If you are going to be listing everything on East Coast standard daylight savings time, then make sure that that is everything that you do and that you always do it the same way. I would encourage all Internet poker sites to stay away from military time and install software that allows the *user* to be able to click on the location on this planet where *they* happen to be, so that everything and all the time frame references are always listed in *their* times, however this applies to their particular location where they happen to be at the moment in which they are playing. This will make the Internet poker–playing experience, and particularly the tournament playing experience, much better and much more pleasant for everyone.

## Slow Action and Disconnects

Everything in cyberspace moves at warp speed. This is the nature of the technology and it makes us think that events in the real world do not appear to be as fast. The perception of speed—and in particular the perception of the speed of action—is significantly skewed in cyberspace, and this is even more acute when playing Internet poker. When playing poker in the real world it would not be considered as "slow" if somebody would take, say, one minute to make a decision. However in cyberspace taking one minute to make a decision is an eternity. This is an interesting exercise in human perception and how we humans adjust and adapt to the world around us, even if in this case the world around us is really only in our minds and exists solely and only in our perception of it. Nevertheless, it is a fact that we have to make decisions in cyberspace and that these decisions take time, and that in cyberspace actions are fast and decisions must be equally as quick. The problem is that many online poker players take forever to make a decision on just about every kind of hand. Fully allowing for the fact that everything in cyberspace happens at warp speed, it is nevertheless extremely annoying to sit there and wait for players who—hand after hand after hand—take as long as they can possibly get away with in order to milk their decision time to its fullest. Even though most online poker sites now limit those decision times to about 30 seconds, this is still far too long. If you are playing Texas Hold'Em, for example, that means that you are sitting at a table with ten positions. You being one of those positions, this means that there are nine other players along with you. If each of these players takes 30 seconds to make a decision that means that it takes 4½ minutes to play that one round. Every poker site that I mention in my book recognizes this problem and limits players to about 15 seconds. This is usually accomplished by the use of a slide bar, similar to the slide bar that you see at the bottom of your screen when you are opening or downloading a page from the Internet. This particular slide bar simply indicates the amount of time that player has left in order to make a decision on his or her hand. On all of the sites that I mention in my book it takes about 15 seconds, and the player is continuously warned by a series of chimes and beeps advising him or her to make a decision. If no decision is made before the end of that 15 seconds, that player's hand is automatically folded. This is a very good tool to expedite decisions in online gaming, and very helpful in online poker. Unfortunately, even though 15 seconds doesn't appear to be long, some sites extend this to 20 seconds, and even that can be extraordinarily long, especially when you consider the multiplicity of so many players at the table taking all of that time on each and every hand. Although the times allowed vary between sites, the median is probably about 15 seconds. Now assume that you have a ten-handed table, where you occupy one position. And let us further assume that on this particular table there are several players who make a decision in a timely manner, but five of those players will take the full allotment of 15 seconds per decision. Therefore, it now takes 1¼ minutes for each round to be completed. This is still extraordinarily too long.

This problem is further complicated and exacerbated by the frequency of player disconnects. This will soon be overcome by the improvement in online technology, in particular high-speed broadband Internet access. However, as of the time of the writing of this book, it is an unfortunate fact that there are still too many players who play on these sophisticated online poker sites using nothing more than basic dial-up service. When we consider that all of the servers that play these poker games are located in countries outside of the United States, this means that the signal has to travel a very long way across a multitude of connections in order for the decisions to be communicated from you to the server and from the server to you. This also means that there are ample and multiple opportunities for this connection to somehow be broken or corrupted along the way. The more primitive your computer and software, and the more primitive your Internet connection, the more problems and disconnects you will suffer. It is understandable that such disconnects will be a problem for you, and all of the online poker sites are doing everything that they possibly can do in order to expand their capacity and the speed of their servers. They have the latest of technology that is currently available in order to allow you to have as much of an uninterrupted experience as possible, but the success of this is highly predicated on your ability to be able to match that commensurately by possessing the kind of equipment and connectivity that will allow you to take full advantage of the technological innovations and expertise that are vested in the servers at these Internet poker sites. Therefore, do yourself and other players a favor by upgrading your computer system and obtaining broadband connection, preferably with some form of a cable modem, if you wish to be a serious Internet poker player.

The problems with disconnects affect your ability to have an enjoyable poker playing experience, and affect other players and their ability to be able to play as *they* wish to play. This becomes even more acute when tournaments are at stake. Particularly large buy-in tournaments. Not only will disconnects cost you money, especially when you enter a tournament and now are disconnected in the middle of a hand, or in the middle of your blind, and even though you might have a very good hand you do not get to win it because the system will fold your hand because you were disconnected. This also costs other players money because they will be faced with delays and decisions and the inability to be able to play against you. The other problem is that whenever you are disconnected, you are usually given about thirty seconds to reconnect and rejoin the table. Everyone else has to sit there and wait for you to get connected, even if you actually are able to find your table after reconnecting to the server. Sometimes being able to reconnect to the server may not be as easy, especially if you are using the old dial-up services. The connections that carry telephone line signals may not be as easily accessible and this may cause compounded problems for all.

Although I understand that this is a problem largely for the players, Internet poker sites can improve their services by not allowing players so much time to reconnect. If someone is disconnected, whatever the reason, that player's hand should automatically be frozen at whatever level of bet that player had made, and the action continued immediately thereafter. That player's hand should not however be folded, because that would be unfair to the player who was so disconnected. That player should be able to participate in the pot up to the level of the amount of wagers that he or she had committed prior to such a disconnect. Even though that player may not have actually gone all in, as that term is traditionally understood, a provision should be made by the online poker sites to allow that players' already committed amount to play in that same manner. That way the action would not be delayed for the other players at the table, and everyone else would be able to go on and compete for the remainder of the pot by making such a side pot. This could resolve such disconnection issues as well as help speed up the games.

Ultimately, of course, it is the player's responsibility to have the required equipment necessary to access the site to play the games as best as they are made possible. If you do not possess the kind of computer or the kind of Internet connection preferable for you to access these poker sites to their fullest potential, then the problem rests with you. Unfortunately, the problem that you are causing for yourself has ramifications for other players at the game. Therefore, my advice to you is to obtain the best possible connection for your computer and only then play Internet poker. I would also like to advise you to please make your decisions quickly. Do not linger and study your cards. The cards that you have received will not change, no matter how long you look at them. Even though you see players on television who seem to study their hands for a long time, remember that these are highly edited TV highlights and in those decisions that player is probably at the final table of some tournament such as the WPT or the WSOP. Therefore their decisions are much more important to that particular hand in progress at that particular stage. On the Internet, the problem I have experienced most often has been that many new players who come to play Internet poker have learned about playing Texas Hold'Em by watching television, and as a result think that they must study each and every hand and look at it for the maximum time available. This is decidedly *not* so. If you are playing Internet poker, and particularly if you are playing in the cash games, you should already know as soon as the cards are dealt to you whether or not you will enter this pot, and if so how you will play. You should already know in your mind exactly which of your decisions will be based upon what kind of flops, what there could be that could either help your hand, or not, or which kinds of cards become indeterminate. You should also know exactly what you will do and under which circumstances you will do it. These are all poker skills that you acquire as you learn what I have written in this book, and in my earlier poker book, *Powerful Profits from Poker*. By reading what I have written in that book, as well as everything in this book should allow you to to make decisions quickly, efficiently, and profitably. Contrary to what you may think by watching poker on television, playing that way in the real world will not earn you many friends. Learn the game, and learn to make your decisions quickly, and that will improve not only your performance and your profitability, but also serve to enhance your image at the Internet poker table. You will find appreciation for taking swift and quick actions. And you will be understood as someone that pays attention to the game and what's going on. All of this serves to enhance your table image and makes it possible for you to play the best poker of which you are capable, based upon your existing skills and abilities and knowledge. Give yourself this advantage, and wherever possible encourage it in your friends and your online opponents. Although I'm not saying that you should try to educate the opponents against whom you are playing, and whom you may perceive to be either novice or unknowledgeable, I do think it won't hurt anyone if you make it plain that a quick decision on Internet poker is a good decision. The only exception to this may be in tournaments, or in high-limit cash games, where you might want to take as much time as the Internet poker site allows you under specific circumstances, particularly in situations where there are significant decisions to be made in marginal situations. No one will deny you this opportunity, and no one will berate you because of it. Just don't do it habitually over hands that don't merit it.

## Playing Cards

Another particular personal peeve of mine is the size of the playing cards and their symbols. Some Internet poker sites seem to take great care to make graphics large, including taking up a lot of space with either a virtual dealer or a virtual rack, or the various other icons and symbols that I discussed previously. However, the one and most crucially important aspect of the graphic display is usually extraordinarily undersized, and very badly designed and displayed. I find it incredible that poker sites do not make it possible for the players to see their cards easily. Many of these cards again try to mirror and mimic the real world, by having them upside down, or displaying them in a very narrow format with difficult-to-identify suit symbols. Of all the graphics that are important to Internet poker players, being able to see the cards is the *most important* thing, crucially and above everything else. Graphic designers should concentrate on these cards first, and everything else second. Cards should be made big. Their designs should not try to mimic the real world, but stand up straight. They should have large numbers and large suit symbols. And, above all, every single site on the Internet should get rid of this idiotic four-color deck. I am absolutely adamant about that because that irks me to no end. My vision is not as good as it used to be, and I find it difficult to stare at my computer monitor for long periods of time, especially for the many hours that are required in playing any kind of an online tournament, particularly tournaments with many hundreds of players. It plainly hurts my eyes and detracts from my ability to concentrate when I have to squint and look at these tiny cards, often displayed in narrow formats, and often in situations where you simply cannot tell one suit from the other.

Even though most of these poker sites give you the option to have what they call "big deck," it is unfortunate that this decision also comes with a restriction of having to accept the four-color deck. Why Internet poker sites would want to do this I don't know, but I can only assume that somehow they think that people who want to see big cards also want to see a four-color deck. We do *not* want to see a four-color deck. We just want to *see the cards.* Poker sites should make them big, or at least give players the choice of being able to select the size of the cards *without also having to accept the four-color deck along with it.* If the site would not waste so much of the server's memory on graphics that do nothing to enhance the Internet poker-playing experience, then they would have the resources to be able to give the player the choice of being able to select exactly how big they want their own cards. The Internet poker–playing experience would improve by giving the player many choices to customize their experience the way *they* want it, instead of the way that the graphic designers chose to do it. Graphic designers are usually artists, and as such they may wish to create something that looks pretty but which is functionally deficient. Instead, perhaps poker sites can instruct their graphic designers to create an Internet poker site with options that *allow the players to customize key* elements, of which the size of the playing cards and how they look is the single-most important factor. If the sites give *players* the opportunity to be able to *choose their own car*ds and *how they look* to suit themselves, then they would enhance the players particular Internet playing experience, and enhance the site's profitability and appeal.

This much said, I once again wish to reiterate that these are my own personal and private opinions and that they are so expressed here with universality in mind. The poker sites I mention in my book are those that I have selected to be included because I personally like the way their designs are functionally enabled. Some sites could perhaps improve on the excellence that they already display, by using in particular my suggestion of allowing the players to choose the way the playing cards look and how big they are. But I want it to be plainly understood that from among all of those tens of thousands of Internet poker sites, the ones that I picked to be included in this book, either as part of the text or in my featured directory of poker rooms, are those that are not only good as they already exist, but whose owners and operators are continuously upgrading and improving them because they have recognized that as familiarity with Internet gambling and Internet poker grows, and as technology improves for both the operators of these sites as well as the players who access them, it is important to continue to improve the service and the performance of the site and the games. I picked these Internet poker rooms for these as well as a variety of other reasons, but primarily because of the overall excellence in performance as they exist now, as well as in the excellence of their continuous upgrades, and their willingness to improve their service to best serve their players at all times.

# Internet Poker and the Law

The legality of Internet gambling in general, and by default Internet poker as well, is still murky at this time. I hope that it will change for the better, not for the worse. Unfortunately, the outlook does not look good. Many legislative and judicial moves are afoot to cause all sorts of problems for the American public and the American consumer, moves made by self-righteous legislators and self-anointed pursuers of law who appear to be exercising their law enforcement authority even though there are currently *no such laws* enacted anywhere in the United States that would provide for them such enforcement authority. The main problem with all of this is that law enforcement agencies, and legislators, are unable to understand the reality of the world in the twenty-first century, and are trying to enforce something that is not only *not* illegal, but that currently has *no law enacted to make it illegal.* Unfortunately, these agencies, such as the U.S. Department of Justice in particular, are nonetheless trying to enforce it by brutal and threatening tactics. At the same time, some misguided legislators in Congress are now trying to legislate to make Internet poker entirely illegal.

There are many problems associated with the legality of Internet poker, the chief of which is the lumping of Internet poker together with something called "Internet gambling." Both the legislators and the U.S. Justice Department equally fail to recognize that poker is not gambling, but is in reality a *game of skill based upon knowledge*. These self-appointed "do-gooders" in the U.S. legislature and U.S. Justice Department are trying to create legislation and laws that would make the application of *all* knowledge through skill illegal. In this same manner, they would make carpentry illegal because the exercise of knowledge as applied to the making of something resulting in a profitable outcome would therefore become illegal everywhere. A carpenter who spends a great deal of his life learning how to be a good carpenter by acquiring great knowledge of carpentry, and then the skills to translate that knowledge into his ability to be able to through his own skills practice the knowledge of carpentry by actually doing it, would now be considered by such legislators and misguided law enforcement officials to have committed an illegal act. A poker player who spends a great deal of his time and his life learning how to be a good poker player by acquiring great knowledge of poker, and then the skills to translate that knowledge into his ability to be able to through his own skills practice the knowledge of poker by actually doing it, would now be considered by such legislators and misguided law enforcement officials to have also committed an illegal act. The problem is that with any such legislation, and such misguided law enforcement efforts by the current representatives of the Justice Department and other various federal and local agencies, would make *any* practice of skill based upon knowledge illegal, no matter what it was. Under such legislation and law enforcement practices, not only poker would be considered illegal, and not only carpentry, but also surgery, science, all public works projects, environmental projects, preservation of endangered species projects, and indeed any and all human activity based upon some exercise of knowledge through skill. If our legislature and law enforcement agencies are allowed to so prevail with these ideas and practices, we can thereafter forgo every human advancement in the annals of intelligence throughout human history, and once again relegate ourselves to thousands of years of "dark ages" where no exercise of intelligence or practice of skill through knowledge will be permitted.

There are currently *no laws* enacted anywhere in the United States, on the federal level as well as on state level, that in any way, shape, manner, or form, prohibit Internet gambling—and that's a fact! Furthermore, there is *absolutely no law*, nor any legislation, that makes your act of playing online poker—as an individual person practicing constitutionally guaranteed freedoms—in any way illegal. Contrary to the opinions that are often being expressed in many texts and columns, and sometimes shown and discussed in Internet poker forums, there are *no such laws currently in effect*, or enacted, in the United States of America on a federal level, or in any state of the union. What laws there are are those that were designed to combat Mafia-style RICO statute crimes on the federal level, and various state efforts whose local legislators have tried to concoct a whole slew and variety of various laws intended to suppress online gambling, which by the strange default also includes the skill-based game of poker. The problem with state legislators has been that they have produced legislation that makes one act illegal in one state, while the same act is perfectly legal in the neighboring state. This adds to the general confusion about the legality of online gambling, and by default online poker.

On the federal level, there are currently several moves afoot to try to create some form of legislation that would ban online gambling altogether. This all began back in the 1990s, and specifically with the introduction of the Internet Gambling Prohibition Act of 1999. This inept piece of legislation was initiated by U.S. Representative Bob Goodlatte (R–Virginia) and Senator Jon Kyl (R–Arizona) to specifically deal with online gambling. Fortunately, the bill died. Unfortunately though, it came back to life, and so did the legislative movement that initially sponsored it.

In 2003, Rep. Spencer Bachus (R–Alabama) introduced House Bill H.R. 2143, which is called the Unlawful Internet

Gambling Funding Prohibition Act, supposedly designed to "ban the use of credit cards, wire transfers, e-Cash, and other forms of payment for funding Internet gambling activities." Not only is this bill insidiously stupid, but what is most dangerous about it is the fact that Rep. Bachus and his cronies were trying to attach this bill to the 911 terrorist legislation mandated by the 2002 law that created a commission to study the intelligence and law enforcement failures that made the United States susceptible to the terrorist attacks on September 11, 2001. By attaching this Internet funding gambling prohibition act to the terrorist bill, Rep. Bachus and his supporters—in particular Rep. Michael Oxley (R–Ohio), who was the chairman of the House Committee on Financial Services and a longtime advocate of the prohibition of Internet gambling—were trying to convince the legislature, and the rest of us, that prohibiting the transference of money to Internet gambling sites, and Internet poker rooms, is somehow necessary to protect us from terrorist attacks.

Fortunately, sanity prevailed, and the more intelligent members of the U.S. Congress recognized the futility and stupidity of these attempts and quickly put a stop to it. Thankfully, the executive leadership of the United States has recognized that if they allowed Rep. Oxley and his supporters to succeed in attaching their gambling funding prohibition act to the 911 terrorist bill, that would not only open the door to everyone else who wanted to attach any kind of special interest bill to any other, but that such an act would have also diluted the impact and value of the terrorism bill and delayed it in Congress likely forever. This bill eventually went before a final congressional vote on September 29, 2004, and was defeated. Sadly, there are continuing efforts by Senator Kyl and others to do this over again.

While these zealous legislators are trying to enact such foolish and foolhardy legislation, and then are equally sneakily trying to attach them to other important bills, there are other, even more insidiously stupid and frightening acts being committed by various officials of the U.S. Department of Justice, and some other law enforcement agencies. Most recently, the Justice Department sent warning letters to publishers, radio stations, and Internet sites that sell advertising around the country, telling them that accepting advertising from online gambling sites—including online poker sites—is a crime, subjecting them to possible prosecution and fines. Although legal experts everywhere have concluded that the Justice Department's position rests on *no fact, no law*, and *on absolutely nothing* other than the pure and blustering threats made by them against lawfully abiding companies and citizens, and persons the world over, including those residing in countries outside of the United States, nevertheless these threats have had the direct effect of forcing otherwise legal companies and the persons who patronize them, as well as other businesses, to stop their activities. Online banking company PayPal was entirely forced out of the Internet banking business altogether, as that applies to the transference of money between Internet poker sites, and Internet gambling sites. Moreover, famed search engines such as Yahoo! and Google have been forced to stop accepting advertising from online poker sites, and online casinos, and to stop their search engines from directing people to them.

However, the most insidiously scary of all of these acts by the U.S. Justice Department was the seizure of $3 million paid by PartyPoker.com to the Discovery Channel for promotional and publicity materials surrounding the PartyPoker.com Million WPT poker tournament. The Justice Department said that "the money was for advertising to promote an illegal purpose." What illegal purpose? The PartyPoker.com server on which the poker is played is located significantly outside of the United States. The PartyPoker.com Million WPT poker tour event is held on a cruise ship several hundred miles outside the shore limits. So, if in accordance with the Justice Department statement the money paid by PartyPoker.com to the Discovery Channel was for advertising to "promote an illegal purpose," *what exactly was* this "illegal purpose" and where exactly did this take place? Herein, of course, lies the greatest problem with any such legislation, and that is precisely the fact that none of this Internet gambling or Internet poker playing, or even the poker cruise, takes place anywhere in the United States. Playing poker on an Internet poker site means that you are playing a poker game located outside of the United States. Playing poker on the PartyPoker Million WPT championships takes place on a cruise ship significantly outside of the sphere of legality and influence of the United States of America, and in particular the Justice Department. None of this is any kind of "illegal activity." What makes this kind of act the most dangerous is not only because the Justice Department has taken it upon themselves to exercise these Gestapo-like techniques, but more so because they have done this *without there ever being any kind of a law*, or any kind of legislation anywhere in the federal statutes that would authorize them to do so.

Nevertheless, as justification for these enforcement activities, the Justice Department, and other such misguided law enforcement agencies, are using the existing state and federal laws in the United States that address the transportation of wagering information over telephone lines and wires, which were legislated in the pre-Internet era, such as the Interstate Wire Act, the Travel Act, the Crime Control Act, and the Interstate Transportation of Wagering Paraphernalia Act. Many experts contend they are outdated, and that their drafters could not have foreseen the advent of the Internet. In other words, their applicability to online gambling is strongly questioned—especially in the case of offshore gambling operations—since these laws provide exceptions to gambling activities between two states or countries that permit gambling.

What we have here is not only a misunderstanding of existing laws, which specifically *allow* exceptions for gambling activities between two states or countries that permit gambling, but more specifically and more dangerously, the complete misinterpretation of such existing laws without any modernizing legislation empowering that clarification to a point where the Justice Department, or any law enforcement agency, can justifiably commit such atrocities in their name. All of the current federal and state legislations specifically permit gambling between states and nations who permit gambling. Therefore, since the United States permits gambling, even though it is limited to specified areas under various individual legislations, the fact remains that Internet gambling is perfectly legal in those *other* countries, and therefore as a direct result of existing laws, neither the Justice Department nor any other law enforcement agency is empowered to in any way seize any property, or stop any commercial activity such as advertising, publicity, or the acts of financial transfers between such institutions and their customers. If this is not plainly stated, and if it is still misunderstood by either the law enforcement agencies, the Justice Department, or the U.S. legislature, or the various state legislatures, then the United States of America is in considerably more trouble than from merely economic problems or world unrest.

The trouble that the United States will be in if these activities are permitted to continue, and the Justice Department and the various other law enforcement agencies that act accordingly to its directives are not curtailed and stopped from targeting online gambling, and specifically Internet poker, is that the United States will no longer be the land of the free and law abiding. It will no longer be a land of the law abiding because even the chief law enforcement agencies such as the Justice Department are acting directly against what is currently legal, and are doing so only because they can and because they command the strength of the federal government, and by so using it instill fear in everyone whom they target.

Let us make no mistake here. Although no act of Internet poker is currently prohibited by any enacted laws or legislation in the United States, nevertheless it is *perceived* to be illegal by some very powerful people in the U.S. government, who apparently don't think the United States Constitution and the Bill of Rights are important. Franklin D. Roosevelt said in his inaugural speech in 1932 that we have nothing to fear but fear itself. Now, we have to fear our very own government whose misguided legislators and law enforcement officials are apparently trying to advance their own personal and private prejudices through agendas designed to curtail the most basic of our freedoms.

We the people are free and self-reliant not because our government permits it, but because we the people *are* the government.

Those elected officials in the executive, legislative, and judicial branches of our government, as well as all government employees and appointees who are paid with public money, are all public servants—and that means that they work for *us*, we the people, and not the other way around. It is therefore prudent to perhaps remind all legislators and all Justice Department officials that they work for us, we the people, and that we the people do not work for them. In America, that particular brand of individual and collective freedom that we all enjoy, and are now trying to export to other places around the world, means that we should never be subject to misguided legislation. Nor should we live in fear of the Justice Department that suddenly decides to wield heavy hands and administer arbitrary justice through selective prosecution and selective persecution, even though there exists no law to so authorize the Department to do it. We the people should not have to live in fear of either such legislative incompetence, or such judicial and law enforcement heavy-handedness.

Finally, in the interest of fairness and to keep myself from being targeted for my personal and private opinions, let me state in no uncertain terms that I have a personal interest in the legality of Internet gambling, and Internet poker. As an author of poker books, and books on casino gambling, including Internet gambling and Internet poker, I have an economic and intellectual and personal interest in the legality and continuation of this form of adult entertainment. Furthermore, let me also categorically state that I in no manner, shape, or form, in any way condone, foster, promote, sanction any activity that is illegal, now, in the past, or that may in the future become illegal. My opinions about the status of legislation and law enforcement as it pertains to Internet gambling and Internet poker, or in any related activities, are purely and only my own personal opinions and stated through the exercise of my freedom of expression, freedom of association under the Bill of Rights, and the First Amendment to the Constitution.

I have strong personal opinions about these issues. They are my opinions, and mine only, and not those of my publisher, nor any person who will distribute, publicize, or in any way commercially transact or transport this book. These opinions are mine and are communicated through this medium of the printed word to the reader, in the same manner as the famous pamphlets of Thomas Jefferson were so distributed to other people who wished to read them for their own purposes.

I hope that this is a sufficient disclaimer to make sure that everyone understands that I have only the best interests of the poker players and the world community at large, and the citizens and residents of the United States of America, at heart. I love poker, and I love playing Internet poker. I don't wish to see this great medium of the world community lost to the world because of the shortsightedness of some misguided and ill-informed persons mired in the distant past.

# Featured Directory of Online Poker Rooms

## PARTYPOKER.COM

PartyPoker.com

World's Largest Poker Room

**GAMES:** Texas Hold'Em, Omaha High, Omaha 8 or Better, Seven Card Stud, Stud 8 or Better

**LIMITS:** From $.50–$1.00 to as high as players wish; pot-limit and no-limit tables also available

**TOURNAMENTS:** Daily, Weekly, and Special, with both scheduled multitable and Sit & Go formats available for all games and limits

**URL:** See online download at: www.partypoker.com

**SECURITY:** 128-bit encryption

**CUSTOMER SERVICE:** 24/7 with telephone, fax, and e-mail

**DESCRIPTION:** PartyPoker.com is the world's largest poker room. With more than 60,000 simultaneous players during peak traffic time every day, PartyPoker. com is larger than all of the land-based poker rooms in the world put together. Known for its highly innovative marketing strategies that attract both new and experienced poker players, PartyPoker.com is the blockbuster success story of online gaming.

**SPECIAL OFFER:** When you open a real-money account, use the Bonus Code: **PARTYCODE**. This will get you a terrific bonus cash amount.

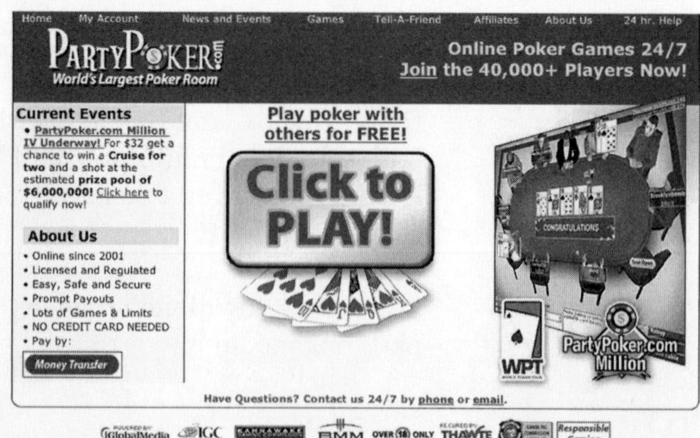


**Photo 12.** When you log on to the URL, this is the Welcome Screen in the main index, which you will see first.

## POKERSTARS.COM

PokerStars.com

| | |
|---|---|
| **GAMES:** | Texas Hold'Em, Omaha High, Omaha High-Low, Seven Card Stud, Seven Card Stud High-Low |
| **LIMITS:** | From $0.01–$0.02 to $100–$200 and higher; pot-limit and no-limit tables also available |
| **TOURNAMENTS:** | Tournaments for all game varieties. Daily, Weekly, and Special, with both multitable and Sit & Go formats available in all games and limits |
| **URL:** | See online download at www.pokerstars.com. The Welcome Screen can be seen on the next page, in Photo 13. |
| **SECURITY:** | 1024-bit RSA key and a Thawte server certificate |
| **CUSTOMER SERVICE:** | 24/7 e-mail support |
| **DESCRIPTION:** | PokerStars.com has become known as the home of the world champions. Each year PokerStars sends hundreds of players to compete on the world's biggest poker stages for millions in prize money. Through thousands of satellites |

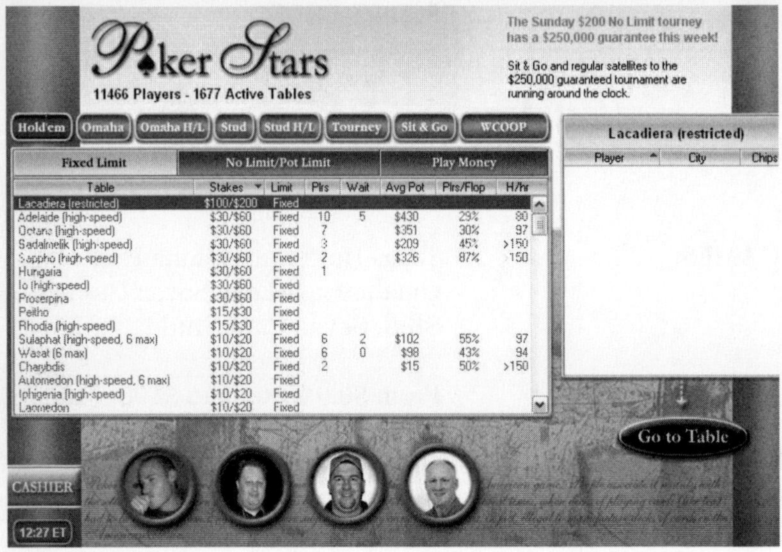


**Photo 13.** When you log on to the PokerStars game site, this is the Welcome Screen in the main lobby, which you will see first.

and qualifying tournaments, PokerStars has made it possible for any player, no matter their bankroll, to get in the game and possibly become the next world champion.

## POKERROOM.COM

**GAMES**: Texas Hold'Em, Omaha High, Omaha High-Low, Seven Card Stud, Seven Card Stud High-Low

| | |
|---|---|
| **LIMITS:** | From \$.50–\$1.00 to as high as players wish; Pot-Limit, No-Limit, and private tables also available |
| **TOURNAMENTS:** | Tournaments for all game varieties. Daily, Weekly, and Special, with both multitable and Sit & Go formats available in all games and limits |
| **URL:** | See online download at www.pokerroom.com |
| **SECURITY:** | 128-bit encryption |
| **CUSTOMER SERVICE:** | 24/7 telephone and e-mail support. 1-888-MY-POKER |
| **DESCRIPTION:** | PokerRoom.com was launched in 1999. As one of the first poker rooms on the Internet, it was launched with "play money" only, but it was all no-download. Since then everything has just grown and improved. PokerRoom.com has become one of the largest online poker rooms in the world, with a stunning selection of safe and secure no-download games, a real sense of community among its members, and a pioneering attitude to the poker industry. Real money games were first introduced in August 2001; since then PokerRoom.com has introduced a number of new games and innovations. At the start of 2004 PokerRoom.com introduced |

spectacular gaming to their players in the form of amazing new software with five different poker games and several fantastic tournaments.

**SPECIAL OFFER**: When you open a real-money account, use the Bonus Code: **WINPPP**. This will get you a terrific bonus cash amount.

**Photo 14.** When you log on to the URL, this is the Welcome Screen in the main lobby, which you will see first.

# General Directory of Online Poker Rooms

**Site Name:** Check n Raise Poker.com
**Site URL:** www.checknraisepoker.com
**Games:** Hold'Em, Omaha, Omaha High-Low, Seven Card Stud and Seven Card Stud High-Low. All are offered in limit form, and Hold'Em and Omaha are offered in pot-limit and no-limit form. Hold'Em is also offered in a spread-limit format.

**Site Name:** Bodog Poker
**Site URL:** www.bodogpoker.com
**Games:** Texas Hold'Em, Omaha, and Omaha High-Low, Seven Card Stud, Seven Card Stud High-Low, Five Card Stud. Bodog Poker features stakes as low as $0.10–$0.25. Multitable Tournaments, Free Rolls, Satellites, Shoot-outs and Re-Buy Tournaments are available.

**Site Name:** InterCasino Poker
**Site URL:** www.InterCasinoPoker.com
**Games:** Texas Hold'Em, Seven Card Stud, Omaha High, Omaha High-Low. Single and Multitable Tournaments, Ring Games. Table types available: 10 seat, 8 seat, 6 seat, Heads Up.

**Site Name:** Full Tilt Poker
**Site URL:** fulltiltpoker.com
**Games:** Texas Hold'Em, Omaha, Omaha High-Low,

Seven Card Stud, Seven Card Stud High-Low, Ring Games, Multitable Tournaments, Sit & Go Tournaments, Big Money Multi-table Tournaments (100 to 1,000+ players), Mini-Tournaments (10 to 30 players), Free Rolls, Special Promotions. Table types available: 10 seat max, 8 seat max, 6 seat max, Heads Up.

**Site Name**: Tropics Poker
**Site URL**: www.tropicspoker.com
**Games**: Texas Hold'Em, Omaha, Five card stud, Seven card stud. Ring Games, Multiplayer Tournaments, Multiday Tournaments, Sit & Go. Table types available: 10 seat, 6 seat, 2 seat.

**Site Name**: TruePoker
**Site URL**: www.TruePoker.com
**Games**: Texas Hold'Em and Omaha High and Omaha High-Low. Ring Games, Multiplayer Tournaments, Sit & Go Tournaments, Heads Up Tournaments. Table types available: short-handed games along with their 10-man tables as well as Heads Up tables.

# Postscript

This is the twelfth book in my *Powerful Profits* series. We have now completed the full circle of discussing every kind of casino game and gaming option currently available. This series of books was specifically designed to provide the most current and up-to-date information about casino games, and casino gaming, as it now exists in the world of twenty-first-century casinos and casino games. As part of this series, I have not only produced books on individual casino games, but I have also written a book about Internet casino gambling, land-based poker, and now this book about the Internet poker phenomenon that has been sweeping the world for the past several years. In all of my books I have provided for you with the most comprehensive analysis of casinos and casino games as they now exist in the casino world, and I have provided easy-to-understand methods and means by which you can maximize your gaming experience. This current book on Internet poker follows those established principles.

Although there are many different books on poker, there are currently only a few about Internet poker. One of the main reasons for this seems to be that those great many terrific poker authors, players, champions, and poker experts who have written books about land-based real-world poker acquired all of that knowledge and experience by playing in the real world under the traditional conditions, and over the years spanning the decades before the advent of Internet poker. Those few books that now exist about Internet poker appeared to me to also be derivatives of the principles that have been established for so many decades about how to play poker in the real world. In my experience, I have found that there is a significant difference between how poker is played in the real world and how it is played on the Internet. It is these differences that I have attempted to capture in this book, in conjunction with my earlier poker book, *Powerful Profits from Poker*. Both books were conceived in tandem and were intended to provide the best overall window into the games themselves—and their applicable strategies and methods of play—as well as to show the differences that are embodied in the way these games are played in their respective worlds. Internet poker resides in cyberspace, in what can probably be best described as cyberworld. Traditional poker games in casino poker rooms and card rooms belong to the real world, which is the world of sight, sound, touch, feel, and taste.

Cyberworld poker exists only in your mind and in your perceptions of the virtual reality. It is not real in itself. Real-world poker exists in the real world, inasmuch as we—human beings—can identify and understand and exist in the world that we perceive through our senses. There are great and many differences between these two worlds. In the way we perceive each world and in the way we exist in it. As far as poker is concerned, the way that we exist in these two worlds is substantially different. When we exist in the real world and play poker, we do so in the casino poker rooms and card rooms where there are real tables, real chairs, real money, real chips, and—most important—real players with whom we can interact, whom we can see and hear and observe. When we exist in cyberworld, we do not exist in that same reality. The reality of playing poker in cyberworld means that the reality in which we exist is in our own home, sitting in our chair, facing our computer wherever it may be, and therefore in a reality nothing like the casino poker rooms or card rooms. Consequently the reality of playing Internet poker means that that world exists not in where we *are*, and not even in the computer at which we are looking, but entirely and only in *our perception* of the reality that actually does not exist. That is what it means to do something in cyberworld, and in virtual reality. Although such virtual reality may actually appear in representations with which we can identify, and which to our minds have some commensurately applicable real-world references, the simple fact remains that these are appearances only. Nothing in cyberworld really exists. As a direct result, the way that we interact with that virtual world is vastly different from the way we conduct ourselves in the real world, and how we interact in it. Consequently, the way that we play poker on the Internet—by its very nature—is significantly different from the way we play poker in the real world.

What I have created in this book is not just the distinction between these two worlds, but also means and methods to navigate between them, in them, and to bridge the transitional gap that spans them. The greatest problem faced by those players who have learned to play poker primarily on the Internet is the transition from Internet poker to real-world poker. That is a difficult transition because, as I have said, these two worlds are very vastly different from each other. Similarly, real-world poker players who have learned to play poker in the real world, in the traditional manner, often find it equally as difficult to play on the Internet. In fact, I know of many real-world poker players who simply cannot play on the Internet at all. Players who regularly win by playing poker in the real world, in a variety of cash games as well as tournaments, equally as regularly find themselves as regular losers whenever they venture into the cyberworld of Internet poker. They find it equally as difficult to make the transition between real-world poker and Internet-based poker as many Internet poker players do when they venture into the real-world arena of land based poker. It is this transitional bridge—and the understanding of it—that I have provided in this book. By understanding what I have written in my book *Powerful Profits from Poker*, and now in this book *Powerful Profits from Internet Poker*, together I provide for you clearly defined knowledge and perspectives that bridge these two worlds, and bring the world of poker into the twenty-first century.

# Acknowledgments

First and foremost, I wish to thank my dear mother, Georgina S. Royer, for her lifetime of help, guidance, and assistance. She is a remarkable lady who fully deserves notice for her tremendous abilities and her steadfast faith in me.

I also wish to thank my literary agents, Greg Dinkin and Frank Scatoni. Greg is an accomplished author in his own right, and Frank a widely respected book editor. Through their agency, Venture Literary, they recognized the value of what I had to offer as an author of books on casino games and gaming. Without their efforts, this book, and the others in this series, would never have come to exist.

My thanks also to Bruce Bender at Kensington Publishing Group, who has published this book and this series. He recognized that this book and this series offer valuable insight into the casino games as they really are, and that this book will enable almost all players to finally realize a happy and profitable casino experience. I thank Bruce and the staff of Kensington for their help in this process, and in particular, my editors Richard Ember and Ann LaFarge.

I extend my gratitude and thanks to my longtime friend Tom Caldwell for the many things he has done to help me and for enriching my life. I also send my thanks to Norreta, Sean, and Brent, for reasons they all know.

My sincere thanks to Bob Dempsey and his company in Las Vegas, Dempsey Graphics, for his help with many illustrations in my books. Bob, thanks also for making that videotape for me for Jay Leno and the *Tonight Show.*

To all my other friends and associates in the gaming business, from owners, managers, senior executives, hosts and supervisors: you all know who you are, and I thank you.

My friends in Australia: Neil and his family, Lilli and little MRM (Mark), Ormond College, University of Melbourne, the governor of Victoria and my former master, Sir Davis McCaughey. Also his Proctorial Eminence R. A. Dwyer, Esq. (I still have the Swiss knife you gave me more than twenty years ago), and the Alumni Association of the University of Wollongong, NSW, Department of Philosophy, and Professor Chipman. Also to the executive, editorial, and display advertising staff of *The Age* newspaper in Melbourne, Australia, and to Fairfax Press in Sydney, with whom I had the pleasure of being associated at one time.

I also extend my grateful appreciation to Laurence E. Levit, C.P.A., of Los Angeles, who has been my steadfast friend, accountant, and adviser for two decades, and whose faith in me and my work has never faltered. A truer friend a man rarely finds. Also to Michael Harrison, attorney-at-law in Beverly Hills, California, whose expertise and help have made my life more secure.

Finally, to all those whose paths have crossed with mine, and who have for one reason or another stopped a while and visited. I may no longer remember your names, but I do remember what it meant to have those moments.

Thank you!

# Index